UNFINISHED MURDER

UNFINISHED MURDER

MURDER

The Capture
of a Serial Rapist

James Neff

POCKET BOOKS

New York   London   Toronto   Sydney   Tokyo   Singapore

POCKET BOOKS, a division of Simon & Schuster Inc.
1230 Avenue of the Americas, New York, NY 10020

Copyright © 1995 by James Neff

Neff, James.
    Unfinished murder : the capture of serial rapist / James
Neff.
        p.   cm.
    ISBN: 0-671-73185-8
    1. Shelton, Ronnie.   2. Rapists—Ohio—Cleveland—
Biography.   3. Rape—Ohio—Case studies.   I. Title.
    HV6568.C54N44   1995
    364.1′532′0977132—dc20   94-34008
                                                          CIP

First Pocket Books hardcover printing April 1995

10 9 8 7 6 5 4 3 2 1

POCKET and colophon are registered trademarks of
Simon & Schuster, Inc.

Printed in the U.S.A.

For the survivors

Acknowledgments

This work of nonfiction owes its creation to a large number of people, whom I would like to thank, however inadequately.

I interviewed most of the identified survivors of the West Side Rapist, including family members, boyfriends, and spouses, and to them I am particularly indebted. Some asked me to protect their privacy, so names will not be listed.

I want to especially thank my editors at Pocket Books: Bill Grose and Molly Allen, whose suggestions vastly improved this book. Their colleague, Tom Cherwin, did a wonderful job of copyediting. Thanks also to my great agent, Esther Newberg of International Creative Management, and her assistant, Amanda Beesley.

The following persons allowed me to interview them or provided other assistance, for which I am very grateful: Carl Anderson, Debbie Baer, Jack Baker, Fred Berlin, Jennifer Borrowman, Anthony Brigano, J. L. Brown, Vernon Brown, Rebecca Buehner, Joseph Cannon, Ed Carter, Andy Charchenko, Richard Chudner, John Corrigan, Valerie Dailey, John E. Douglas, William Dungan, John Dunn, Lucie J. Duvall, Patrick Evans, Martin Flask, Josie George, Ed Gray, William Hanton, Mark Hastings, Frank Hickman, Ray Hill, Arnold Hovan, Robert Howell, Paul Jones, Bea Kelly, John T. Kenney, Carla Kole, Edward Kovacic, Victor Kovacic, Dorothy Lochner, Bob Matuszny, Larry McCormick, Gerald McFaul, Tim McGinty, Maria McGivern, David McQuirk, Richard McMonagle, Jay Milano, Jerry Milano, Steve Monroe, Joseph New, Patrick

ACKNOWLEDGMENTS

Nicolino, Barbara Parker, Robert K. Ressler, Michael Rhoades, Candace Risen, Howard Rudolph, Ross Santamaria, James Schotten, Bob Schroeder, Jim Simone, Charles Stuart, John Stuckbauer, Emanuel Tanay, Champ Thomas, Danny Trovato, Frank Viola, Kevin Whelan, Jennifer Wise, Chester Zembala, and Larry Zukerman.

The Dick Goldensohn Fund, Inc., provided a crucial grant at an early stage of this project.

I deeply appreciate the efforts of Stephanie Saul, Walt Bogdanich, Margaret Lynch, Abby Mann, and Joseph Neff, who read the first draft and whose suggestions made *Unfinished Murder* a better book.

My love and thanks go to my mother and father and, especially, to my wife Maureen and the boys.

Note

Many of the rape survivors of Ronnie Shelton wanted me to use their real names in this book, saying they had nothing to be ashamed of. Other survivors (and two of Shelton's former girlfriends) wanted their privacy protected; to them I assigned pseudonyms, which are footnoted in the text at first reference.

Every other detail in this book is true, based on more than one hundred and fifty interviews. Among those interviewed were most of the rape suriviors, their spouses, boyfriends, and family members. Four women had kept journals before or after being raped and shared them with me. In addition, prosecutor Tim McGinty and defense lawyer Jerry Milano cooperated fully; they let me read their trial notes and files. Maria Shelton showed me the diary she kept during the trial and allowed me full access to her brother's papers and memorabilia. Ronnie Shelton gave me a series of signed releases, which I used to pry lose school, medical, psychiatric, juvenile, and nearly every other private and public record pertaining to his life. In all I compiled a seven-foot stack of records, including jail visiting logs, emergency room records, nurses' notes, IQ tests, probation reports, incident reports, confessions, victim statements, letters, photographs, psychiatric evaluations, trial transcripts, even grade school report cards.

With these records and interviews I was able to reconstruct key scenes and conversations, taking into account individual speech patterns, which made the direct quotes more accurate than anything paraphrasing could ever accomplish.

Neither Ronnie Shelton nor anyone else in this book was paid for their cooperation.

Thin Ice

Mommy I'm sorry
I know I'm your baby

I'm not what you wanted, Dad
I could never amount to anything

I may look normal
but look harder (something's wrong)
Can't you see it?

I live my life on thin ice
Someday I know the ice will break
but when?

—Ronnie Shelton

CONTENTS

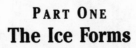

PART ONE
The Ice Forms
1

PART TWO
Skater's Waltz
25

PART THREE
A Crack in the Ice
127

PART FOUR
The Ice Breaks
207

PART FIVE
"Unfinished Murder" Revenged
263

Author's Epilogue
339

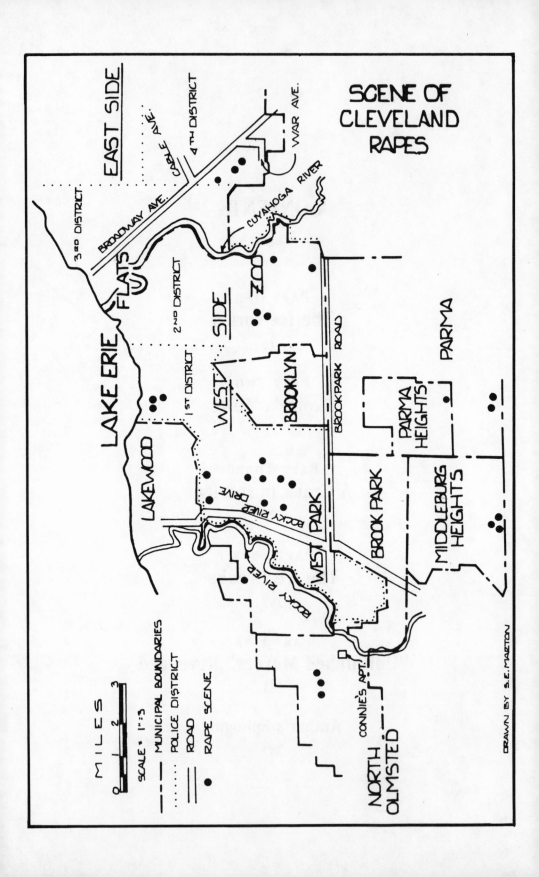

PART ONE

The Ice Forms

Cleveland, Ohio

April 13, 1983

He turned back the covers and sat for a moment on the edge of a well-pounded mattress.

The young woman beside him stirred under the rumpled sheets. "What're you doing?" she asked sleepily.

It was four in the morning. From the corner of his eye he watched her stretch, her toned muscles loose and relaxed from a night of lovemaking. He had gone out of his way to satisfy her and could tell from her responses that her previous lovers had not been very skilled in bed.

He lighted a cigarette and pulled black jeans over his slim hips.

"Come back here," she said. "I need you." She was blond, nineteen, with the look of a soap opera nymphet.

"Gotta get some air. I'll be back." He knew she was annoyed at being turned down, but fuck it. He believed in playing hard to get. In his experience it made the girls want him all the more.

Besides, he had things to do before daybreak.

In the predawn dark he drove his car down West 117th Street, Cleveland's most heavily traveled thoroughfare. He welcomed the sprinkling of traffic; it made him less conspicuous.

He told himself he was driving aimlessly, but in fact he was drawn to a block on Marne Avenue, a narrow residential street of identical bungalows.

He parked one street away and sat for a minute. He retrieved a handgun from under the front seat, tucked it in his waist, and pulled on a yellow baseball cap. He left the car and slipped down a driveway into the backyards of a group of one-story frame houses. Light-headed, staying close to shadows cast by trees against streetlights, he crept toward one of the houses.

Once there he crouched near a rear window, his mind ablaze. He had seen her before through this lighted window, tall, slim, with a strong chin and cheekbones, blond-streaked brown hair down to her shoulders. He had watched her long enough to know her patterns and those of her housemates. Now he imagined her in her bed, sleeping on her back, naked, her breasts spread across her chest. He decided to go in.

Until this moment, it had been a typical week night for Kathy Bond. She waitressed until ten at Casey's Family Restaurant on West 117th, made about $30 in tips—more than the other waitresses, as usual—and hurried home. Her roommate, Michelle, who was divorced and owned the tiny house, had to leave soon for her midnight shift at Tony's Diner. Kathy was going to watch Michelle's six-year-old daughter and four-year-old son.

Kathy wanted to get married and have children someday. Over the past six months she had become close to Michelle's kids and loved them as if they were her own. Tonight both were asleep when she arrived—Michael in the lower bunk in the children's bedroom, and Missy, as was usual lately, in Kathy's double bed.

After Michelle left for work, Kathy drank a beer in front of the TV, stripped to panties and a T-shirt, then moved Missy to one side of the double bed and climbed in. She fell asleep quickly and woke only when Missy began crying that her leg was asleep. Half-asleep, Kathy carried the child to her mother's bed, where a heating pad was plugged in. She tucked in the girl, kissed her softly, and turned on the pad. Missy had only recently started complaining about her leg, and Kathy wondered whether the heating pad really helped or if Missy was simply comforted by the attention.

Kathy had been back in her own bed for a few minutes when

she heard the kitchen window rattle. She listened for a min
Silence. Must be the wind, she decided as she drifted off.

He had pulled off the screen and jimmied the window
quietly as he could. He climbed inside and froze for a minu
listening in case anyone had heard him. All right, he thoug
not a peep.

This was his favorite part. The buildup. He was inside and r
one knew. He took his time, wanting to figure out her lif
studying the furniture and decorations and dishes in the sink. H
wanted to connect with this woman he had never met.

He tiptoed to the narrow hallway, his brain awash in pleasure.
She would wake up, her eyes wide, terrified, and beg him not to
hurt her. She would do what he said—they always did. And she
could not hurt him or his feelings, not in any way.

He checked a bedroom and saw bunk beds with rumpled
covers. Kids. Good, he thought. That would make things easier.
He found a little girl in another bed in another room. Then he
crept into the woman's bedroom and watched her sleep, her
breathing quiet, her hair fanned on the pillow like flower petals.

Blood flooded his groin, tightening his crotch. He picked up
the purse from the dresser and delicately rummaged for money.
He found her tip money in a cigarette case, which also held an
empty pack and her driver's license. He turned the laminated
license to catch a sliver of light from the window: Kathleen Bond,
twenty years old, five-foot-eight, 124 pounds. Great face, he
observed.

He pulled out the gun and moved in. "Kathy," he said softly.
"Kathy."

She opened her eyes and an icy terror constricted her chest.
She heard herself scream.

A hand was clamped over her mouth and a gun thrust in her
face. "Do what I say," a voice said softly, "and the kids won't get
hurt. Don't look at me."

The house was silent. Kathy nodded that she understood. She
felt as if she was about to vomit.

5

"Take off your clothes."

Trembling, her skin prickling, afraid she had only seconds left to live, she stripped. Suddenly she thought of the little girl, forgetting she had moved her. "Where's Missy? What've you done to her?" She started to look up.

The intruder drew the brim of his baseball cap down over his face. "Don't look at me," he ordered.

"The little girl was in my bed!"

"There's no kid. I don't know what you're talking about."

"Please, where is she?"

"There's one kid in one bedroom and another in another. Now shut up and they won't get hurt."

He pushed down his pants and immediately forced his way into her mouth. A few minutes later, he stretched out on the bed, the gun in his hand, and made her get on top. "Don't look at me!" he said as he bucked between her legs.

She felt him ejaculate. She wanted to kill him but was too afraid to move.

"Okay, you can get dressed. But stay in the bed and don't move. Now, where is your money?"

"In my cigarette case."

"I already got that."

"That's it. That's all I got."

She listened as he walked from room to room, then heard him stop at the refrigerator, open it, and pop the top of a can of beer. Oh my God, she thought, he's not leaving. He's going to stay until he kills us all.

He took a swig of the beer. He couldn't believe how calm he was. He was taking his time, dallying deliberately. He liked her.

A storm window rattled somewhere and, worried that she was making an escape, he ran back to the bedroom, the gun held clamped in both hands, arms out straight.

"I said don't move," he hissed.

She was still under the covers. "It wasn't me, it wasn't me, I didn't move, I didn't." He could hear panic in her voice.

He lowered the gun and continued his search, opening drawers and cupboards, looking for cash. So far all he had found

were two Mickey Mouse piggy banks full of change. But a desk drawer in the other bedroom was locked and he couldn't snap it open. He came back and pointed his gun at the woman.

"Where's your friend's money? Don't lie."

"I don't know.

He decided to take her word for it. "I need a suitcase to carry things with," he told her.

"Up in the attic."

She heard him shuffling around upstairs but couldn't force herself to run. She was pinned there by the children. He had said he'd hurt them if she screamed. Imagine what he'd do to them if she ran.

Suddenly he was in the bedroom again, pointing the gun at her from a crouching position like a cop in a television drama. Kathy put up her hands. "I didn't move," she said, shaking.

He unzipped his pants. "Don't look at me," he commanded, and climbed on the bed and forced oral sex again, then a few minutes later pushed her legs apart and raped her.

"I need to get a drink of water," she said when it was over. What Kathy really wanted was an excuse to get out of bed. Anything would be better than the hopeless feeling of lying flat on her back.

"I'll get it for you," he said brightly. When he came back the baseball cap was low over his face. He handed her the glass. "Okay, go in the bathroom and put your hand on the window. I'm going outside and if I don't see your hand there I'm coming back in. And don't call the cops. I know every car in this neighborhood. If there's a strange car here, I'll be back, and the two kids will get it first. Then you."

Terrified, Kathy nodded, afraid to look at him. Before he left, he lighted a Marlboro cigarette, then as an afterthought tapped out a few more from his pack onto the counter for her. "Here," he said, his tone friendly. "I know you're out."

With his dark jeans and jacket, he knew he blended into the night, and he forced himself to walk slowly to his car. He was slick with a fine sheen of sweat, slightly shaky, drifting down from an intense, pulse-pounding high. He sauntered with exaggerated casualness.

He hoped no one had seen him. He had taken another big chance tonight. The police might even be on their way here now, sirens off, a husky V-8 roaring. That would be exciting. They'd screech up, doors slamming. Then they'd brace him, screaming, shoving their silly police-issue .38s in his face.

Moments later the thrill faded. He lighted another cigarette and rehearsed a cover story in case the police stopped him. Fat chance in Cleveland, he thought. All these times stalking, breaking in, and it hadn't happened yet. He got in his car, slid his handgun under the front seat, and drove off.

KATHY BOND

For a few minutes after being raped, Kathy Bond thought of keeping it all a horrible secret, as the rapist wanted—of carrying on her life as if nothing had happened. But the idea made her gag. She had to do something.

Sobbing, she called Michelle at Tony's Diner and choked out what had happened, assuring her the kids were okay. Michelle called the police, then raced home.

It didn't take long for two officers to get to Marne Avenue. Behind them came a police beat reporter for the Cleveland *Plain Dealer;* he had overheard the radioed assignment on the scanner in the newspaper's tiny office at police headquarters.

"This isn't going in the paper, is it?" Kathy said, her voice cracking with fear. "The guy who did this told me not to call the cops. For sure he'll know if you do a write-up." The reporter mumbled and moved to another room.

After hearing Kathy's account, one of the cops carefully dusted for fingerprints on the beer can and water glass handled by the rapist.

Later, Kathy called an old friend, told him what happened, and asked for protection. He said he would drive right over. That evening she felt completely out of control. She couldn't sit still. When Michelle or the kids said something to her, she didn't hear or couldn't hold the thought. She struggled to keep from crying. By midnight she had drunk enough beer to dull her shattered nerves and fall asleep. Her friend sat up in the living room, watching TV with a shotgun resting on his thighs.

Kathy woke up crying a few times and came out to talk. "I can't stay in that bedroom. I think I'll have to move out."

Good idea, he said.

"I feel bad leaving Michelle and the kids. I'm abandoning her, and that guy might come back."

The next day, she saw a headline on page 10 of the newspaper: "West Side Woman Raped." That decided it. "Oh my God, he's going to come back and kill me," Kathy said. She packed and moved out a few hours later.

Until the rape, Kathy had been full of energy, quick to laugh, a fun companion for a night of club hopping as well as a devoted surrogate mother to Michelle's kids. She lived on coffee and cigarettes, and maybe a quick sandwich at work, sitting in the kitchen, chatting with the cooks.

But now that someone had raped her, she lived in fear in her own apartment, afraid to be alone at night. She couldn't sleep. Nor could she explain her fears—she thought they made her sound crazy—to the young man she was dating. She was not ready to have sex, and manufactured excuses when he made overtures. It was just too painful to explain.

She felt herself growing apart from her family. When one of her younger brother's friends insensitively kidded her that she'd probably enjoyed sex with the rapist, she punched him in the face, then burst into tears. She was surprised at how easily her rage flashed into violence. She never had been like that before, and had hated that quality in her first husband, who she'd left two years earlier at eighteen, after seven months of marriage, when he had hit her for a second time. She had told herself long ago that she would never stay with a wife beater. Watching her mom put up with being a punching bag had been torment enough.

Along with the rage came moments of panic. Not long after Kathy moved to a new apartment, her boss mentioned that a Cleveland detective named Miller had called the restaurant, wanting to know where she had moved, explaining that he had to talk to her about the case.

Kathy screamed at her boss, convinced that the caller was really the rapist trying to find her to kill her for calling the cops, as he had promised. That night she stayed with a friend, and the next day she moved out of her new apartment. She would have to find another one.

Back at work, Kathy was like a raw nerve ending. Before the rape, she had been Casey's best waitress, a natural with customers. She had built up a loyal crew of regulars: a handful of older couples, truck drivers, workers from the nearby discount stores and factories, and several Cleveland cops from the First District station house.

But now everything seemed to spook her. One evening, she noticed a shadowy figure pass by the restaurant's front window, and instinctively she dropped to the floor, trying to make herself as tiny a target as possible for what she was sure was a gunman.

Moments later, she stood up, sweating, shaky, embarrassed. "I can't believe I did this," she said. By then the figure passing the window had walked in and asked for a table; he was just a hungry older man.

Over the next week, whenever someone outside passed the restaurant windows in a certain way, Kathy dove to the floor in fear. Unaware of why she was doing it, other waitresses also dropped to the floor, thinking they too were in danger. Then Kathy would apologize and reveal she had been raped, explaining, "He said he'd come back and kill me."

Her erratic behavior began to hurt business and her manager

insisted that she get help at the Cleveland Rape Crisis Center, a nonprofit social services agency.

There she met with a counselor, an older woman, who explained that her behavior and her feeling of rage were normal responses for women who had been raped. There was, in fact, no "normal response" to the trauma of being raped, but she was not crazy if she had flashbacks, couldn't sleep, got depressed, suffered panic attacks, or felt guilt, shame, and self-loathing. Some rape victims mutilate themselves, Kathy was told. Others go on crash diets or binge on drugs or food. Whatever the response to being raped, the counselor explained, it was okay to feel that way. Kathy learned that anywhere from one in ten to one in four women end up being victims of sexual violence, and that a lot of women who have survived rape are out there to talk about it.

The counselor, worried that Kathy did not have a healthy release for her anger, brought out foam rubber paddles and told her to bash whatever she wanted to in the office. At home, she suggested pillow fights to get out anger.

A pillow fight? Kathy wondered what the hell good a pillow fight was when what she really wanted was to tear off the guy's face.

THE RAPIST

He parked his motorcycle on a hill perched above the Flats, Cleveland's industrial zone flanking the Cuyahoga River as it snaked south from downtown. Here the black sky covered him like a quilt. In the distance, forges and foundries cast an orange glow, softened by a haze of steam and smoke that was barely discernible at night. The exhale of steel mills.

In the dark the hum of tow motors and the low-gear rumble of semitrailers tumbled up the brush-covered slopes, the constant, purposeful sound of men at work, a reassuring lullaby. Some nights, if the wind was right, he could taste chalky soot on his teeth.

It seemed as if it had taken him forever to learn to sit in the dark on this hill. As a boy, he used to feel terrified at night, when a sudden clank or shop whistle or a rat rustling in the scraggly sumac bushes would detonate a terror that pounded across his chest. Even tonight he felt vulnerable, as if he had been swallowed by a hulking mechanical beast.

Opposite his perch, across a tangle of freight tracks and up the brambles to the north, were the housing projects, a foreign land. He imagined their residents as people with shiny skin and the blackest faces, their looks as angry as his father's. He had been taught to hate them.

The projects made him think of one warm summer night when his mother and he were driving in their old car, windows down. They were going to the mill to pick up his father after shift

12

change at the Jones and Laughlin Steel Corporation, in the Flats, where his father had worked as an electrician since 1964. On the way there, at a stoplight on Broadway Avenue, a black man jumped into the car. He was young and didn't know what rape was, but somehow he knew how the man was going to hurt his mother. She shrieked, a sound more piercing than a whistle at shift change. His ears rang now just thinking about it. Panicked, the man bolted from the car and ran across two lanes of traffic.

The recurring nightmare came when he was older: He walks alone at night up Broadway Avenue and climbs the porch stairs to a nondescript house. He steps inside a smoky living room packed with sweaty black men, and there on the floor, her skirt up to her waist, thrashing, her wrists pinned, is his mother. They are raping her, repeatedly, and she screams, screams, screams. . . . And then he wakes up.

But now the dark had finally become his friend. It had stopped re-creating the terror of his childhood on War Avenue, just off Broadway, a narrow street of small frame houses crowded together like cartons in a storeroom, where, trying to sleep in his attic bedroom, he would hear his parents fighting below him.

Tonight, out on the hill, he thought about how he had hated the War Avenue house. Painted two dull tones of green, it sagged behind a grass patch the size of a truck bed. He wanted to burn down the place, to watch the fire rage, a dirty orange flame-ball on a dead-end street.

He hated that house, yet here he was at twenty-two living in it by himself. His father had kept it as a rental property after moving the family to suburban Brunswick Hills. His sister, Maria, two years younger, lived there with their parents.

It was close to ten o'clock. He went inside the War Avenue house and began the nightly ritual: getting showered and dressed to go out to the nightclubs. He toweled dry, shaved carefully, and splashed on cologne. He pulled on tight jeans and snapped them over his tiny waist, then climbed into western boots that boosted his five-foot-seven height a couple of inches. He put on an expensive casual shirt, leaving the top few buttons unfastened. He was a wiry 135 pounds; no amount of weight lifting or diet supplements could bulk him up.

13

He looked into the mirror and smiled. He knew he was handsome—long rock-star hair, dark-lashed eyes, cleft chin. His girlfriends loved his hair: thick, dark brown, with body and wave that responded like modeling clay to the touch of a blow-dryer. He would take forever in carefully styling it to frame his face perfectly, puffing it up on the crown to make himself appear taller. A girlfriend once hid his hair dryer as a joke. Wet from a shower, his hair starting to dry untamed, he demanded it back with a terrifying fury.

He slipped on a faded blue jean jacket, left the house, and climbed on his motorcycle, a cigarette in the corner of his mouth. He felt he looked perfect: the Marlboro man meets Richard Gere. First impressions were vital when meeting a good-looking woman in a nightclub, he believed. He liked to practice glances and smiles and low-key pickup patter. But first he was meeting his best friend, Danny, a handsome male stripper. They needed each other at the nightclubs, since nearly all single, unattached women went to bars in pairs. Pickup etiquette required that you didn't leave a girlfriend alone if you met someone you liked. So men, even loners like himself, traveled in pairs as well. He and Danny were a team.

Tonight the two young men made an entrance at the Mining Company: pounding music, clouds of cigarette smoke, teenaged women in tank tops and tight jeans and young men in cowboy boots and muscle T-shirts, playing a nightly mating game. The Mining Company featured male go-go dancers one night, cheap drinks for women the next. The nightclub was a runaway success, always crowded and loud, patrolled out of necessity by off-duty Cleveland policemen. He loved the place, and tonight dozens of pretty young women were on the prowl.

He noticed an attractive woman being pulled outside by her enraged boyfriend and knew from experience that the woman was going to get hit. She seemed to sense his concern and gave him a look that he felt said, "Save me."

He ran after them to the parking lot and dove headfirst at the woman's boyfriend, knocked him down, and repeatedly smashed the man's head into the wheel rim of a car. One of the off-duty policemen broke up the fight.

14

He was scratched and bruised, but didn't care. He felt he had protected a woman, just as his father had always instructed him, and he went back inside the nightclub to take a victory lap around the bar. He would actually make a pretty good cop, he decided. Maybe he should apply. That would make his father respect him.

As a small boy he had been driven to earn his father's approval. He remembered the thrill of once being lifted high by his dad to unscrew a burned-out lightbulb in a ceiling fixture, his tiny hands unsteady from the rare excitement of his father's touch. He had even thought later of breaking the lights somehow so he could be close to his father again, but he realized he would get a whipping instead.

To this day his father thought of him as a mama's boy, with a girlish preoccupation with his looks. To please his burly, hot-tempered dad, he became a fighter, starting as a boy on War Avenue in their deteriorating neighborhood close to the mills.

As a junior high school student, he had been beaten up by an older bully on the block, and he ran home crying to his father. His dad hired a tougher, bigger boy from outside the neighborhood to come in and thrash the bully.

But two weeks later, the bully of War Avenue again beat up his younger neighbor. This time when he ran home crying, his father pulled him outside and said, "Let's go." He never forgot his father's next words. "You hit, you kick, you bite, you find a place on his body and you don't let go. Whatever it takes."

He walked with his dad to a baseball field at the end of the street and felt ice in his chest when he saw the bully with his back to them, watching the game through the fence.

"Do it!" his father told him, and he sucker-punched the bigger boy. They grappled and went down in the grass, rolling, grunting, while his father yelled, "You better whip him or you'll get it from me." Then he told his son to bite. The boy clamped his teeth on the bully's wrist, and a shriek was heard down War Avenue.

His father yelled to let go, but he wouldn't; he had something to prove. When the bully finally pulled loose he had to be treated at the emergency room of nearby St. Alexis Hospital.

With this encounter he broke through his fear of getting hurt and became a fighter. He felt himself turn around, walking to school confidently, even though biting wasn't the traditional manly way to settle disputes. In his eyes, he had shown his father that he could fight, that he wouldn't back down, that despite being small he would tackle a good-sized opponent.

Weeks later at school, knowing his father's dislike of blacks, he took on a black student during music class. He broke his hand during the fight and had it splinted and bandaged. He counted on his father being proud of him, but lost confidence on the way home. So instead he told his sister Maria to tell their mother that he had tripped on a curb and fallen against a fire hydrant outside school.

But his father didn't believe the story. He was taken to school, where he and his father met with the principal and the truth came out. "Swats or detentions," the principal offered. He chose the detentions, but his father said give him the swats. And then his father took the paddle and, with the window blinds open, spanked him in full view of his junior high friends, who were watching through the glass.

That night his father cut off his hair, shaving his head into a burr cut. He felt humiliated. He wished his father would be run over by a truck.

KATHY BOND

Not long after she was raped, Kathy Bond and a girlfriend visited Michelle on Marne Avenue. Kathy had felt terrible about moving out so abruptly, but was unable to explain to Michelle why she just could not live there another instant.

During the visit, Kathy's friend thought she recognized a young man a few houses down the street. "Let's go and see him," she said. "He's a nice guy." Kathy agreed.

But when the young man came to the door, dressed in shorts and a T-shirt, a tattoo on his biceps, Kathy froze. It was the man who had raped her! She was sure. Same size, same look, and from the way he gazed at her, he seemed to know who she was. Trying to hide her panic, Kathy tugged on her friend's arm. "C'mon, let's go."

Her friend said no, but Kathy was firm. She sprinted back to Michelle's home. "Call the police, Michelle!" she yelled. "It's the guy that raped me!"

Within a half hour, uniformed police and detectives stationed themselves at the doors of the man's house while a detective walked Kathy to the front yard. There they had the suspect on the porch. His name was Larry McCormick and the police were running a criminal-records check on him.

"Is this the guy who raped you?" an officer asked.

"Hey, I don't know her, I never saw her!" the man shouted.

Kathy looked him over—the small build, the handsome face,

the tattoo on his arm, the skinny legs, the longish brown hair.
She nodded. "He did it."

"This is bullshit!"

"Look, Mr. McCormick," one policeman said. "We might be
able to clear you if you let us search your house and don't find
anything. Otherwise we'll have to arrest you." The police hoped
to find the piggy banks that had been stolen from Michelle's
house.

"I'm not letting you search it," McCormick retorted.

With that the police arrested him, handcuffed him, and
transported him in a squad car to the city jail.

Kathy felt relieved by McCormick's capture. Now she
wouldn't have to look over her shoulder for the rest of her life
waiting for some rapist to come back and terrorize her because
she had called the police. She went out with her pals that night to
celebrate and got deliciously drunk.

Two days after the police arrested Larry McCormick, Kathy
Bond returned to her old house to visit Michelle and the kids,
only to spot McCormick in front of his house. "What the hell is
he doing out!" she said. "I'm calling the police."

She remembers a detective explaining: It was her word against
his, and that doesn't make for a very good case. The detective
said he was sorry, but nine times out of ten at trial you get
dragged through the mud and lose the case because the defense
creates a reasonable doubt.

Kathy slammed down the phone. She did not think to ask if
McCormick's fingerprints matched those on the beer can police
dusted the night of the rape. In fact, they did not.

Late that night at a popular bar, she told some friends what
had happened. As the drinking and the hour progressed they all
grew furious. The system had cut loose a rapist, and it wasn't
fair. It was time for frontier justice. Near closing time, Kathy, two
guys, and a girlfriend were breathing fire and, pumped up for
revenge, drove to McCormick's house.

Kathy clomped up onto the porch in her platform clogs and
banged on the door. Lights flicked on. "Hi," she told Larry,
"would you step outside, please?"

"I was told not to talk to you," he said through the screen door.

"How do you know who I am, you coward?" she replied. "You told the cops you didn't know me."

She saw him peer out. He must have figured out that she had some young guys as her backup, hiding to the side. "Get off the property," he said. He and his roommate picked up softball bats.

"C'mon out here."

"Hey, I didn't touch you."

"Just come out," she said. "Why aren't you coming out? Afraid you'll get beat up by a girl?"

"Get off the property or we're calling the police," he said.

"Go ahead, call 'em, you little chickenshit. You're really bad when you got a gun on somebody, aren't you."

McCormick stayed inside, looking like he was afraid she and her friends would storm the house. A minute later, Kathy kicked the door and yelled loud enough for the whole neighborhood to hear, "Chickenshit! Rapist!" She stomped off the porch and drove off with her friends.

Only later did she realize what had driven her that night: She wanted to handle McCormick herself in order to take back her life, to establish control, to restore what she felt he had taken from her. She wished she could go back to the way she had been before she was raped, when life seemed so carefree. Now she was a tangle of nerves. Many days she felt she could not last another hour. The only thing that made her feel better about herself was simply talking about being raped with her friends.

For the next several months, Kathy drove herself crazy thinking of McCormick walking free, with his cocky smile and skinny ass, making himself out to be the innocent victim of her accusations. The only time she wasn't tormented by thoughts of the rape was after downing half a dozen drinks; then she could fall into a soggy sleep. But sleep did little to refresh her. She suffered nightmares, flashbacks to the attack. She bolted awake at the slightest sound, sweating, pulse racing, wondering if she should get out of bed to check the house.

When this happened, she reached under her pillow for the tiny .22-caliber handgun given to her by one of the cop regulars at

Casey's Restaurant, then checked around her apartment. Although she was nervous about not having a permit, she carried the gun everywhere—to work, in the car, even taking a bath.

A gun really wasn't the answer, Kathy realized. She didn't know if she had the guts to fire it. She hoped no one ever put her in that position.

September 1983

RADA STOVICH*

He had seen her in the clubs before: an attractive twenty-year-old woman whose dark looks came alive on the dance floor. Fast or slow, she danced with passion, laughing, spinning, not afraid to work up a sweat. Three or four nights a week she frequented West Side nightclubs.

One night at the Rampant Lion, a bar near the Baldwin-Wallace College campus in suburban Berea, a friend introduced them. Her name was Rada Stovich, and she was a second-generation Serb. He could tell she was not particularly impressed with him as she checked out his long hair and thin mustache. He was disappointed, because he felt he looked pretty hot, with a white Spanish-style shirt that bloused open to show off his deeply tanned chest.

He liked what he saw. Rada didn't wear a lot of makeup. Her outfit was modest, not the tight miniskirts and revealing halter tops worn by many of the women—"sluts," he called them, muttering the insult as the young women passed him in the bar

---

*Not her real name.

or on the dance floor. He was searching for a "good girl," someone to impress his parents and maybe even marry. At least that's what he told himself. He saw no contradiction in sleeping with women from both categories, but only if *he* approached them first. He had standards. No woman was going to pick him up. He was the man and he had to make the first move.

Just before closing time at the Rampant Lion, he asked Rada to drive him to his parents' home in Brunswick Hills. "It's storming and I've got my bike," he said. He couldn't ride his motorcycle in the rain he explained; he'd leave it and come back for it later.

She had known him all of two hours and was a cautious woman. He struck her as the Latin lover type, not her taste in men. But he came on soft and low-key, with almost exaggerated politeness, casting himself as a victim of forces beyond his control, the weather. He was totally disarming, a polite young man. She took pity and said yes.

In the parking lot, Rada unlocked her car and he opened the driver's side door for her with a courtly flourish. "What do you do?" he asked her on the drive to his parents' home.

"I'm a bill collector; I call people on the phone for an agency," she said.

"You're kidding. Maybe you've been calling me," he said. "I've got lots of bills I can't pay."

He told her about undergoing ten thousand dollars' worth of emergency surgery the past summer after falling off a ladder at a temporary construction job. He was helping to build a garage and had fallen from a joist beam, perhaps nine feet up, and had landed forehead first. The fall punched out a piece of frontal skull bone, knocking him unconscious for three days. Doctors performed emergency surgery to remove a blood clot inside the skull that was creating life-threatening pressure.

It sounded awful. Rada gave him some ideas on how to deal with the bill collectors. They turned to other topics, moving smoothly from work to pop music to family, and suddenly it was three in the morning. By now Rada was impressed with him.

Over the next week, he made a point of running into her at the Mining Company and at her other haunts. Soon he asked her for a date. She was flattered by his attention, because by now she realized he had dated many women more beautiful than she. In the nightclubs, many women stared at him with either desire or contempt. Of the ones who shot him dagger eyes, he explained, "I used to go out with her." To Rada, barely twenty years old, his honesty seemed charming, even mature.

He courted her with romance-novel manners—opening car doors, pantomiming to radio love songs. Within a week, he took her to his parents' home for dinner. His parents seemed nice enough to her. His father, Rodney, was a millworker, built like a stump, handsome in a beefy way. But he rarely met her eyes; he ate silently, then went off to smoke cigarettes in the living room. Katy, his mother, was one of fifteen children of a Mexican migrant worker, Rada learned that evening. With long black hair and electric brown eyes, it was clear she had once been a beautiful girl, but now her nervous smile showed silver-filled teeth in an aging face. She skittered through the kitchen nervously, speaking broken English.

When dinner was over, he took Rada home. After a month of courtship, she still couldn't believe he hadn't tried to sleep with her. She said to a girlfriend: "His name is Ronnie Shelton and he's perfect. He's honest. He's straight. He talks about his feelings."

"You're kidding. Like what?"

"You know how guys don't show feelings about their family," Rada said. "He told me he loves his sister. He's concerned. Very protective."

"I've got to meet this man," said her friend.

After their first or second date, Ronnie gave Rada a key to the house he rented from his parents on War Avenue and insisted that she drop in whenever she wanted. Soon Rada made a practice of stopping in after night classes at Cleveland State University. If Ronnie wasn't around, she studied her premed courses, then fell asleep. If he was home, they'd talk.

"I like to listen to you talk," he would say.

"Why?"

"Because you're smart. You're interesting."

She was captivated, and he could tell no man had ever flattered her for her brains.

"You're too nice," he said.

"What's wrong with that?"

"Nothing. You're just a nice girl."

From their soul-searching talks, Ronnie learned that Rada was straight as far as sex went. Most guys at the Rampant Lion or the Mining Company or the other clubs expected sex after a first date, and many women as well were disappointed when things didn't progress that fast. He decided Rada was a "good girl," and he was glad. She was the kind of woman his father would approve of.

Without directly saying anything about it, Ronnie encouraged her to be as attractive as possible, and she lost the last few pounds that had kept her from having a perfect figure. He knew she was hooked on him, but Ronnie felt they didn't have a future together. They were too different. He was more comfortable taking Rada one block down on War Avenue to Mike and Gloria's, a shot-and-a-beer bar with country music on the jukebox. But she had higher aspirations: a college degree. Ronnie, who had dropped out of high school, hated it when she decided to pledge at a Cleveland State University sorority. He knew all about frats and sororities from television, he told her, and didn't like them. People in them were stuck-up and probably thought they were better than he was (which he secretly felt they were). One night he saw Rada costumed for a Halloween frat party to which he was not invited. She was going as a flapper, sheathed in a red dress with a tassled hem, wearing sexy black stockings. Ronnie hated it. "It makes you look like a whore," he told her.

Weeks later, after a night of barhopping, Ronnie arrived at the War Avenue house and found Rada asleep in his double bed. They had dated for two months and he was tired of her. Now he told himself it was okay to fuck her. He woke her up and in ten

23

minutes it was over. Then he fell asleep. He didn't know that Rada stayed awake for hours, upset about the encounter.

Within days, Ronnie picked a fight with her, their first, over something insignificant. But Ronnie wouldn't let it drop, escalating the disagreement into an ugly scene. They never dated again.

Rada had seen a dark side to him, and it scared her.

PART TWO

Skater's Waltz

April 1984

RONNIE

In the hour before dawn, Ronnie drove along residential West Side streets, swiveling his head, scanning the first floors of houses for lighted windows. From inside one, a light was turned on, near the back. Good. He parked his car around the corner and slipped over on foot.

He made a pass by the house on foot. It was a two-family home, an up-and-down, with a few shrubs. He crept around the back in the dark, listening for dogs, then pushed up against the side of the house and crouched.

Tingling with excitement, he slowly raised his face inches from the kitchen window, giving him a clear view through a thin space along the bottom edge of a shade. Perfect. A woman stood at an ironing board, wearing a bathrobe. She had it loosely cinched to cover her panties and bra. She was ironing a blue postal carrier's uniform, and from her movements Ronnie could catch a glimpse of her body inside the robe.

He fired up a Marlboro, cupping it with his left hand to hide the ember, then unzipped his pants and worked on himself, gazing intently. She had a lush body and straight black hair that fell to her waist. She was quite a find, and he memorized every detail, adding her to his mental list of anonymous targets.

For more than a decade, well before his first orgasm, Ronnie had been creeping along the backs of houses in the dark and peering inside. He would never forget the first time. He was still a boy, maybe twelve, living on War Avenue, when he slipped out

27

of the house early one night. He hid next to a nearby home where a young woman rented the bottom half of a tiny two-family house. Through a first-floor window covered by cheap curtains came the soft flickering light from a television screen. It drew him like a beacon. He peeked inside and saw her stretched on a wide couch. She was naked, watching TV, the glow of the screen illuminating her skin. Snuggled behind her, facing the television, was the man who lived upstairs. He appeared to be naked too.

Ronnie stared at her breasts and her black tangled patch and her blue-white skin. He was frozen for what seemed like forever. Oh, so this is what it's all about, he said to himself. He could not remember ever feeling so wonderful, his crotch warm and tight. At that moment, he felt closer to this stranger than to anyone else in the world. He had seen her exposed, vulnerable, and it seemed a perfect relationship: He knew her and her secrets but she did not see him and could not hurt him. As often as he could, he crept in the dark to his neighbor's window, but it was never as gratifying as that first time.

Part of his attraction was wanting to know how other people lived. Did they live as he did at his home, with screaming fights and family secrets and strict rules? Or did they live like the families he saw on TV shows, or in some entirely different way? He wondered especially about women and what they did at night when they thought no one was watching.

Now, like a hawk swooping and snatching whatever caught its eye, the grown-up Ronnie hunted through backyards nearly every night, addicted to the voyeuristic thrill of secretly knowing a woman. With favorite targets he acted out a pathological form of foreplay. He broke in when his surveillance told him the woman was at work or on a date. He fondled her slips and bras. He opened closets and stared at her clothes and imagined what she would look like in them. Would I like to go out with her if I saw her in a nightclub? he wondered. He studied snapshots tucked around mirrors or pinned with magnets to the refrigerator. He noticed how clean she kept the place. He took his time after he broke in, because he was getting to know her; he wanted to connect. Would she like me if we met? he always asked himself.

Sometimes he unlocked a window before he left. Later, when the unsuspecting woman was asleep, he would break in. He would find her wallet to learn her name and stare at the photo on her driver's license, checking the license for height and weight. If it indicated he made a mistake, that she was heavy, he would think "fat bitch," steal her money, and sneak out. Sometimes he would just lightly touch the sleeping woman and leave.

The black-haired woman who carried the mail intrigued him, and he began watching her regularly. She kept the house neat and left for work punctually. He liked that. And she loved her little boy. Ronnie never saw her spank him. She seemed like a perfect mother.

One morning, while spying on her through the kitchen window, Ronnie watched and stroked himself as she finished ironing her uniform. Then she took off her robe. He caught his breath. It seemed like he could feel blood pumping to his muscles, making him powerful, a superman. Like the times he had been whacked on coke, only ten times as intense.

Should I go inside?

Ronnie was still amazed that many women didn't take even the simplest precautions. They left windows and doors unlocked. They left first-floor windows open. In warm weather all he had to do was make a hand-sized slit in a screen with his knife and open the window.

Outside the kitchen window he stood in a trancelike high. His penis stung from a friction burn that would raise a scab. Should I do it?

A moment later, the woman pulled on the crisp blue uniform and went into another room. Ronnie zipped up and left. At the sidewalk he whispered to himself, as he always did when nothing terrible happened, "Thank you, God."

BETTY OCILKA

Betty Ocilka heard the clunk and figured it was the paperboy throwing the *Plain Dealer* up against the screen door on her back porch. It was about 5:40 A.M., April 13, 1984, and she came downstairs to the kitchen in a fluffy terry cloth robe and started ironing her mail carrier's uniform. Some mail carriers didn't care how their uniforms looked, but Betty always wanted to look sharp. She had started delivering mail at nineteen, trudging twelve miles a day, shouldering a sack that might weigh forty-five pounds at the start of her route. Few women carried mail then, and now, more than a decade later, she still took pride in her job.

She turned off the hot steam iron and stepped away from the board. As she pulled up the uniform pants under her bathrobe, a man with a pink and blue stocking cap pulled over his face rushed from the tiny pantry and put a choke lock around her neck with his left arm. His right hand pointed a knife at her neck. Betty screamed, and instantly he clamped her windpipe tight.

"I'll kill you if you make any noise," he said.

She gasped for air, shaking, the knife now at her sternum. This can't be happening, she thought. He walked her into the living room in what seemed to be slow motion. She felt wiry hands push her to the couch, fondle her breasts, and yank down her pants.

She had to do something. "I'm having my period." She squirmed, then went limp, and tried again to break free.

"Don't move," he hissed. "I don't want to hurt you, but I will."

Betty tried not to cry. She didn't want her three-year-old son to hear her. Whenever he heard her cry, he ran up and hugged her and tried to make her feel better. If her boy toddled downstairs and the attacker moved to him, Betty knew she would try to kill the bastard. It would be his body or hers when the police arrived.

Now she felt the edge of the blade press into her neck, pulling the skin tight across her voice box. She trembled and prayed, God, I want to see my baby grow up. She wasn't ready to die, and she found herself submitting. He forced her head down, his touch making her flesh crawl, then a moment later told her to swallow.

"I need money," he said as he let her up. She left and went in the kitchen and found all her cash—$21. He was behind her with the knife.

"I'll write you a blank check," she said. She just wanted him to go. She would do anything, as long as it did not wake up her son.

He shut her in the bathroom. "Don't come out and don't call the police. If you do, I'll know and I'll come back."

She heard steps, a door being opened, then silence. She felt vulnerable standing there, but it was a couple of minutes before she ran out and called the Cleveland police. She vaulted the stairs, looking for her son. He was not in his crib, and she panicked. The bastard kidnapped him!

She ran frantically from room to room. The second time through her room she threw aside the bunched-up quilt on her bed, and there was her boy, asleep. He had never before climbed out of his crib and into her empty bed. Now she was even more devastated. He must have heard something frightening and sought comfort. Thank God he didn't come downstairs.

Betty wanted a stiff drink, something to calm her down, but instead brewed some coffee. She quickly drank two cups, black, rinsing her mouth repeatedly. She felt defiled and wanted to flush out every trace of what had happened.

Soon two Cleveland police patrolmen from the nearby Second

District station arrived and said they would take her and her son to Deaconess Hospital, only a few minutes away.

In the hospital examining room, Betty told a nurse what had happened. "Did you shower or use mouthwash?" the nurse asked.

"No, but I drank about ten cups of hot coffee to rinse my mouth."

"That was evidence. You rinsed away the evidence."

The remark made Betty mad. "What was I supposed to do?"

"You could have spit it out, into a cup maybe."

"How do you spit it out when he's holding a knife at your throat?"

Betty felt the nurse's manner soften as she went through the checklist of rape victim procedures. The trauma room nurses at Deaconess Hospital treated several rape victims a week, using Mark-It rape kits to collect evidence. In the examining room, a nurse cut a piece of Betty's hair to include in the kit. She also collected pubic hair specimens and asked her to urinate in a cup.

Then she turned off the lights and flicked on an ultraviolet light that bathed Betty's mouth and lower body in a purple glow. "Semen shines under this light," the nurse explained as she wiped the inside of Betty's throat with a long swab.

Betty felt as if she were being tuned up by a mechanic in a garage. Everything was cold as steel.

BOB MATUSZNY

Detective Bob Matuszny slapped his briefcase down on the punched-out metal desk in the detective squad room at the Second District police headquarters. The lieutenant looked up. Bob was hard to miss: six-foot-two, 220 pounds, a thick brown mustache that stretched ear to ear, a massive chest, and arms that had bench-pressed 400 pounds until he tore up a shoulder.

"We got another rape early this morning," the lieutenant told him.

Bob found a copy of a Form 10 on the top of a stack of daily felony reports. As he read through the field report made out by the patrolmen who handled Betty Ocilka's call, he felt his guts tighten. Oh, Christ, not Betty. She delivered mail on the side streets around Second District headquarters, and Bob occasionally saw her on break at C&J Donuts, a popular cop stop just across from the station house.

Bob had also known Betty's late husband, a Cleveland policeman in the Second who had killed himself, a not uncommon occupational hazard for big-city cops weary of the unrelenting misery. Bob was glad he had developed his own defense against the toxic by-products of the job—he power-lifted almost daily, with the heaviest weights he could manage.

There was another reason the rape report chilled Bob: It was familiar. A week earlier, he and his partner, Phil Parrish, had investigated the rape of a forty-one-year-old waitress, Joy Vandella,* who lived two blocks from Betty Ocilka. He mentally noted the similarities:

Young guy, white, thin.

Uses a knife.

Attacks in the early morning.

Speaks quietly, says, "I need money. I'm not going to hurt you if you do what I say."

Forces oral sex first, all the time fondling breasts, saying, "Don't look at me."

Takes their money, then locks them in the bathroom.

The waitress told them the rapist had a raised scar or bump on his penis. Betty Ocilka's preliminary report did not mention this.

Minutes later, Phil Parrish arrived. Matuszny and Parrish were probably the best, most experienced team of detectives in the Second District. Both grew up on the rough South Side, and they had gone to South High School together. Their personalities complemented each other. Bob was quiet and headstrong, intense almost to the point of being high-strung. Red-haired and stocky, Phil could gab for hours to a total stranger. He liked to clown around, finding it a good way to break up the drudgery and horror of the job.

"Hey, look at this." Bob flipped the hour-old crime report to Phil.

Phil scanned the two-page complaint. "You think this is the same guy?"

"I sure do."

By nine o'clock that morning, they located Betty Ocilka in the Deaconess emergency room, talking to a friend, somewhat calmer from the 10 milligrams of Valium a doctor had given her.

"Sorry about what happened to you," Bob told her. "We're here to help you all we can. If there is anything you need, just tell us."

They carefully took Betty through a moment-by-moment account of the rape. She seemed annoyed at having to describe

---

*Not her real name.

the crime again. She had already narrated it to the two uniformed policemen, to a nurse, to a doctor, and to a friend.

"We have to ask these questions to help us catch him. Please don't be offended," Bob said, "but we have to know exactly what he did to you and exactly what he said."

Unlike the patrol officers who made the initial report, the detectives needed to know the attacker's precise words, when he said them, the exact order of his sexual predations.

"Anything unusual about his genitals?" Bob wanted to know.

"He had a bump or something near the end of it," Betty said. "A rough area, kind of raised up or something."

That cinched it. They knew dead solid certain they were dealing with a serial rapist.

"I wonder if he's hitting anywhere else?" Phil mused after they left the hospital.

Bob had a vague memory of a similar case. Back at the detective bureau he hunted for the report in the unsolved-felony folders in a battered tower of file drawers, until he found what he was looking for—the Jane Lamb* case, October 5, 1983.

He glanced through it, and remembered that he had done the initial spadework. She was a nice-looking woman, twenty-three, her boyfriend a Teamsters business agent at the factory where they worked. She had just moved into the Fulton Parkway apartments, a first-floor unit, and hadn't put up drapes or unpacked. She hadn't wanted to go to the emergency room, but Bob had gradually persuaded her to do it. He had lifted fingerprints and canvassed the neighbors, quickly exhausting all leads.

Now Jane Lamb's address caught his eye. She lived only a few blocks from these two recent rapes. Each was only a few dozen steps from the woods surrounding Brookside Park.

"One guy is doing all this," he said to Phil. "This one has gotta be his. We got a serial rapist out there."

Bob and Phil talked and decided to take their suspicions to their boss, Lieutenant Robert Howell. Maybe he would free them up and they could work pretty much full-time on this case.

---

*Not her real name.

As far as supervisors went, the two detectives liked Howell. He didn't hand out an assignment and forget about it. He read, analyzed, and stayed on top of all their reports. He gave plenty of rein to the self-starters, and ran herd on the rest.

In Howell's office, Phil gave him a brief sketch of the cases. Howell didn't need to hear much. He had already picked up on the remarkable similarities in the two recent rape cases when he read the Ocilka crime report that morning.

"Any lifts?" Howell asked.

"We lifted prints on all of them, but we haven't heard if they're the suspect's."

After listening to them for a few minutes, Howell asked, "Well, what do you really think?"

"The guy is going to be a problem in our district," Bob said.

"Okay, do what you have to do," Howell said.

"Work the case exclusively?"

"Whatever it takes," the lieutenant said.

BETTY OCILKA

The month before she was raped, Betty Ocilka completed an alcohol abuse program and was working her way through thirteen weeks of group meetings. The day after the rape, her counselor called, wanting to know why she'd missed a session.

Betty told him about the rape. After responding supportively, he asked, "Did you have alcohol in the house?"

"Yes."

"Did you take a drink?"

"Yeah, I had something to drink. Coffee. I drank black coffee."

The counselor said he was impressed. Here she was, fresh out of treatment, subjected to terrible trauma, and still sober, even though she had a bottle of booze within reach. She was one tough lady.

On her first day back at work, her coworkers presented her with a small decorative wooden box. They had taken up a collection, and the box held $80 in folded bills. There was also a beautiful basket of flowers. Betty cried and thanked everybody.

At her next counseling session, a week later, the doctor who had supervised her treatment asked her to come into his office. She owed him $600, the deductible amount not covered by her health insurance plan.

"If you had liquor in the house and didn't touch it after what you went through, you're very far along," the doctor said. "You're going to make it, Betty."

She didn't know what to say.

"I'm really proud of you," he said. "Forget about your bill. It's been taken care of."

Betty was moved. The man had just erased a $600 debt. Everybody was being so nice to her.

Vic Kovacic

A day or two later, Cleveland Police Sergeant Vic Kovacic, supervisor of the Scientific Investigations Unit, came to work to find, as usual, a stack of emergency room rape kits on a counter. The stack of kits, looking like a pile of box lunches, held the sex crimes evidence compiled in emergency rooms over the past three days. Soon Kovacic's serologists and technicians would be up to their rubber gloves in the blood, hair, sputum, and secretions of strangers, analyzing the kits' contents, performing the unheralded work that cracks criminal cases.

Kovacic, trim, handsome, and nattily dressed for a cop, had grown up in Cleveland's Slovenian neighborhood along St. Clair Avenue. He had dreamed of being a big-league pitcher, but after a couple of years in the minors, he turned to police work. Now he ran the SIU, which occupied half a floor at the Cleveland police headquarters. Its rooms and labs were filled with expensive gear: microscopes, polygraph equipment, tiny refrigerators lined with tubes of blood and sputum, ballistics tanks to identify bullets, X-ray machines, image enhancers that detected forgeries, and other sorts of high-tech gadgets.

Janet Chariac,* a serologist, had started on one of the new rape kits. She took the crime report number off the kit's property tag and called the report up on the SIU computer terminal. Kovacic insisted that all the techs read the crime reports before analyzing forensic specimens collected from victims.

---

*Not her real name.

Janet found such reports tremendously useful. They helped her decide where to look for trace evidence. Depending on how the crime was committed, she might look for semen on a victim's hair sample or on a piece of clothing. If the report noted a struggle, she'd make sure to look for skin or blood traces on fingernail trimmings.

This latest report frightened her. The victim, Betty Ocilka, was raped in her home only a couple of blocks from where Janet lived with her parents in what was supposed to be a safe neighborhood. And the week before, one block over, another woman was raped under similar circumstances. Janet worked with crime reports all day, and it did not bother her, but now her job was reaching into her home life and that made her nervous.

Janet broke the seal on the rape kit, signed her initials, and removed two test tubes that held cotton swabs of the victim's vaginal fluid. She cut off a piece of cotton and placed it on white filter paper in a dish on her desk.

She dribbled on a few drops of acid phosphatase, a reagent that identified a protein found in semen. The paper turned deep purple. Good—probably a positive specimen.

She smeared a glass slide with the swab and slipped it under her microscope lens. In a moment, she had some immobile sperm cells in focus. Great—evidence. Now she wouldn't have to fool with the more difficult and time-consuming sperm detection tests.

She dribbled another reagent on the sperm slide and came up with the blood type of whoever left the sperm. It was Type O blood, the most common, with an ABO secretor status.

She didn't need to analyze hair and saliva samples, since she already had a positive sperm result and the blood type of its secretor. She resealed the forensic kit with tape, initialed it, and sent it to the main police property room for cataloging and storage. She labeled the stains and vaginal swabs with the rape case number and stored that evidence in the massive Scientific Unit freezer.

That was the easy part. Now she had to share her worries.

She dropped into Vic's office. The latest forensic science journals were piled neatly on a bookcase. Parts of homemade bombs sat on the top shelf. She had heard stories of how her boss, during the city's Mafia wars several years back, had defused three live bombs in a twenty-four-hour period. His expertise made him fearless.

"There was another rape in the Second last night," she told him. "They're all right in my neighborhood and it looks like the same guy is doing it. Everything is the same."

Vic called up the reports and noted the similarities. It was uncanny. But he also knew that *all* stranger rapists were serial rapists. The only difference was how soon you caught them in their chain of crimes.

"I think you're right," he said. He saw Matuszny's name on two of the reports, and smiled. The department had three hundred detectives, but only two dozen were top-notch. Bob Matuszny was definitely top-notch.

"We're going to keep an eye on this," Vic told her. She felt better. After she left his office Vic took a blank file folder and wrote "West Side Rapist" across the top.

RONNIE

Ronnie pulled his motorcycle into the driveway behind his parents' home. He wasn't expected, but he needed a shower and something to eat.

In the kitchen were his sister Maria and Rada, whom he hadn't seen in months. Since Ronnie had introduced her to his family, Rada had been the recipient of his sister's smothering attention. Rada found Maria Shelton to be a sweet woman, concerned about clothes and hair and finding a husband, but incredibly naive about sex. She was very religious, accompanying her mother every Sunday to services at the fundamentalist Church of God of Prophecy. She and Rada often went out together, but Maria was oddly unreliable. Many times after they made plans Maria never showed up; nor did she call or apologize. Maria also talked about wanting to lose weight so her breasts would be smaller and had even asked Rada to help her shop for a minimizer bra. Whereas Ronnie was fixated on women's breasts, Maria seemed to hate them.

Ronnie said hello to the two women and made himself a sandwich. He was standing in the kitchen, eating, when his mother, Katy, rushed in, screaming. She slapped Ronnie and he backed away, the sandwich in his hand, his other arm up to ward off her blows. She yelled about crumbs on the floor, the mess he was making in the kitchen she had just cleaned. He let her vent her anger. He had been through these inexplicable flare-ups hundreds of times.

"Look, I'm just going to take a shower and leave," he told her.

That set off Katy once more. She hit him again and screamed, "You get the towels wet, the floor wet. You make a mess." She tried to hit him, but he danced away and locked the bathroom door.

The blowup with his mother must have triggered something in Ronnie. After his shower, he found Rada talking to his sister in Maria's bedroom and broke in on their conversation.

"Who are you dating?" Ronnie asked Maria.

"Nobody in particular," she replied.

Her answer angered him and he moved in closer. "Are you sleeping with somebody?"

Maria hated this routine. "Leave me alone, Ron. We're talking."

"Are you still a virgin?" he demanded.

41

She was, but she also was sick of her brother's possessiveness. "None of your business."

"You answer me."

She threw a Kleenex box at him and he grabbed her wrist and started slapping her face. She screamed.

Rada stood up, mouth open, wanting to do something.

"Stay out of this, Rada," Ronnie warned. "This is family business. Stay out." Ever since he was a child, Ronnie had felt it was his job to punish Maria. He had to keep her under control. It was his business to insure her virginity for the Shelton family honor.

Maria broke loose and ran out, crying. Ronnie turned to Rada and said, "I'll kill anyone who has sex with my sister."

Ronnie had always been overwhelmingly protective of his sister and never liked anyone she dated. To outsiders, though, he probably seemed more like a jealous lover than a brother. Maria hated it. Once, after a bitter fight, she went to the living room and scratched out the eyes in a large studio portrait of Ronnie.

When they were children, Maria had been a mystery to him. Two years younger, she was nearly his size. In stores or at church, strangers remarked how pretty she was, and even as a young boy, he felt that his parents favored her. Standing in the side yard one summer day, Ronnie got Maria to pull down her pants. The two young children sat looking at each other, his hands exploring, until their mother's screams pierced the morning and they both jumped up. She was in the upstairs window, looking down, her face twisted, her mouth wide. Ronnie had never heard such a shriek. Its tone and fury told him something terrible had happened. In a moment, she was outside. She jerked his arm and pulled him toward the house, her free hand slapping his face. He did not completely understand her screams, half of which were in Spanish, but he knew he had been bad to make his mother this upset.

After she beat him, she sent him to his room. There he worried about what his father would do when he got home from the mill, but hours later, when Ronnie was called down to dinner, his father didn't raise a hand or say a word. For the moment Ronnie was happy. Later he figured out that what he had done was so terrible that his mom couldn't bring herself to tell his dad, fearing he'd go crazy. Ronnie looked at her and prayed that this would always be one of their special secrets.

His mother's lesson never left him: He had done something dirty and shameful that day, and he deserved what he had gotten. He told himself to try to be a good boy.

BOB MATUSZNY

In the first days after his lieutenant approved the full-time manhunt, Detective Bob Matuszny felt a strange exhilaration. He was free from nickel-and-dime assignments and could focus on one major case.

His euphoria was tempered by the knowledge that if he and his partner didn't come up with something solid in a few weeks, there would be pressure to at least show something worthwhile for all the time spent. Phil Parrish was under less pressure than Bob, because Phil was a short-timer: He had passed the sergeant's examination and was waiting for a June assignment, six weeks away. He would leave behind Bob and the life of a detective, which he regretted, but Phil had a big family and felt compelled to climb the ranks.

Bob and Phil canvassed the city's five other district detective bureaus. They asked each bureau's "office man" (a sergeant in charge of assigning and tracking cases) to alert them to recent unsolved rapes that fit the modus operandi of the young man they were now calling "the West Side Rapist," in particular those in which a victim described her attacker as having a bump on his penis.

Within a day, Bob heard of two rape cases from Sergeant Paul Jones in the Fourth District, which included the Slavic Village neighborhood just east of the Flats and the steel mills. Jones supervised uniformed officers who worked in the department's black-and-white zone cars.

First, Jones told them about an older woman raped on Covert Street, a fairly well-kept residential street of mostly older couples of Eastern European descent: "White male breaks in, rapes white female, age fifty-one, then locks her and her granddaughter, age three, in a bathroom." It had happened only a couple of months before, on February 2, 1984.

Jones said he thought he had seen everything in his twenty-five years on the job, but this rape upset him so much it made him feel like a rookie cop. "Raping a grandmother with her granddaughter right there," he said in disgust.

"No signs of a break-in, nothing," Jones went on. "The house was a two-story, windows and screens intact. No pry marks. Just a bunch of her bras and panties thrown all over at the bottom of the stairs in the living room."

"Sounds like the guy's got an underwear fetish," Bob said. "Anything unusual about him physically?"

"She said he had a bump at the end of his penis. A growth or something."

"Hey, so did our guy," Bob said.

"Her daughter lives there and said her ex-husband has a little growth on his prick. I think he might be the perpetrator. She says he's the crazy-jealous type. Counted her underpanties when he got home from work to make sure she wasn't stepping out on him, crap like that."

Bob asked Jones about the second case.

"Same description, same everything," the sergeant said. A twenty-five-year-old woman on Rosewood, Christy Cosimen.*

---

*Not her real name.

Only she won't talk to the detectives. She got a good look at the suspect, but her husband says no, don't talk about it."

Bob thanked him for the fill-in. He and Phil talked about the two new cases and decided it now seemed likely that one suspect was responsible for these two as well as for the three rapes in their own district. It made sense to consolidate all five cases and work them together. That meant they had five chances for an eyewitness or a lucky break.

They gave their lieutenant an update. "The guy is going to make a mistake," Bob said. "We'll catch him before summer. We've got some good eyewitness descriptions. And there's that bump."

"That could be the breakthrough," Phil said. "We get a suspect, someone who matches the composite, we make him expose his prick and see if there's a boil on it. Hit him with that and—bam—he'll fold."

"Probably confess before he pulls his pants back up," Bob said.

"I hope so," the lieutenant said. He cleared it for them to take over the two Fourth District rape cases. The detectives in the Fourth were happy to dump the cases, since their district had the highest crime rate in the city.

The next day, Bob and Phil arrived at the Second District squad room early, eager to hit the streets. First, for identification purposes, they needed a diagram of a penis to show victims. They went to the Cleveland Public Library, where they asked a short, silver-haired librarian for help.

"Oh, yes," she said enthusiastically. "I think we can find it." After a few minutes, she opened a medical book and called across the crowded reading room, "Oh, Officer." The room of patrons looked up and saw her displaying a diagram of a large penis. "Here's a nice one!" she said to the detectives.

Embarrassed by all the stares, Matuszny thanked her, took the book, and ran off copies on the duplicating machine. Later that day copies of the diagram were given to two victims, Betty Ocilka and Joy Vandella. The detectives sequestered them and asked each to mark the location of the rapist's penile wart.

The two women circled the same spot.

Things were coming together well, Bob felt. On April 15, 1984, he and Phil brought Betty Ocilka and Joy Vandella to police headquarters to meet Detective Andrew Charchenko. Charchenko, short and roly-poly, was a university-trained artist. He politely escorted the women into a darkened room with a slide projector and chairs. Charchenko clicked through a dozen carousels of slides of different shapes of heads, eyes, noses, mouths, and chins. Slowly, painfully, struggling with imprecise recollections, the two rape victims picked out the composite parts.

Later that day Charchenko went to work. Using a soft-lead pencil, referring to notes and the slides, he crafted a composite sketch. It took about an hour.

That night, Bob and Phil made dozens of copies of the composite sketch and distributed them in taverns, bowling alleys, and pizza parlors on the West Side. A few of the five rape victims had noted that their attacker had professionally cut hair, long and feathered in the back, not the kind of cut you would get at a barbershop. The detectives posted the composite sketch at dozens of hair salons, too.

Sooner or later, they felt, the asshole was going to make a mistake, and they'd be there waiting.

A week later, about eleven at night, Detective Charchenko had a taste for cabbage pierogies and stopped at the BKS Tavern, a bar owned by a Ukrainian family who served authentic pierogies and stews. The BKS, located across the street from the Second District station, was often full of cops unwinding after second shift.

In the middle of his meal, Charchenko looked up. A man walked in who looked just like the composite he had drawn of the West Side Rapist. The man was wearing dirty white tennis shoes with blue stripes, just as Betty Ocilka had described.

Charchenko calmly went to the telephone and called across

the street to Second District headquarters. "This guy looks like the composite. I think it's him. He's wanted for five rapes."

"Andy, it's shift change now," the deskman said. "I don't have anybody to arrest him."

Charchenko decided he'd have to enjoy pierogies later. He walked over and arrested the man, telling him he was a suspect in a rape case.

The man said his name was Espiridion Feliciano and insisted they had the wrong man.

In a while, Matuszny and Parrish came on shift, heard of the arrest, and hurried excitedly to the Second District jail. There they questioned Feliciano about what he did for a living, where he lived, and where he was at the times of the rapes.

He had alibis for everything, and Bob felt his hopes dim. But might as well go the whole nine yards, he figured.

"The guy we're looking for has something a little different about his penis, okay, so . . . we'd like you to drop your pants and show us your penis so we can make a determination."

"What if I don't feel like it?" Feliciano asked.

"Then you're still an active suspect and we'll continue to investigate you. I think you'll want to help yourself out by eliminating yourself as a suspect."

Feliciano said okay and they took him into the men's room. No bump. The detectives let him go.

May–June 1984

BOB MATUSZNY

By early May, Bob Matuszny and his partner had worked a couple of weeks full-time chasing the West Side Rapist. Already they were heading into dead ends in the two cases the Fourth District detectives sent over.

The prime suspect in the rape of the fifty-one-year-old woman was her wacky former son-in-law with the penile wart. When it turned out he was at work at the time of the crime, he was dropped as a suspect.

In the other case, twenty-five-year-old Christy Cosimen was now willing to tell police that her attacker knocked on her door, pushed his way in with a knife, and raped her. He was thin, white, and spoke with a quiet voice, saying, "Do what I say and you won't get hurt." And, on his penis, the telltale bump.

What excited Bob was that the woman got a long look at the rapist. Depending on her eye for detail, she could help the police artist make an accurate sketch. She represented the first significant breakthrough in the case. Unfortunately, the victim's husband, struggling with the trauma of what had happened to his wife, was still telling her not to get involved.

When he heard this, Bob wasn't surprised. He had often seen a husband or boyfriend show more shame and embarrassment than the victim. For rape investigators, it was a frequent and frustrating development. But Bob pressed on. He asked a female detective in the Fourth District to interview the reluctant victim, to try to draw her out in a low-key way.

"Promise her anything," Bob instructed. "Tell her she won't have to testify, she won't have to come to court, nothing. If she'll just sit down with the artist for a few minutes."

But the victim—still terrified, her husband resolute—refused to meet with the artist.

Bob wasn't happy with the news. Well, nothing to lose by coming on strong, he figured. He called the victim. "Please, just give us a few minutes with our artist," he pleaded. "I promise you no involvement. No name. You don't have to testify. Help us nail him before he attacks another woman like yourself."

She didn't say anything, and Bob took this as a good sign. "I've seen this kind of criminal," he went on. "He keeps going until he gets caught. You've got to help us. You've got to help the other women out there. You're the only hope. Please, help us make a sketch."

It was working—she was staying on the phone. Then a man's voice came across the line. "Leave her alone!" Click.

Bob slammed the phone. "Dammit!" He felt like kicking a hole in his desk. He couldn't wait to pump iron after work.

On May 6, late in the evening, two Second District patrolmen spotted a man waiting for a bus that went over the Harvard-Denison Bridge, a huge span that connects the banks of the Cuyahoga River, two hundred feet above a tangle of steel mills and slag mounds and railroad tracks. He looked like the rape suspect that they had been briefed about at the daily roll call: white male, not too tall, thin build, brown hair, possibly Hispanic. Moreover, the bus cut through Slavic Village, near the site of several crime scenes. They arrested him and notified the detective bureau.

Bob and Phil came in the next day and, in a glance, Bob knew in his gut the man was not the West Side Rapist. But rather than cut him loose, the two detectives decided to conduct a lineup and let the rape victims look at the suspect. This was smart office politics. They remembered their days as patrolmen when they felt mistreated by the detective bureau. They would make a collar on a detective bureau case, based on a composite sketch or an ID disseminated at roll call, and often the detectives never thanked them or even told them what happened to their collar. Sometimes detectives would cut the suspect loose without any explanation to the arresting team in the patrol car.

It wasn't until Bob became a detective that he realized that a skilled investigator immersed in the details of a major case could immediately spot clashes and inconsistencies and eliminate a suspect in minutes.

So on May 7, he and Phil Parrish brought in Betty Ocilka and Joy Vandella to a lineup room. Then the detectives brought in two other men from the district jail who were white and roughly the suspect's age. The suspect was five-foot-nine, 150 pounds, and nervous.

On command, he and the other two men stood and turned to their right, then left. Behind the one-way glass, the two women looked them over, safe from the men's stone-cold stares. They were unable to make an identification.

By now Bob and Phil were checking about two West Side Rapist look-alikes a week, men that roughly fit the composite and were turned in by police in patrol cars or by callers who had seen the composite sketch in a bowling alley or beauty shop. It seemed as if every other day Bob and Phil had some guy in the men's room with his pants down, proving himself to be wart-free. Before long, the other detectives began razzing Bob and Phil, calling them the "pecker checkers."

Bob was weary of inspecting the privates of every rape suspect who surfaced, but felt the informal inspections were a quick, if unorthodox, way to eliminate possible suspects. No one outside the police district knew about the bump on the suspect's penis, and all the detectives and supervisors knew enough to keep it that way. It was their unique identifier, their secret ace in the hole.

RONNIE

When he wasn't staying overnight with a girlfriend, Ronnie slept at War Avenue in the downstairs bedroom that had been his parents'. The place was a mess. He never cooked or cleaned. Once every other week, his sister or mother came over with food and vacuumed and scrubbed.

Ronnie did not have a job. In the spring he had worked briefly as a counterman at an auto parts store and behind the cash register at a pizza parlor, but he always quit or got fired. Because he prowled all night, he couldn't get up early enough in the morning for a regular job.

When he did get up before evening, he drove a few minutes to his friend Danny Todd's house and hung out. When Ronnie had met him, he'd learned Danny had something going he didn't want anyone to know about. Danny worked sometimes as a carpenter, and had home security that was unusual for his block in Slavic Village. He had installed double-locked Andersen windows throughout the house, a rarity in the neighborhood, and had reinforced the front door with a steel jamb and dead bolts. Later he would surround his lot with an eight-foot board-on-board fence, and on its driveway gate hang a warning sign: "Premises patrolled by K-9 dog." It wasn't true, but who would take the chance to find out? Then Danny built a new garage, with padlocked doors, where he stored his tools. That's why he needed security—the tools—Danny would explain.

But as Ronnie learned, Danny Todd cultivated marijuana

plants in the basement under powerful grow lights. He also fenced tools and electronic gear. Soon Ronnie was bringing over VCRs and TVs and other valuable items for Danny to fence.

During this time, Ronnie went out on the small remodeling jobs Danny scared up, working as a carpenter's helper for $5 an hour. Ronnie was proud to be learning a skill and used it to explain to his father what he did during the days.

Ronnie knew he confounded Danny. He was broke one day and flush the next. Sometimes he'd stop in at Danny's house in the early morning, looking haggard, after a night of peeping in windows or worse. When Danny came back in the late afternoon, he'd find Ronnie still sleeping on a couch.

On days when Danny didn't work, he and Ronnie would have girlfriends over for the afternoon. If weather permitted, the women sunbathed in the backyard while the two young men worked out on the bench and weight racks Danny set up in the empty dining room. With the stereo playing soft funk, the two bare-chested men grunted through sets of presses and squats. After showers, he and Danny took turns bringing their dates into the bedroom for sex. Afterward Ronnie had his girlfriend of the week give him a bath.

Ronnie was obsessed with cleanliness. He recalled that his mother had bathed him until he was a teenager, checking to make sure he was clean, even between his legs. But it made him uncomfortable to think about it, so he never mentioned it to Danny. He just knew he liked to be clean for the girls and he wanted them to be clean for him. He wasn't going to make love to a woman with some other guy's touch on her.

Bob Matuszny

By mid-May 1984 Detectives Matuszny and Parrish had no progress to report on the hunt for the West Side Rapist. So they decided to cast a wider net. Bob and Phil sent a bulletin about the rapist to police departments in the suburbs that hemmed in the West Side. In it they described the West Side Rapist and asked for cases that appeared to be similar, especially those in which victims, in describing their attacker, mentioned anything "abnormal about his genitals."

Within a week, they heard from Parma, Parma Heights, and Middleburg Heights, middle-class suburbs southwest of Cleveland. Each suburb had unsolved rape cases that fit the modus operandi of the West Side Rapist: Parma had two, the others one each.

A few days later, Bob, Phil, and detectives from the other departments met at the Parma police station and shared information. Afterward, Bob photocopied all their reports.

Matuszny noted that the two Parma rapes were at the same apartment complex, the Pleasant Lake Apartments off York Road. One victim, a pregnant woman, Jeannine Graham,* was attacked about 3 A.M. The other, a fifty-four-year-old woman, was raped while her granddaughter slept in the next room.

With the four additional suburban rape cases, Bob and Phil now had nine crimes strongly linked to the same suspect.

---

*Not her real name.

Further, a complete review of all unsolved rapes from the Second and Fourth Districts turned up three more rapes the West Side Rapist had possibly committed. Now they decided to design a surveillance plan to sell to their supervisors. It would take hours of overtime, and the city's budget was strapped, but they knew that the number, a dozen rapes, would soften up the police brass.

The story of a serial rapist hitting the West Side and nearby suburbs had not yet been exposed in the Cleveland *Plain Dealer* or on local TV stations. However, at crime watch meetings in the "raping" zones of Cleveland, people knew of rapes near their own blocks, and they were increasingly frightened. Cleveland City Councilman Joe Cannon, who represented the middle-class area around the Cleveland Metropolitan Zoo, complained about the rapist to the Second District police commander. Cannon said his constituents were demanding more police protection.

There was little police brass could say except that they were working on it. Actually, apart from rapes, Cleveland was becoming safer. Car thefts, burglaries, and other serious felonies were down. The homicide rate was at a seventeen-year low. But rapes were up 18 percent, and even that figure missed the mark—the Cleveland Rape Crisis Center said the number of women calling in to report they had been raped was twice that of the official Cleveland police statistic.

For a tangle of troubling reasons, rape victims still were not calling the police. If they had, Detective Matuszny probably would have had twenty-five cases linked to the West Side Rapist at this point.

Responding to neighborhood fears, as well as recognizing the merit of Matuszny and Parrish's plan, the Second District commander approved an expensive surveillance detail. The surveillance would concentrate on what police dispatchers termed Zone 223, the sixty-block area where the rapist was hitting. From midnight to early morning, three two-man detective teams would work the area in unmarked cars. The zone cars, "black-and-whites," would cruise the area as usual but would not respond to call-in complaints about rapes, burglaries, break-ins, trespassing, suspicious people, and so on. Instead, Matuszny and Parrish and the other detectives would slip in silently in unmarked cars. The first car in would cover the house or apartment. The other unmarked cars on the scene would go directly to woods or gullies or natural cover, if any, or search a two-block perimeter of the crime scene, hunting for anyone on foot or walking to a car. They would grab everything that moved.

"If the asshole hits during this detail, we'll nail him," Matuszny said.

By late May, Bob and Phil sat at night in an unmarked car parked on crime-scene streets such as Muriel or Fulton Parkway, watching, waiting. Some nights, on the side streets, sitting in the car with the windows down and trees rustling overhead, Bob swore he could feel the rapist's presence. "He's right out there watching us wait for him," he told Parrish.

"He ain't that smart."

"Then how come he hasn't hit anyone since we've been out here?"

Matuszny had a point.

The surveillance detail dragged on for the next several weeks: night after night of sitting in an unmarked car, moving from residential street to street, talking about the case. During one such night, after brainstorming, Bob and Phil came up with a new tactic that was based on two unrelated facts of the case:

Fact one, a large number of the attacks were a few blocks from the No. 79 bus route, which started downtown, came up Fulton Road through the West Side, and ended its run at the Pleasant Lake Apartments. Two rapes had occurred there. Fact two, none of the rape victims or their neighbors reported hearing or seeing a car leave the crime scene.

Hunch: Maybe the guy rode the bus.

Phil and Bob started tailing the No. 79 bus at night and in the early morning, checking out all the men boarding it. If a lone white male who fit the description climbed aboard, Bob got on the bus, dropping in his fare like a regular rider, and sat behind the suspect, scrutinizing him. A few stops later Bob got off and Phil picked him up. They did this time after time, without success.

Bob and Phil even interviewed each of the No. 79 bus drivers at the end of the run at the Pleasant Lake Apartments, a complex in Parma. They showed the pencil-sketch composite, but not one of the drivers could recall such a passenger.

Matuszny was coming in early, staying late, and not putting in for overtime because he knew it would not be approved. The police budget was strapped. None of his Second District supervisors was complaining, but Bob felt pressure to come up with something. By mid-June, after six weeks of surveillance, he and Phil had run into a dead end. There were no more leads to track down. At the same time, newspapers and TV stations started nibbling around the story, and public pressure to crack the case intensified. Publicity about a crime wave cut both ways. It flushed out tipsters, but it also frightened the citizenry.

At home, desperate to unwind, Bob couldn't keep from going over the case constantly. He knew he shouldn't be taking the case so personally, but he couldn't help it. He found himself driving around the crime scenes, again and again, grasping for anything he might have missed the first time, his mood darkening.

In late June of 1984, the brass decided to pull in the special rape detail. It hadn't turned up anything. The decision was correct, Bob felt, but still he was frustrated.

At the same time, Phil, now officially a sergeant, was reassigned to the downtown district. The split was more painful than Bob had expected. The guy knew him better than anyone else, and he was going to miss him.

Now, Bob realized, the West Side Rapist was truly his case; it rode his shoulders, and his alone. He would become the hero for cracking the case, or the chump detective outwitted by a sex freak hiding out in the bushes.

MARIAN BUTLER

On June 22, Marian Butler was relaxing in her living room, watching television with her friend Sue, when a handsome newscaster caught their attention. He gravely told of a young man, possibly Hispanic, who was raping women throughout Cleveland's West Side.

"One look at this body and he'd run the other way," Marian Butler said, laughing. She had a stout trunk that dropped straight down from broad shoulders. She did not wear makeup or attempt much with her short hair.

Sue laughed nervously. "You live on the first floor, Marian. You of all people shouldn't laugh."

Marian, a divorced office worker, was glad to have such a good friend living half a block away, but Sue worried too much. Marian felt she could handle whatever raw deal came her way. Like her mother, she was as stubborn as a stump. When she was sixteen she and her mother had had a fight, and Marian had moved out of the house, taken a job, and finished high school on her own.

Now, twenty-one years later, she lived in a one-bedroom apartment with cathedral ceilings on Valley Forge Drive in Parma Heights, a middle-class suburb of bungalows and retail stores that sprang up in the 1960s to house the autoworkers at the nearby Ford and Chevrolet plants.

On this hot June Friday, Marian spent the early evening planting marigolds in a bed that ran underneath her living room

57

window. All the windows were open because the building's cooling system circulated only a faint stream of chilled air. About midnight, she stubbed out a final cigarette in a tray beside her bed and fell asleep. *Star Trek II: the Wrath of Khan* flickered on the television.

Four hours later, the sound of a door closing jolted her awake. Marian opened her eyes, saw a stranger, and shrieked. The man flew across the room and clamped his hand on her jaw.

"I've got a knife in my pocket and I'll use it if you don't shut up. Don't look at me. Do what I say and you won't get hurt."

His voice was steely calm and soft, the most evil sound Marian had ever heard.

"Where's your money? I need money. Where's your purse?" he demanded. "Do you have any jewelry?"

Good, he's a robber, Marian thought. Maybe he won't kill me.

He began rubbing her under her thin summer nightgown and slid a hand down to her crotch. It seemed like every few seconds he battered her with the threat, "Don't look at me. Look at me and I'll kill you."

Marian felt ice cold all over. "I just had an operation there," Marian said. "The doctors said I can't have sex yet. It'll hurt me." Three weeks earlier, a surgeon had excised a cyst on her pelvis.

"Then you're going to have to give me a hell of blow job, bitch," he said, and pressed his knife.

She decided to do everything he said, fearing that otherwise he would probably kill her. As if a switch had been thrown, Marian felt her eyes and brain floating above her body, calmly memorizing each detail of the rapist: no belt, faded blue jeans, black suede rubber-soled shoes, a waist-length fake leather jacket. Right hand wrapped in an Ace bandage starting at the third knuckle; looks professionally done. Thin, maybe five-foot-eight. Breath that smells like he just ate a mint. She was determined to make the best damn crime report the police had ever seen, even though she quaked with fear and was afraid to let him see her looking at him above his waist.

After the rape she got a chance to look at him. He was sitting on the side of the bed, his profile visible, yanking on the cord to the clock radio. The cord was jammed in tight behind the end table. He got flustered and turned on a light for a moment. Marian burned his face in her memory.

"I want all the money in the house," he said.

Marian got up and found $15 in her purse in the kitchen. Then he grabbed her and pushed her to the bathroom. "Stay in here. Don't come out until I tell you it's okay."

She heard the drawers of her dressers being emptied, then a crash. It sounded like he had kicked out a window screen. She opened the door and ran to the bedroom window.

Now her rage was kindled, and she pushed her head through the curtains. She looked left and right, scanning the dark for a fleeing figure, then dialed the Parma Heights police. "I've just been raped by your friendly Parma Heights rapist," she said sarcastically. Then she called Sue.

Parma police cars roared up before Sue could walk over. Two uniformed men fanned out and looked behind and around the apartment buildings. A few minutes later Detective Ray Hill walked in.

"Would you like coffee? I've made coffee," Marian said. It was just after four in the morning, and she was moving through her morning routine, clinging to everyday motions as if performing them would somehow help her survive.

Hill said thanks for the offer, but declined. A patrolman came in the apartment and said, "He stood in the flowerbed, took out the screen in the living room, and came in."

"Oh, my God, the flowers," Marian cried. "Not my flowers." She was verging on hysteria. "How many did he ruin?"

The patrolman said he wasn't sure.

Marian seized on the flowers. "I have to know. How many? Could you tell me how many?"

He had seen rape victims react like this before and knew to do whatever they wanted to reassure them. The uniformed man went back outside and took a look. "Three, I think," he called in.

Somehow, in getting his answer, Marian felt she had accomplished something, that she was taking back the control the rapist had just wrenched from her.

Hill started a gentle questioning, and Marian gave him a

detailed description. The detective said he was impressed with her precise recall. Later on, he told her, "I think this is the same criminal we've been seeing on the West Side."

"I heard about him on TV," Marian said. "I can't believe it."

Marian got dressed and walked out to the patrol car for the trip to the hospital. She felt as if a neon sign were flashing over her head with huge letters that said, "I was raped." Within minutes, she began to blame herself for the attack. "Why didn't I lock the windows? I should have fought back." She replayed the rape, asking herself what she could have said to make the outcome different. Only later would she learn that such self-destructive behavior is typical among rape victims.

After collecting swabs of possible evidence, the emergency room doctor gave Marian a Valium to help her sleep. Back at her apartment Marian took the pill and stretched out on the couch while Sue stood guard. A few hours later, Marian woke up, surprised she had been able to relax enough to sleep.

"Someday," she said to Sue, "I'm going to testify against that bastard."

Years earlier, Marian had made a tough decision that still haunted her. In 1968, in the days before liberalized abortion, she was single, twenty-two years old, and about to give birth. She let her boyfriend convince her to give up their day-old daughter for adoption. Months later, she married him, but instead of happiness she felt anger and tremendous guilt for having given away her baby. She turned these destructive emotions onto herself and her soon-to-be-former husband.

Being raped changed her emptiness. Within hours of the attack, Marian found a target that masked her pain. Her anger formed a crosshairs on a thin, five-foot-seven young man with a bandaged hand and minty breath. She was obsessed with his capture. She longed to point to him from across a crowded courtroom and shout, "That's the man! He . . . raped . . . ME!" She dreamed of castrating him on a butcher's block.

But first she had to learn to sleep alone in her bedroom. For the first few nights, Marian dozed on the living room couch. And she was afraid to use the closet in the bedroom.

The bastard's won if I keep this up, she told herself one

morning after waking. That night she made the bed and forced herself to lie down on the fresh linens. She thrashed about for a while, her mind wandering back to the attack. But she refused to get up.

The next thing she remembered was waking up in the bedroom, daylight filtering through the blinds. Her body felt okay, signaling her that she must have slept for several hours. "Hey, wait a minute, I slept. I slept!"

Marian jumped up, exhilarated. She felt like she had soloed the Atlantic in a rowboat. "I slept in my bed all night! I'm going to beat that bastard."

But her upbeat mood soon faded. She still was too afraid to go out at night. After work she drove straight to her apartment, arriving about six, then locked the door. Her fright was suffocating, but she couldn't shake free.

Her fear took other forms. If anyone stepped too close to her at work, Marian jumped back. Every man was a suspect. Her once-full social life shriveled. She dropped out of community college because she could not force herself to attend night classes.

Hiding out in her apartment, she felt as if she was losing her mind. She had to do something. After some soul-searching, she decided to buy a gun. With this reassuring hardware in her purse, she felt powerful and scared at the same time. But finally she was able to go out at night, driving with the gun on her lap. In a few weeks, she started taking night classes again.

One of her friends warned her that the gun was too dangerous to carry. "What if you pulled it out on some guy and didn't use it?" the friend asked. "He could take it away and shoot you."

"Look, I know I would use it, I know it in my heart," Marian said. "I've always got a bullet in the pipe, ready to go. I just have the safety on."

One night while driving home from a night class Marian passed a car that was traveling in the opposite direction. The men inside hooted at her and the driver turned the car around quickly through a red light. In her rearview mirror, Marian saw that the men were tailing her. She gripped the gun in her right hand as the car came up behind her. She thought, They want to gang-rape me. She was intensely alert and clammy with fear as she clicked off the gun's safety.

Soon as they try anything, she told herself, empty the clip into them. Shoot first, ask questions later.

After a moment, the car dropped back and turned onto another street. Marian slowed down, shaken by the knowledge that she could shoot to kill.

RONNIE

One afternoon Ronnie slept in his parents' old bedroom at the War Avenue house, exhausted from a full night of club hopping and an early-morning round of voyeurism. He awoke to the sound of a car crunching gravel in the driveway. He cracked the shade. Shit. Dad. His father, Rodney, often showed up at War Avenue on either side of his 3 P.M. shift change at the nearby steel mill.

Ronnie was embarrassed to be found in bed. He could just hear his father: What are you, sleeping? When you gonna get a real job, bud? Ronnie hated it when his dad asked him about work. As an excuse Ronnie would remind his dad about the headaches he suffered after his near-fatal fall the previous summer and the doctor's orders to take it easy. Ronnie had filed a worker's compensation suit against the auto body shop and hoped to get a five-figure settlement from the state.

Ronnie wasn't always embarrassed to see his father. Sometimes he told him about the remodeling jobs he had with Danny Todd and Rodney would show up at the job site. Once in a while

Rodney would find his son sleeping inside Danny's truck. "He said he's got a headache," Danny would explain. Rodney Shelton was grateful Danny was apprenticing his son, but made it clear he didn't think Ronnie would ever amount to much.

Today Ronnie didn't want to face his father, so he ran to the basement. Hiding from his father reminded Ronnie of being a kid again, lying in his bed, fearing the moment when his dad came home from the mill and would hear from Mom about his misbehavior. A week didn't go by when he wasn't hit by his mom or dad, or both, with a board or extension cord or belt.

His mother was the worst. She was erratic, enforcing a rule one day and ignoring it the next. Spurred by his fear of the beatings, he quickly learned to lie. One time when he knew he was in for a switching, he pulled on an extra pair of long pants, a trick he had learned from watching Spanky, Alfalfa, and the rest of the "Little Rascals" on television. His father swung the belt, and, when he heard dull thuds instead of the usual sharp smacks, told Ronnie to pull down his pants. It stung much worse on his bare legs, and Ronnie focused on counting the swipes—"eleven, twelve, thirteen"—to distract himself from the pain.

When it was over he crept off to his upstairs room, a dark, lonely place that had served as the attic, and escaped into a favorite fantasy: His dad was walking across a parking lot to the steel mill with his electrician's tools. A semi-trailer roared through the parking lot and barreled over his father, crushing him like a bug under a boot. With each whipping Ronnie locked tighter and tighter onto this fantasy, a dream as soft and comforting as a baby's blanket. He would make the sign of the cross and pray silently: "I believe in you, God. I hope you're listening. Please have my father run over by a truck. Don't hurt him, just do it real fast. Thank you, amen."

Ronnie felt a tiny thrill after saying this prayer. If God answered it, he alone would be man of the house; he would have his mother all to himself.

On other days, he was sure he wanted her to die, too. Once, when he was a boy, Katy whipped him outside where the neighbors could see. From the distance it probably looked as if Ronnie and his mom were playing a game. Her hand was clamped to his wrist, and he ran in a circle, pinwheeling around her. But up close, you could hear screams and sharp smacks. Dressed in short pants and a T-shirt, whimpering, Ronnie tried to pull free. Katy flailed her arm, again and again, whipping the back of his calves and buttocks with a doubled-up electrical cord.

Ronnie remembered a woman screaming, "Stop it, Katy! Stop hitting him!" His mom stopped, looked up . . . and resumed the punishment.

She sent him to his room. Later, when his father came home and saw the welts, he walked out. A moment later, his mother came in and said she was sorry and hugged him. Ronnie held his arms down, his sullen face showing fear and fury.

She was inconsistent. She would whip him for talking back or coming home several minutes late from school, then inform her husband. As soon as Rodney would take off his belt and start swinging, she'd run in, intercepting the blows, cursing her husband, casting herself as Ronnie's protector. He was confused. Finally he decided his mother was a witch and that she and his father weren't really his parents.

Now, half-naked in the basement, Ronnie heard his father's boots thump on the thin carpet above. He could imagine his father lighting a cigarette, surveying the slovenly house, scowling. Ronnie told himself to get Mom over to clean.

Come on, come on, leave. Go.

Ronnie couldn't get back to sleep after his father left. He hated being made to feel like a little boy.

July 1984

Bob Matuszny

On Saturday, July 7, one of his days off, Bob got a morning call from district headquarters. "Your pal showed up again," said one of the detectives.

"Who?" Bob asked.

"Another rape. On West Tenth off Brookpark Road. Same M.O. as the ones you're working on: bumps on his dick, cuts the phone cord, everything."

Bob was sick. Weeks and weeks of stakeouts and as soon as he shuts it down, the asshole strikes. "I'll be there soon as I get dressed."

He roared north on Interstate 71 in the Oldsmobile Cutlass he had rebuilt, expertly weaving through a swell of early-morning traffic. At the crime scene, Bob noted the woods in the back of the houses on the east side of West 10th, which separated the residential street from an apartment building a block over. That was the asshole's cover, he thought.

Two zone car patrolmen had already taken a statement from the twenty-three-year-old victim, Roxanne Lincoln. They held a brown paper evidence bag that contained what looked like a girdle.

In the living room Bob saw a big, blond man sitting next to Roxanne, whose hazel eyes were tired and puffy. Before he sat down, Bob asked one of the patrolmen, "What did she say happened?"

"She was sleeping on the couch with her son, three weeks old,

65

when an unknown male woke her up by playing with her breasts. He held a knife and said if she did what he said, her kid wouldn't get hurt."

Bob glanced at the beefy young man with Roxanne and quickly back at the patrolman.

"Her husband," the patrolman said softly. "He left for work at six-thirty A.M. She went next door and called him after it happened. The telephone cord was cut."

Bob introduced himself to Roxanne and her husband and started a low-key questioning. Her answers thudded into his brain with sickening familiarity: white man, slim, thick curly hair and a mustache, wearing blue jeans and a black waist-length jacket. Soft hands, soft-spoken, no accent. Forced oral sex only because she complained she'd just had a baby. Bump on penis. Wipes himself dry with her girdle. She asked what she had done to deserve this and the rapist replied it wasn't her fault, it was her husband's.

The crime spurred Bob's anger beyond the usual outrage he felt as a detective taking a statement from a pathetic victim. It wasn't just the rape and the infant and the frustration. It had turned intensely personal. This slick little shithead is sitting out there laughing at me. Soon as surveillance is off, the asshole hits. Right in the same goddamn zone. He's sticking it in my face. Daring me to figure out who he is.

Bob began canvassing the neighbors. He was determined to work until something turned up. He didn't care how long it took—this crime wave had to stop.

Matuszny, five other detectives, a few supervisors, and three pairs of uniformed patrol officers knocked on every door on West 10th and the surrounding streets. A Scientific Investigations Unit technician processed the Lincolns' bungalow, dusting door-frames for prints. Among the tangled sheets, he found an unlighted Marlboro cigarette. Roxanne Lincoln and her husband smoked Winstons. The SIU tech put the cigarette in a small evidence bag and labeled it for the crime lab. If the rapist had held it in his mouth, the lab could determine his blood type from saliva residue.

In the forty-five minutes it had taken the police to arrive,

66

Roxanne's husband had roamed the block, knocking on doors. They had moved in only a month earlier and didn't know the neighbors. He had to introduce himself and say, Sorry, but my wife was just raped. Did you see anything?

Now, on the corner at the top of the street, a woman told the police she'd noticed a young man in jeans and dark jacket cutting down West 10th about a half hour before. "He cut through two yards up on Spring. He turned up West Tenth and then turned in a few houses up."

"About which house?" Bob Matuszny asked.

She pointed to the brick bungalow. "Right there."

Bob's pulse quickened. The Lincoln house!

"About twenty minutes later he came back the same way and cut through again."

"Where did you last see him?"

"Going up the driveway of those apartments. See it?" She pointed to the Jennings Commons a block away, a series of low apartment buildings at the corner of Spring and Jennings Roads.

Bob carefully took down her name, phone number, and address. With any luck, she might be a prosecution witness someday.

RONNIE

On July 20, 1984, Ronnie found his way to the office of Ross Santamaria, Ph.D., in the Medina County Administration Building, about fifteen minutes from his parents' house.

Ronnie wasn't looking forward to the visit. Two years earlier, when he was living in Colorado, he and his girlfriend had tried to pull an inside job at a money exchange and got caught with $32,000. When the case finally wound its way through the Colorado courts, Ronnie was fined and given a suspended sentence. Colorado transferred probation authority to Ohio when he moved back home, and Ronnie had been ordered to get counseling.

He knew he needed help, but not for the nonviolent crime that the probation authority was supervising. This visit would be a waste of time. What was he supposed to do, tell the doctor he was peering into windows nearly every night and sometimes raping the women he saw?

In the office, Ronnie sat down and stared. Santamaria looked like a social worker type. He wore eyeglasses but seemed streetwise and in good shape. He had a confident, slightly macho attitude. Right away, Ronnie decided he didn't like him.

"You've been referred to us by the State of Colorado as a condition of your parole on a robbery of a money exchange and another incident where you took a hundred dollars. Is that right?"

"Yes."

"What happened?"

"I left home with a buddy and went out to Denver and was living with a girlfriend. She worked for a check-cashing place. She told us about the code on the safe, and me and her and another guy took the money. It was right when she opened up in the morning."

"She faked it, said it was a robbery?"

"Right."

"How much?"

"Thirty-two thousand dollars." Ronnie looked to see if Santamaria was impressed. He didn't show a thing.

"Are you working?"

"I'm a landscaper. I work in Parma."

"You like the work?"

"For four bucks an hour, no. And I got all these bills."

"Tell me about that."

"I fell off a ladder at work. I had to have brain surgery. I got a hole in my head. See, right here."

Ronnie turned his head and pushed the hair off his forehead, displaying a quarter-sized indentation in his skull. "There's no bone there. I've got to have more surgery."

Santamaria took notes. "What do you think we have to work on?"

"I get in fights. I was a boxer in Denver. I fought professionally. I had three fights and won them all."

Actually, Ronnie had shown promise as a fighter. He worked with widely known Denver trainer Champ Thomas, who liked what he saw: a raw fighter with fast hands, fair power, and a streak of exhibitionism that could be molded into self-promoting showmanship. Most of all Champ could see that Ronnie was full of rage. You had to be angry to be a good boxer. Thomas put him on several undercards and the crowd loved him. Thomas thought Ronnie had the potential to be a world champion, but he didn't listen and didn't train hard for fights. Last Thomas heard, Ronnie had been arrested for something.

"Why do you think you fight?" Santamaria asked.

"I got a temper. I get it from my father."

Soon the fifty-minute session was over and Ronnie and Santamaria arranged to meet again on August 1. Ronnie left, kicked his motorcycle to life, and headed north to Cleveland. He knew he'd never show up for another session. That guy didn't care about him. He didn't want to help him. Fuck it, he thought. If missing the next appointment was a violation, they could just come get him.

Kathy Bond

In the year that had passed, Kathy Bond had quit taking her handgun to work at Casey's Restaurant. The gun made her feel more nervous than safe. She gave it back and bought a black Labrador retriever that quickly learned to worship her and growl at strangers. But even the dog didn't help her sleep. Every sound in the night set her off. Meeting new men was a problem too. In the supposed prime of her dating life, Kathy found herself unable to trust men. The thought of sex frightened her.

At a restaurant one night, she was introduced to a huge, muscular, soft-spoken man, a few years older than she, who said his name was Rex. He was a psychology graduate of the University of Michigan, which he had attended on a football scholarship as a standout linebacker until he injured his shoulder in his junior year. Now he used his bearlike strength as an in-city hauler for Central Cartage. They clicked immediately and talked until the early morning over coffee at an all-night diner. There she found herself telling him about being raped, and the psychology major took it in, responding sympathetically. A few hours before dawn, Rex walked her to her car, gallantly kissed her hand, and said good night. Kathy couldn't believe it. She had finally found a guy she liked, and he hadn't even asked for her phone number.

Rex knew Kathy worked as a waitress at Casey's Restaurant on West 117th Street. He visited her there the next day and began an insistent courtship. He couldn't believe this beautiful woman had suffered so much pain; he wanted to protect her, to save her, to help her fall asleep at night. Within three months, he asked her to marry him, and she agreed.

On their honeymoon, Kathy and Rex camped near Galveston at a pristine, peaceful national seashore park on the Gulf of Mexico, a thousand miles from Cleveland. Outside the tent, waves lapped soothingly on white sands, a dreamy postcard vista.

Kathy awoke that night, crying, reliving the rape, feeling she was losing her mind. "Did I do the right thing?" she sobbed.

"Of course you did," Rex said, holding her.

"I should have fought. I should have run. They would have caught him."

"Think of Michelle's kids," Rex said. "They're alive. You did the right thing."

She knew he was right. But then why couldn't she sleep?

BOB MATUSZNY

One of Bob Matuszny's supervisors, who had taken courses at the FBI Academy, told the detective about its Behavioral Science profiling unit, which helped local authorities track serial criminals.

Bob was unfamiliar with the FBI profiling unit but was ready to try anything. He had submerged himself for the past several months in a tricky rape investigation and had nothing to show for it except a long list of cleared suspects. It was late July, and the number of rapes linked to the West Side Rapist now stood at seventeen. He needed some luck. Maybe it was time to call on the FBI for assistance.

The Behavioral Science Unit, which has studied the patterns and motivations and rituals of hundreds of serial criminals, is tucked into the basement at the FBI Academy in Quantico, Virginia.

There FBI profiler Blaine E. McIlwaine sifted through the materials submitted by Matuszny and the suburban police departments working the case of the West Side Rapist. He had seventeen rape reports, complete with follow-up investigations, summaries of physical evidence, and pictures of the crime scenes. He had also looked at victim statements and located addresses on a Cuyahoga County street guide.

He carefully considered the victims, their backgrounds, ages, and occupations. A serial rapist might change his modus operandi or place of attack, but he still selected the same type of victim, and this selection revealed much about him and his motives.

Was this a criminal enterprise to gain money? the agent considered. Obviously, no. Was it an opportunity rape coming after a successful break-in and robbery? No again. Was the attacker acting alone or as part of a group? Was he after a sexual high? How much of a risk was the rapist taking? What did the time of the crime—early morning—indicate? What did the locations reveal?

A few days later, the FBI profiler sent Matuszny a four-page psychological profile of the West Side Rapist.

Bob Matuszny took his time reading the offender profile. It noted that the earliest cluster of rapes was near the Cleveland Zoo, and that the first rapes by this kind of rapist "will be committed within walking distance of where he lives." The rapist spied on potential victims, then selected single women or women with small children—"a safe bet inasmuch as the victim's concern for her children gives him added leverage."

This was all fairly obvious to Bob. The "offender profile" section had a few new insights, however: The rapist, it said, had a definite connection to the first cluster around the Cleveland

Zoo and felt comfortable there, probably because he lived or worked in the area. Because the rapes took place around 5 A.M., the suspect most likely didn't have a regular daytime job. Normally, this sort of rapist has a poor self-image and works in a menial job without much public contact, the profile went on. "This offender is committing these rapes to convince himself that he is capable of sexual performance."

The profile noted that the victims described the rapist as "extremely clean," which was unusual. "It is likely that this individual is employed in a capacity that requires him to be clean, such as food preparation or possibly a technician in a hospital or factory. We noted that Deaconess Hospital lies within the first cluster."

Bob made a mental note to pay attention to the hospital's employees. He read on.

"Socially this individual is considered a loner with few positive social traits. If he dates at all, it will be with a significantly younger female. He is probably dominated by a female figure with whom he resides (i.e., mother, aunt) and due to the conflict with her is under a great deal of stress. This stress is also related to doubts about his masculinity. This individual will engage in a great deal of fantasy and collect pornography."

The rapist has a juvenile record for voyeurism, panty thefts, or breaking and entering, the profile said. He may ride a motorcycle or drive a dark, older vehicle in poor condition. Often such a rapist keeps a written record of locations and habits of victims. He may have a diary of his rape experiences.

In its "post-offense behavior" section, the FBI profile said the offender feels pride, relief, and disgust after the rapes and "sees himself as inadequate." He continues to rape to reassure himself of his sexual prowess. "He may feel some pride as a result of media impact." He may save newspaper clippings of his crimes.

"Your offender may be a very religious person and has possibly increased his 'religiosity' to help cope with his crimes. If he is a user/abuser of drug or alcohol, he may have increased in this regard.

"Your offender may have gained some little amount of self-esteem back in his role as a Cleveland area rapist," the profile

73

concluded. "His impulsiveness will lead to his downfall however and if properly interviewed he will readily confess to all his crimes."

Bob sure hoped the asshole would confess when they caught him. Great way to tie up a slew of cases. He stood up and went to make a photocopy of the FBI profile for his boss.

RONNIE

The summer of 1984 marked four years since Ronnie's grandfather had died. He still had not gotten over it. He thought of Grandpa Harvey every time he passed his grandfather's favorite tavern, the Wooden Nickel Saloon, a smoke-choked blue-collar beer joint on East 77th Street in Slavic Village.

His grandfather was the only man who had ever shown Ronnie affection. Harvey Shelton was a skilled machinist—as well as an alcoholic. He had never remarried after his wife, Daisy, was murdered in 1963.

All Ronnie knew of his grandmother came from an old black-and-white photograph: Grandma Daisy was holding him in her lap, a tiny, pretty woman, only forty-two, with wispy gray and brown hair that fell in waves to her shoulders. He was two years old, and she was killed several months after the photo was snapped. Ronnie's father didn't say much about his mother, particularly about how she died. Like so many important matters in the Shelton family, her death was cloaked in mystery. Rodney Shelton sloughed off his son's queries. When pressed, Rodney said she had been killed in the hill country of southern Ohio by bootleggers; he was in the navy at the time, in Texas, and didn't really know what had happened.

Ronnie always knew where he stood with his grandpa, and loved him above all others. He'd find him in the saloon, and Harvey, after a few belts, would sing along with the country tunes on the jukebox, making Ronnie laugh. Ronnie wished Harvey had been his father. He made him feel safe. Once when Ronnie crept out at night without permission, his father caught him. Saying he was afraid of what he'd do to Ronnie, he dropped the boy off with his grandfather. The next morning Grandpa Harvey fed Ronnie doughnuts and milk.

In the spring of 1980 Grandpa Harvey retired from a tool-and-die factory and moved to Minford, Ohio, a tiny town on the Ohio River in the Appalachian foothills where he had grown up. Harvey Shelton promised Ronnie that once he got his house set up, he would send for him. It was their secret plan and Ronnie, at nineteen, dreamed of spending his days in the woods of southern Ohio or finding a job in town, miles from his parents and the troubles of War Avenue. But a month after retiring to Minford, at sixty-two, Harvey Shelton suffered a fatal heart attack.

His family was surprised by how tearful Ronnie was on the five-hour drive from Cleveland to Minford. While his parents and sister received family at the funeral home, Ronnie crept off with a bouquet from the wake and walked to the cemetery. There he found the freshly dug grave that would swallow his grandfather's casket in the morning. He placed the flowers on the grass surrounding the grave and climbed down, trying not to soil his good clothes. On the clay walls of the pit, he scratched, "I love you, Grandpa."

He lay in the grave and looked up at the stars, sparkling brighter than any he'd ever seen in Cleveland, and cried intermittently in the flower-scented dark, "You cheated me, Grandpa! Goddammit, you cheated me!"

It was as though his own life were over, too.

September–October 1984

In Parma Heights Rapes:
Is It the Same Man?
By Julie Washington

Parma Heights police have few clues to help them solve a pair of unusual rapes within the past five weeks.

In each case, the rapist's method was the same, leading police to believe they are seeking the same man for both. The man took a small amount of money from the women's purses, which is unusual behavior for a rapist, said Parma Heights police Sgt. Richard Rob.

"I've never seen it happen before," Rob said. "It's kind of a trademark, I would say."

Both work in the same store at Parmatown Mall in Parma, although they did not know each other previously, and live only a quarter-mile from the mall.

The first rape occurred July 26, between 4:30 and 5 a.m. in the 6700 block of York Ave. The rapist cut through a living room window screen while the victim, 27, slept in a bedroom. The man showed a knife and threatened to kill her, Rob said.

The woman was treated at Parma Community Hospital. She told police she might have heard a motorcycle as the man left.

A rapist struck again Aug. 17, this time entering an apartment in the 9000 block of N. Church Dr. about 12:30 a.m., apparently cutting a screen door. He sexually molested a woman, 60, who was sleeping in the bedroom, Rob said.

—*Cleveland Plain Dealer*, September 4, 1984

KAREN HOLZTRAGER

The telephone jangled and Karen Holztrager grabbed it quickly. With three preschool boys and a husband working the overnight shift, it seemed as if someone was always asleep in their tiny apartment.

Her husband's sister was calling with a bit of disturbing news. A woman had been raped near their apartment. The story was in the paper.

"You better be careful."

"We'll be out of here soon," Karen said.

She was concerned. Break-ins and rapes seemed to be on the rise near Tarrytown Apartments, where she lived, just a stone's throw from one of the biggest General Motors plants in the country. She had not expected to feel creepy about the neighborhood when she moved to Parma, a suburb of 89,000 people where police protection was supposed to be excellent.

She took comfort in their planned move next month into their first home, a modest three-bedroom ranch in Lagrange, nearly forty miles from the crime and hustle of the city.

They had scraped together every cent to make the move, she selling Avon products, her husband Lee working nights at a grocery warehouse, loading and stacking pallets. Karen hated being home at night alone. Their apartment was on the first floor, and she never felt completely safe. Three of the window latches were so caked from being repainted that they did not lock.

She had been preoccupied with safety since she was a girl. Two things had always terrified her—a house fire and rape. In grade school, when her family lived in the upstairs suite of a two-family home, she tied a rope to her bed frame and kept it ready in case of a fire so she could drop it out the window and shimmy down. That helped her sleep more securely.

And ten years ago, when she was thirteen, she had been molested at a church service. She had left her family in the crowded pew to use the rest room, which was in the basement. A man slipped into the rest room, exposed himself, and made Karen stroke his penis. Later, when she finally told her parents about it, her dad blew up, saying he was going to kill the bastard. Karen felt guilty, like somehow it had been her fault.

Afterward, Karen made sure to keep a heavy lamp or statue on her nightstand. If anyone attacked her she would smash him bloody, whatever it took. No man was ever going to violate her again.

After talking to Lee's sister, Karen phoned the Tarrytown's building manager and complained, again, about the damn window latches. "Don't worry," he told her. "We'll get to it soon."

Well after midnight he hid in the shadows along the side of the apartment building and made sure the woman's husband had left for work. He liked what he saw: early twenties, blond hair, pixieish face, nice body, and a clean apartment. Clean house, clean body, he thought.

Tonight another woman was visiting and sat with her in the living room. They were watching television and eating popcorn. He did not even think about going inside with two adults there. Too risky. He was happy just to watch, to get to know her. He switched positions when the woman stood up. She came to the window and looked right at him, and he went to his car. She seemed to continue to stare at him, and he drove off quickly. Had she seen him?

A few days later, September 13, 1984, Karen saw Lee off to work at 11 P.M., then did the dishes. The boys were asleep.

A while later she climbed under the sheets and stretched out in just her panties. The building's brick walls had been baking all day in the sun, making the apartment muggy and hot. It'd be nice to feel the breeze, Karen thought. But I'd better keep the windows shut to be safe.

Soon she fell asleep. A few hours later she felt pressure on her hand. She awoke and saw the outlines of a man sitting on the edge of the bed. She felt ice cold and wanted to scream.

"Be quiet," he said softly. He waved a knife near her face. "Don't worry, your kids are okay. I checked on them. I closed your door, so they won't hear anything."

Oh Jesus, the door is shut. He's not kidding.

"I'm not going to hurt you if you do what I say." His voice sounded nervous. "Pull down the sheet."

She trembled as the sheet slipped over her breasts. She felt his hands, cold and soft and smallish, like those of a scared boy, which made him seem weird and even more terrifying. Then one hand slid to her crotch.

"Do you know me?" the voice said.

"No," she said, wondering, Do I?

"Well, I know you. I've been watching you. Now make yourself wet. Take my hand and use it."

She couldn't stand to touch his skin. Suddenly he had his pants down and the knife on the bedstand and he was forcing his way inside.

This can't be happening, she thought, and her mind focused on the sheets, now crumpled around her. They were only two days old, their first new ones since she and Lee had gotten married. They felt thick and crunchy and smelled so fresh. Now I'll have to throw them out, she thought.

When he was through, he picked up the knife and said, "I need money. You gotta have money around here."

Karen said she had over a hundred dollars from Avon sales.

"Get it," he said. "No, wait. I'll go with you."

She surprised herself. "Give me my robe." All of a sudden she was goddamned if she was going to walk naked with this guy through her own apartment so he could run off with her earnings.

"Give me my bathrobe," she said again.

"Where is it?"

She pointed in the dark. "Right there."

He threw her a shirt. Karen threw it back at him. "That's not it."

He threw her a T-shirt.

She said, "That's not it."

"Just put it on!" He sounded mad.

The streetlights shone through the curtains and in the soft illumination Karen saw a slender young man with olive skin. His nylon windbreaker swished as he moved, making the same sound Lee's windbreaker made. Oh, Lee will kill this guy when he finds out, Karen told herself.

"I've got a jar of pennies," she said.

"Fuck the pennies."

She opened her eyes and looked at him.

"Close your eyes. Don't look at me."

She found her money pouch in the kitchen cabinet and handed it to him. He took out $180, then told her to stay in the bathroom.

"If you call the police, I'll know. I'll come back here and kill you—and your kids."

A few minutes after he slipped out, Karen called Lee at the warehouse. He dropped the lunchroom phone and darted for his car, its tires squealing as he left the parking lot. His boss wondered what the hell was going on.

He was home in ten minutes, shortly before the police arrived. Lee stayed inside for a moment, made sure that Karen was all right, then ran out to the parking lot to see if he could find the rapist.

A few minutes later, Karen was choking out her story to two Parma policemen.

"Do you think you know your attacker?" one asked.

"No, but he said he knew me. He said he was watching me."

"What did he look like?"

"Thin build, brown hair. He wore a ski jacket. I think it was burnt orange, just like my husband's. It made the same sound when he walked."

One of them turned to Lee. "Can you prove you were at work?"

Lee bit off his words. "Of course I can prove I was at work. What the hell is that supposed to mean?"

Lee stormed around the Parma Community Hospital emergency room, his anger pouring out. He wanted to kill whoever did this to Karen, but that was impossible at the moment. When the emergency room doctor wouldn't let Lee stay with Karen during the examination, he stomped off to call Karen's parents and tell them what had happened. Meanwhile, his wife sat alone in the examining room, shivering under the harsh light.

"Are you her husband?" one of the nurses asked him in the hallway.

"Yes."

"Well, could you fill out these insurance forms?"

Lee wanted to tear up the papers; they wouldn't let him comfort his wife, but they sure were quick to make him show his Blue Cross insurance card. He heard his father-in-law running down the corridor, yelling, "Where's my daughter? Where's my daughter?"

His voice put Lee on edge. His father-in-law always seemed to suggest that Lee wasn't good enough for Karen, that she should have married a lawyer or a doctor.

"You can see her in a minute," a nurse said.

When they finally let Lee and his in-laws into the room, Karen seemed disoriented. Her father was incoherent, which frightened her. Her mother hugged her and said, "Honey, you survived. At least you're alive."

Somehow, her mother's remark struck Karen profoundly. She calmed down like magic. Years later, she would remember holding that thought in her head right then and telling herself to try to put her life back together.

RONNIE

In early October, Ronnie decided once again that he had to do something about the hole in his skull. Using a mirror, he looked at the quarter-sized indentation in the hairline above his left temple. You couldn't really see anything, just a dent in the scalp, shallow as a bottle cap. But he felt it was his Achilles' heel. All it would take would be a lucky punch from some asshole at a nightclub and he could be killed. At least that's what the doctor told him.

There'd be more fights, he knew, usually in front of an audience. It was odd, but he enjoyed losing control. His rages blasted him to an intoxicating high, and afterward he felt cleansed and relaxed.

He was irritated that Dr. Ling hadn't installed the protective plate yet. Ling had prescribed an anticonvulsant as a temporary safeguard, but it had given him a rash and he'd quit taking it. Ling always warned him about drinking and about driving carefully. He said to stay off the motorcycle, take it easy. How the hell was he supposed to get around? Ronnie thought.

Ling's office was near St. Alexis Hospital, in Ronnie's old neighborhood. During the visit, Ronnie complained about feeling dizzy off and on.

Are you taking your phenobarbital?

"No."

Why not?

"I don't like it."

Ling consulted Ronnie's medical charts. So far he had pre-scribed Dilantin, then Mysoline, and now phenobarbital for Ronnie Shelton. Dilantin had given him a rash. Mysoline made him a bit dizzy. Now he wasn't taking the phenobarbital. Last November, according to emergency room records in the file, the patient had gotten into a fight at a bar and needed nine stitches to close a gash over his right eyebrow.

Dr. Ling felt Ronnie was at tremendous risk if he kept brawling. He hated patients like this. They got angry and lashed out with a lawsuit. They didn't take responsibility for their care.

After Ronnie left, Dr. Ling dictated his notes carefully, making sure to record that the young man wasn't following his advice: "It appears Mr. Shelton has discontinued to use the phenobarbital on his own because 'He didn't like it.' He came in here demanding that a plate be put in his head primarily because he has just recently gotten into another fight and now seems to be concerned about his personal safety. . . . If this patient contin-ues to refuse medical treatment I will have to refuse to be responsible for his medical care."

BOB MATUSZNY

By October 1984, Detective Bob Matuszny had spent half a year chasing the West Side Rapist. The rapes kept mounting, and he was no closer to catching him than when he'd gotten the first composite sketch last spring. He felt subtle pressure from his superiors to come up with something, but all he had was the FBI profile, his own chart of crime patterns, and a list of nearly a hundred cleared suspects, eliminated usually through alibis or informal "pecker checks."

Much of the pressure he felt came from within. He possessed as much pride and discipline as one could find in a detective. He worked long hours, handled other assignments as well, and came home cranky, the investigation never far from his mind. Who was this serial pervert? What did he look like? Why was he doing all this? Where did he work? Where was he going to hit next?

Throughout October, Bob Matuszny continued to distribute fact sheets about the West Side Rapist to the six Cleveland police districts, and he asked that it be read to everyone at roll calls. The idea was to blanket Cleveland, get all 1,800 members of the police force on the lookout. Something was bound to break.

On October 21, 1984, two patrolmen in a zone car took a radio call for assistance at a downtown flophouse. A twenty-seven-year-old Latino, dressed up like a heavy-metal rocker and whacked on something, was acting crazy and tearing up the place. He looked just like the composite sketch of the West Side Rapist. The police ran a records check, which showed he had been arrested before on charges of indecent exposure, felonious assault, and gross sexual imposition. They immediately arrested him.

Questioned by the police, the man freely admitted carrying a knife, owning guns, and knowing the West Side streets where the victims were raped.

They drove the suspect to the secure psychiatric unit of Cleveland Metropolitan General Hospital. "Oh, I like this place so much," he said when he arrived. "Last time I was here, man, there was plenty of chicks. My dick was always wet."

The next day, Bob drove over to Cleveland Psychiatric to talk to the suspect. Later he called the two zone car cops who made the arrest, even though he didn't have to. "I appreciate what you did," he said, "but he's not the guy."

Bob wanted the patrolmen to feel appreciated for trying to make a good arrest. He wanted to motivate every policeman in the district to be on the lookout for the West Side Rapist.

Spring 1985

CONNIE BELLINI*

Closing time loomed at O'Malley's nightclub, one of Ronnie's favorite pickup places. He felt the nightly mating dance heat up. He had played it cool earlier in the evening, scoping out pretty young women, chatting with friends, sipping a mixed drink. He made the rounds with his eyes, gazing at each woman he found sexy. If he caught her eye for an instant, he glanced away quickly, smiling. He made sure to look back a second later, as surreptitiously as possible, to see if she was looking back at him. If she was, he knew she was interested. He had her. Then it was up to him to make the move.

He had his eye on a short, black-haired beauty with olive skin, who reminded him of his mother. She wasn't wearing tight clothes, though from what he could tell she had the body for it. She was modest, well dressed. Ronnie could tell by the way she danced that she didn't think of herself as a fox, which pleased him.

He fluffed his hair, walked up to her, and softly asked, "Would you like to dance?"

Connie Bellini didn't seem surprised at his move. He had been staring at her for the past hour. She had already decided that he wasn't her type. He was too short. She liked tall men.

"Oh, I don't think so," she said, letting him down softly.

Ronnie was not fazed. "I just got back from an Air Supply

*Not her real name.

85

concert," he said. "I really like their songs. Do you like the band?"

Connie happened to enjoy the mushy pop ballads of Air Supply. Well, she thought, he can't be too terrible if he likes Air Supply. "Okay, I'll dance," she told him.

He was soft and polite, almost annoyingly so. Connie couldn't believe it. Usually the short guys in the nightclubs felt they had something to prove and adopted more of a macho pose. This guy seemed different. They danced a few more times before the bar closed. Ronnie asked her if she'd meet him here tomorrow, Sunday night. Connie said, sure, she'd be there.

The next night at O'Malley's, Ronnie repeated his smooth moves with her and afterward took her to a private party thrown by a friend who was a male go-go dancer at the Rampant Lion. It was a crowd of good-looking men and women, dancing, drinking, casually taking drugs. Connie was not used to such fast company and shyly hung on Ronnie's arm the rest of the night.

He took her back to her apartment, and she invited him in. Ronnie had misgivings. He didn't want to move too fast with her. What if she turned out to be another easy conquest? This woman seemed special, and sex would ruin everything, he felt.

Everything they said and did the rest of the night seemed to mesh perfectly. He made a move, she responded. He told a joke, she laughed. He ended up staying the night, and the next and the next. He took her for rides in the country on his motorcycle, zooming down deserted lanes that cut through corn and soybean fields in Medina County near his parents' home. He came off like a dreamy romantic, whose idea of a date was to stay at her apartment, watch rental movies on the VCR, and talk. He insisted that he didn't like to go to bars, even though she had met him at one. But that didn't strike Connie as odd, because she was falling for him.

Early on, he brought Connie to his parents' house for dinner. He introduced her proudly, knowing this pretty, well-spoken woman who didn't smoke or wear trashy clothes would meet with his parents' approval.

Connie was surprised that he had dragged her to Brunswick

Hills so early in their relationship. He really seemed to care about his family and what they thought of her. He seemed to be the sort of man she was looking for.

During one visit to Brunswick Hills, Ronnie took Connie into his bedroom where he sometimes stayed when he was on good terms with his parents. On a dresser was a fishbowl filled with cutesy greeting cards, love letters, and cocktail napkins with telephone numbers and women's names. "These are some of the girls I dated," he said.

He dug his hands into the bowl, churning its contents like a bingo operator pulling the next lucky number, and came up repeatedly with photos of old girlfriends. Connie could see that they were all cute.

Normally a stunt like that would have turned her against a man. Instead Connie felt flattered. Of all these women, she thought, he wants me.

In June, Connie moved into an apartment in a high-rise in suburban North Olmsted. It was a secure building, newly decorated, with indoor parking. As an executive assistant at British Petroleum's SOHIO division, she earned a good salary for a twenty-six-year-old woman who hadn't finished college.

Ronnie helped her move her furniture into her new place, stayed the night, and never left. That was fine with Connie; she found herself depending on him.

At first, he couldn't get enough of her and swamped her with attention. He had to have sex every day. Once in bed, he dwelled obsessively on her breasts. Connie came from a strict Italian home and was inexperienced sexually. She still was too embarrassed to talk about birth control, so she let Ronnie handle it. During intercourse, he stayed hard inside her for what seemed an impressively long time, and just before climax pulled out and ejaculated on her stomach. It was a crude form of contraception, but to Connie it seemed as if he was a master at it.

Even though she was falling in love with Ronnie, Connie didn't feel comfortable enough with him to tell him how to help her reach an orgasm. And then there was the matter of his penis.

Sometimes, near the tip of his shaft, large bumps or warts appeared. Over several weeks, the bumps would disappear, only to crop up again. She hated the sight of them.

To Ronnie, being able to provoke jealousy in a girlfriend meant that she cared for him. He put Connie to the test. It didn't concern him that she might not appreciate being manipulated. In a checkout line at a store, in a nightclub, wherever he encountered a pretty young woman, Ronnie flirted and Connie fell for the bait. She retaliated without words, instead silently digging her fingernails into the flesh of his arm. It hurt like hell, but Ronnie glowed when she did it. It reminded him of how his mom used to punish him with her nails. Only Connie's clawing never drew blood.

Now, at twenty-four, Ronnie felt in love for the first time. To prove it to himself, he insisted on reacting with sudden fury whenever another man so much as glanced at Connie when they were together at the clubs. "What the fuck are you looking at?" became Ronnie's refrain, and a few times he touched off fights. His violence both frightened and impressed her.

LUCIE DUVALL

Lieutenant Lucie J. Duvall was on the telephone with her friend, Cleveland Chief of Police Bill Hanton. "Really? A sex crimes unit? Sure, of course. I'd love to run it." Prone to giggling when nervous, she laughed. "You know me—I'll try anything."

Duvall, one of the highest-ranking women in the Cleveland

Police Department, had flourished under the command of Hanton, becoming the first female officer to command a vice squad. The novelty of her rank, her assignment, and her looks—she was barely a hundred pounds, with eye-catching red hair—gave her a high public profile. Cleveland television viewers became accustomed to seeing news clips of her in her office, wearing bright plum or red blazers and matching lipstick, explaining the latest vice bust.

"Good," Chief Bill Hanton replied. "I knew you'd say that. Now let's see if we can get it past city hall."

The idea of a centralized police unit to handle all sex crimes was not just Hanton's. Each month he met informally with his three deputy chiefs and the commanders of the six districts to talk about crime problems and to kick around new tactics. At one of these meetings, someone came up with the idea of forming a specialized detective unit just to handle sex crimes.

It made good sense to Hanton. Public awareness and concern about child abuse was growing, almost hysterically. Further, women were reporting rapes with increasing frequency now that some of the stigma was fading. And, of course, the West Side Rapist still roamed free.

A sex crimes unit had been tried before. In the 1970s, the Cleveland Police Department fielded a specialized unit that handled rape cases and other sex crimes. But by 1979, the city had fallen on tougher times and cuts were made across the board within the police department. Its 2,000-officer force dropped to about 1,800. Detectives from the sex crimes and juvenile units were dispersed to the six districts, where they worked general detective duty, handling whatever was assigned. Some detectives even ended up back in uniform and in zone cars.

Hanton felt Duvall was nearly the perfect choice for the job. She was loyal and he trusted her. She was also capable, ambitious, and more than a match for male cops who chafed at the idea of being commanded by a woman. She had made a name for herself a few years earlier acting as a miniskirted decoy in prostitute stings, arresting their johns and pimps, and had climbed up to supervising the large, all-male downtown vice squad, the first woman in the country to do so.

Duvall did have a weak spot: She had never investigated a rape case. So Hanton sent her to a child sex abuse seminar at the Federal Law Enforcement Center in Glynco, Georgia. Duvall was glad to have an expenses-paid assignment that broke her routine. She enjoyed the classes, even knowing that the Sex Crimes Unit, as it now was officially called, might never materialize. Cleveland City Council had to approve it first.

RONNIE

It was a matter of dumb luck that in the late spring of 1985, just as the Cleveland Police Department was marshaling forces to combat rape, Ronnie moved his base of operations to Connie's apartment in suburban North Olmsted, twelve miles to the west. A prospering greenhouse and truck gardening community, North Olmsted by the 1970s had seen much of its farmlands graded and paved to build a sprawling shopping mall rimmed by apartment towers and busy six-lane thoroughfares. Immodestly named Great Northern Shopping Mall, it served as the nerve center of North Olmsted. Each day it was flooded with shoppers and workers who had to navigate a confusing tangle of access roads to the mall and nearby strips of stores and fast-food places. The area was a voyeur's paradise; anyone might have reason to be there.

North Olmsted's police department enjoyed a good reputation, with a quick response time that was never an issue. Felony crime in the city consisted mostly of auto thefts and burglaries. In an average year, North Olmsted detectives investigated a handful of rapes. That statistic was soon to change.

Ronnie got a job in North Olmsted after meeting and charming the manager of a Scandinavian Health Club there. The manager, an attractive henna-haired woman in her early thirties, hired him as a sales instructor, a commissioned position. As part of his duties, Ronnie gave potential customers a tour of the pool, the bar, and the workout rooms. He gave his best sales pitch to the young women who came through the door. Using a polished manner and a lot of eye contact, he tried to convince them that a membership in the club could transform them into stunning hardbodies in virtually no time at all.

Ronnie loved the idea of working at Scandinavian, a national health club chain with sexy ads of famous actresses in skimpy leotards, all cleavage and shapely thighs, pouting among the high-tech exercise gear. And Scandinavian's walls were covered with mirrors, so he could indulge his passion for girl watching. It was a great pickup place. As an instructor, he had an excuse to walk up and talk to any woman he wanted.

Best of all, he had a key to the huge health club. A few times that spring, after the bars emptied out at two in the morning, he brought dates and friends to the club. He ushered them in proudly, flipped on the lights and sound system, then persuaded everyone to strip and go swimming. He felt like a big shot.

It was nine o'clock, a crisp early-summer night, when Ronnie cut through a field near a golf course in North Olmsted and walked toward the apartment buildings on Country Club Boulevard. He moved back and forth along one side of a building, looking into lighted ground-floor apartment windows. It was early and he had plenty of time to locate a target. If he found someone enticing, he planned to come back later, after the nightclubs closed.

In apartment 204, a second-floor unit, a woman spotted someone lurking outside and called the North Olmsted police. "There's a guy out there looking in windows."

"What's he look like?"

"About seventeen years old, white, with dark hair. He's got sunglasses on top of his head. Looks like brown pants and a leather jacket."

"Okay, we'll send a car right over," the dispatcher said.

The patrol car pulled into the back of the apartments as Ronnie walked nonchalantly across the parking lot. The police officer got out of the car, aimed a flashlight at Ronnie's face, and said, "Let's see a driver's license."

Ronnie pulled it out. "What's wrong, Officer?" he said calmly, eyeing the man's gun.

"What are you doing here?"

"I was looking for an address," he said. "I think this girl I met gave me the wrong address."

Over the squad car radio the patrolman called in Ronnie's name and social security number to check for outstanding arrest warrants on the state and national crime computers.

Ronnie sized up the fence around the back of the parking lot. He could scale that pretty easily. The cop wouldn't shoot him in the back if he ran.

A minute later, the dispatcher radioed back. Negative. No warrants or arrests. The patrolman told him he could go.

Ronnie got into his old car. His legs were shaking so much he could barely drive.

Ronnie didn't let a close call with the cops tame his criminal behavior, even temporarily. He risked arrest almost daily, as if he wanted to get caught. At closing time a few days after his close encounter with the North Olmsted police, he provoked a fight with a man, David Olson, in the parking lot of Streamer's, a club on the Brookpark Road strip near the airport.

Ronnie charged Olson, swearing, swinging furiously, and Olson fought back, landing power punches to the chest and jaw. Ronnie landed a left that bounced off Olson's skull. Olson smashed him again.

Ronnie pulled out a handgun. "I'll blow off your fucking face!"

Olson backed up, hands up.

The crowd around them had been enjoying the show but now,

with a gun visible, moved back. Ronnie closed in on Olson, who froze, trying not to provoke him. Ronnie smashed the gun backhanded across Olson's mouth, splashing blood and bits of teeth across his face.

Ronnie got in a car with two women and they sped out of the parking lot. He asked them to take him to Southwest General Hospital's emergency room. There a technician x-rayed his jaw, ribs, and hand.

"You better take it easy for a while," the technician said.

"Yeah," Ronnie said. "Sure."

Connie had been with Ronnie a couple of months when she mentioned a guy she had dated whom Ronnie knew a little about.

"You were naive," he told her. "It was a mistake. He was wrong for you."

She could not figure out why he seemed to be getting so jealous. Didn't he know she loved him? "He was okay. There was nothing wrong with going out with him," she said.

"Yes, there was. He used you. I can't believe you let him touch you. That makes me sick."

Connie would not admit something she didn't believe, even to pacify the man she had fallen in love with. "No, Ronnie, you're wrong—"

He punched her squarely in the left eye. Then he started to cry. Tears slid down his cheeks, which he made no effort to wipe, "I'm sorry, Connie. I don't know what happened."

She ran to the apartment door, her face red and her eye socket swelling, the makings of an ugly black eye.

"I won't do it again. Don't hate me," he said as she left in tears.

Connie wandered around for a few hours. Why is this happening to me? she asked herself. What did I do to deserve this? Is it my fault for bringing up an old boyfriend?

She returned to her apartment. Inside she saw Ronnie with his head slumped on her dining room table. She knew he had heard her come in. He raised his head; his eyes looked red, as if he had been rubbing them. Shards of a broken water glass decorated the floor.

"I couldn't stand what I did," Ronnie said, his voice cracking. He gestured to the floor. "I was so mad at myself I smashed the glass."

He was watching her face. "I'll never do it again, Connie. I promise."

Connie began to weep. "I believe you, Ronnie."

"I love you."

"I love you, too."

He ran and hugged her hard.

August–September 1985

BOB MATUSZNY

In early August, Bob Matuszny read a memo on the district headquarters bulletin board that stopped him short. A new unit was being created that would handle all rape and child molestation cases out of downtown police headquarters. Lieutenant Lucie J. Duvall would be in charge.

If the West Side Rapist kept striking, Bob realized, the fresh rapes would be assigned to the new unit. He'd be cut out of the case.

He was upset at the possibility of having the biggest case of his career yanked away by bureaucratic reshuffling. His other option, of course, was to join the Sex Crimes Unit. But he knew he'd be miserable working downtown. Parking and traffic were a bitch, and would cut into his workout time at the gym. Even worse, the job description said half the time would be spent on child abuse cases. Bob already knew he didn't have the stomach or temperament to question young victims. Some of his pals in the Second District detective bureau did ask for transfers to the new unit, including Bob's friend Ed Gray.

Just before Labor Day 1985, Duvall selected fifteen Cleveland detectives for transfer into the unit. They were to be responsible for investigating some 1,500 new sex crimes a year. That worked out to four new cases a week for each two-detective team. In such an emotionally numbing job, four new cases a week would make for a crushing workload.

A few weeks later, Detective Ed Gray and his rookie partner were assigned to a rape that had occurred on San Diego Street on the West Side. Gray glanced at the victim's first statement, given to Cleveland police the day of the rape. It seemed familiar to him: a thin, young white man surprised the victim just after her boyfriend left for work. He held a knife at her throat and said, "I've been watching you. I want you to give me a blow job like you give your husband." The victim described bumps at the end of the rapist's penis.

Gray finished reading the report and remembered Bob Matuszny's West Side Rapist investigation. Gray called him and asked him to join them at the victim interview. You'll know right away if this is tied to your guy, he told Bob.

Bob said, sure, he'd love to help, that he had already heard about the rape.

San Diego was a street of older homes, many of them two-family houses, a fairly safe area. Gray and his rookie partner, Andrea "Zeb" Zbydniewski, pulled in just ahead of Bob. Together they questioned the victim, a waitress, and her boyfriend.

"I saw a guy right when I was going to work," the boyfriend said.

"What did he look like?" Gray asked.

"Short, skinny. A white guy."

"What was he doing?"

"It was weird. He was walking real slow on the street and he looked at me. I didn't think anything of it. Then she ran out of the house to tell me something. It only took a second. When I went back, the guy was gone."

They turned to the victim, Lorraine Kaye,* and she struggled through the interview. "I don't know if I was asleep or what, but I turned over and he had a knife right there and he said, 'Shut up, don't say anything.' He already had his pants down."

Matuszny was convinced it was the same rapist he had tracked for two years. I wish I was running this investigation, he thought.

"He pulled off the covers and said, 'I want to see you,'" Lorraine said. As she went through the grisly details, Bob felt he could have interrupted and told the others what she was going to say next: played with her breasts, forced oral sex, forced vaginal sex, demanded her money.

"What do you remember from his face?" Gray asked.

"Nothing. He had panty hose over his head. He just looked scary."

After the interviews, Gray asked Matuszny what he thought. "It's the same one, I'm sure of it," Bob said.

Back downtown at Sex Crimes, Gray realized that to really do the investigation right, he would have to ask Bob for his files on the case. It was a sensitive request. Gray knew that the case had been Bob's baby for two years, that he had dumped his guts into it. Now he was being pushed aside.

Gray was uncomfortable when he phoned Bob and asked for his files. If he said he had lost them or couldn't find them, Gray would have understood.

After a moment, Bob said okay. Except Gray would have to do the copying, and Bob wanted the files back.

When Gray came to the Second District detectives room, Bob produced three inches of reports, filled with detailed legwork. "Man, you've really laid a foundation," Gray said.

Later, back at headquarters, as he started to photocopy the files, Gray felt sorry for Bob. It had to be tearing out his heart, being pulled off a case like this.

---

*Not her real name.

RONNIE

Ronnie knew he had to charm Connie Bellini's parents if he was going to marry their daughter. They were born in Italy, and watched over their four beautiful daughters with Old World strictness. He knew Connie would never marry him without their blessing.

Since he was not working, he occasionally dropped in at her parents' Parma home in the morning and had coffee with her mother. He offered to do chores in the yard, chop wood—anything to get them to like him.

He was usually good at making favorable first impressions. But he could tell he was having a tough sell. (Only later did Connie's mother tell her that Ronnie did not impress her favorably. She had seen this sort of man, the gigolo, in the Rome of her girlhood: smooth, helpful, handsome, charming on the surface, with nothing better to do during the day than to flatter an older woman so she would bless her daughter's relationship.)

He had had a previous spectacular failure with a friend's parents, and though it was a dozen years earlier he still felt shame when he thought about it. He was about twelve years old, staying overnight at a friend's house. In the middle of the night he awoke and crept quietly toward the bedroom of his pal's parents. He had been fascinated by the older woman, and in the dark he found her and her husband asleep in a double bed.

Ronnie moved quietly along her side of the bed, near the wall. He wedged himself between the mattress and the wall and watched her breathe, her chest rising and falling, covered by a thin gown. He put his hands on her breasts, then tried to slip his hands inside the top of her nightgown. She woke up, realized it was Ronnie, and stifled a scream.

Ronnie was ordered back to the other bedroom, and the next morning Rodney Shelton was told about the incident.

Now Ronnie wondered why his father had not taken him for help back then. He had to know he had a messed-up kid. Instead he threw the incident up to him—"I know what you did"—and threatened to humiliate him by telling his mother.

If Connie or her parents ever learned about this, they would never welcome him into the family. Ronnie knew he had many secrets to keep.

October–December 1985

LUCIE DUVALL

By October 1985 Lucie Duvall needed help. After only a month in the new unit, two of the original fifteen Sex Crimes detectives had asked to be reassigned. They were good street cops who just couldn't stand the constant flood of gruesome rapes and stomach-wrenching child abuse cases. And the West Side rape case was developing a higher public profile with each passing week. The number of rapes believed to be committed by the West Side Rapist now stood at twenty-four. If the investigation dragged on, it had the potential of making Duvall and her new unit look inept.

Based on what Ed Gray had told her, Bob Matuszny was the expert on the West Side Rapist. Duvall knew what she had to do. She got the police chief to temporarily reassign Bob to her unit.

Bob wasn't pleased with the reassignment. He had heard Duvall was tough to work under. The first day in his new assignment, she gave him a list of things she wanted done differently. Among them was the way he filed investigative reports.

In the Second District, all reports were entered into the computer, but Duvall wanted only written reports, with a copy sent to her. She didn't want any cop who felt like it to be able to punch up a case and find out how the rape investigations were going.

Matuszny said he had no problem with that. He could be as secretive as the best of them. "Who's gonna be my partner?" he asked.

"You're it," she said.

"I'm working this alone?"

"If you need someone for something, ask Gray or Zeb, or one of us can help out," she said.

He struggled to keep his mouth shut. This is bullshit, he thought. I can't run the whole investigation myself. There are two dozen rapes all over the West Side and in three or four suburbs. Plus, Gray and Zeb are swamped with new cases. I can't ask them to help. What the hell is going on?

He didn't complain. Duvall was tight with the chief, and Bob didn't want to antagonize her. Having been forced into the unit, he decided to make the best of it. At least he would get to work the case.

One of the first things he did was to send out a teletype to police departments across the country describing the modus operandi of the West Side Rapist, and asking for reports on similar rapes. Bob was flooded with calls and teletypes from all over—Laramie, Wyoming; Murfreesboro, Tennessee—but none of the out-of-state crimes fitted the Cleveland pattern. In fact, most were wildly dissimilar, and he soon began to feel he was wasting time talking to these other detectives, that he should be out on the street talking to neighbors and passing out composite photos.

Soon, he switched over to checking new leads and suspects connected with the Lorraine Kaye rape case. As usual when he got a suspect who fit the composite and seemed promising, Bob performed an informal check for penile warts. Before long Duvall heard about his unorthodox procedure and angrily put a stop to it.

This is crazy, she told him. Unless you've got a medical degree I'm not aware of, the police doctor will handle all inspections in the future. No more pecker checks.

Bob said all right, fine.

BOB MATUSZNY

About a month later, November 9, 1985, in the early Saturday morning dark, Ronnie was skulking in back of some houses along Elsetta Avenue on the West Side. He pulled up the ski mask hiding his face, lighted a cigarette, and turned down a sidewalk. He didn't notice the fourteen-year-old newspaper carrier watching him.

Suddenly, the boy came up behind him, startling him. "Hi," Ronnie said. "Hey, have you seen a collie?"

"No, I didn't see anything," the boy said. Ronnie cut across Elsetta and hurried off.

On November 11, Bob Matuszny finished his report on the Lorraine Kaye rape, tidying up the dozen or so leads he had pursued in the past month that had gone nowhere. In the four-page report, he also listed the suspects he had checked and eliminated. On the last page, he typed: "I have no further investigative leads into this crime. In the event a new lead does arise, this matter will be reopened."

With that he asked the chief's office for a transfer out of Sex Crimes, and it was approved. Bob was pleased. He would be back in the Second, able to investigate on his own time if another rape occurred in the Second District. He alerted Gray and Zeb about what he was going to do. Bob didn't want to make waves with other detectives.

BECKY ROTH

It was still dark on December 13, 1985, when Becky Roth's husband pulled on jeans, boots, and a flannel shirt and headed to his construction job in a beat-up van.

Inside the house on Elsetta Avenue, Becky sat on the couch, trying to wake up. She stripped off her nightgown and went in the bathroom and turned on the shower.

Becky didn't have to be at work until 7:30 A.M., so she had time to fix her long hair. She plugged in a curling iron while she waited for the water to warm up. A short woman with a Mona Lisa smile, she tutored mentally handicapped children for the state. She had patience, but even so her work sometimes left her frustrated. The water was hot and she stepped in and adjusted the spray.

Lurking in the bushes, Ronnie couldn't believe his luck. He had been about to abandon his voyeur's perch because the woman didn't turn him on. The house was sloppy and her husband looked like a grubby biker, which to Ronnie meant his wife was dirty, too. But he could hear her taking a shower! Rape in the shower, a favorite fantasy! She would smell fresh, her husband's touch scrubbed from her skin. Ronnie's hand shook a little as he jimmied the back door with his knife. He slipped inside silently and crept to the bathroom.

Ronnie quietly pushed open the bathroom door, smelled the tang of soap, and saw steam, which seemed to rush out and flood the entire house. Everything was bathed in shades of gray, made up of tiny dots like in a blown-up newspaper photo. Time stopped and he floated light-headedly. He was at peak excitement, sweating. He knew exactly what he was going to do.

He opened the shower door and she jumped. He had his pants down and a mesh T-shirt over his face. In his right hand he clenched a knife. "If you do what I say, I won't hurt you."

Then he pushed her to her knees and raped her every way he knew how while she cried hysterically. During the ordeal he commanded her, "Say 'I love you.'"

She could not. She was crying too hard.

"Say 'I love you'!"

Finally she said it, and he flushed with pleasure. She was the type of victim he most enjoyed: scared, small, pretty. Her sobbing knocked him out of his usual rape trance, and for the first time he felt as if he were attacking a real person. Even though her cries made it more difficult, he kept up the torment. Afterward, he warned her not to call the police or he'd come back and kill her.

As he started to leave, she said, "Be careful of the curling iron; it's hot." He took that as a sign of concern. Maybe she liked him. He stepped over it, shut the bathroom door, and took off. He drove to a twenty-four-hour diner, went into its deserted men's room, and scrubbed his penis in the sink.

Of all his rapes so far, Ronnie Shelton decided that this one had been the most satisfying.

Ed Gray

Detective Ed Gray steered an unmarked maroon police car down Brookpark Road near the Cleveland airport, a stretch of honky-tonks, diners, discos, porn shops, and adult video stores—the sleazy all-night entertainment strip at the southern border of the West Side. On the front seat of the police cruiser sat his partner, Andrea "Zeb" Zbydniewski, and a stack of photocopied composites of the West Side Rapist.

Gray admired the fresh composite, which had been based on the memory of the newspaper carrier on Elsetta Avenue whom the detectives located the day after Becky Roth was raped. The boy recalled a man prowling around one morning wearing a ski mask, then taking it off to smoke a cigarette. His face closely resembled earlier composite sketches. The boy described the prowler right down to the stripes on his running shoes and the color of his disposable lighter. Gray wished every witness were as observant.

The two detectives figured it made sense to blanket the sex spots with the new composite. Gray believed the rapist was a sex and power freak. Maybe he got supercharged with smut, then went out and did his dirty work. Who knows? It was worth a shot. After dropping off what seemed like a hundred composite fliers, they ended their shift with no new leads.

The day after Christmas, Gray took a telephone call in the squad room from a cashier at Brookpark News & Books, a ratty porn shop with peep-show booths and a wide assortment of hard-core smut. The cashier said one of her regular customers looked just like the composite. The guy was a cook on the midnight shift at one of the all-night restaurants on Brookpark.

Gray thanked her. Before their afternoon shift was over, he and Zeb interviewed the day managers at half a dozen diners, without success.

Later, Gray typed up a report for Lieutenant Duvall, thinking, No wonder this case has been around for two years.

As head of the new high-profile unit, Duvall had a lot at stake. So far her unit's four-month investigation into the case had been tremendously frustrating. Gray and Zeb were working it, but not exclusively. They were also assigned other rape cases and child abuse cases that flooded into the office, a total of more than thirty new ones a week. Along with everyone else in the unit, they couldn't keep up with the new investigations.

Furthermore, Duvall was feeling political heat from West Side City Council members and neighborhood groups, who repeatedly asked her whether her detectives were making progress. As did everybody else connected to the West Side rape case, she wanted it solved yesterday.

Two days later, Gray and Zeb got a break. A sixteen-year-old waitress at the Country Kitchen saw the composite picture taped on the cash register and said, "That looks like Wade Elmore." She called the detectives. She told them Elmore drove an old blue Ford Fairmont and she once saw a knife on its floor.

Gray checked Elmore through the computerized motor vehicle records and found a Parma address. "That's near those Parma rapes," Gray said. "Damn, let's find this guy."

RONNIE

Connie had bugged Ronnie about getting a job ever since she found out he had quit working at Scandinavian. But he felt everything she suggested was beneath him. He had to have a job that paid more than hers at SOHIO did. He wasn't going to be humiliated by having his woman bringing home more money than he did. Meanwhile, he was comfortable living off her paycheck, having her cook his meals and do his laundry.

He occasionally read the want ads, and one day spotted a job that sounded interesting: collection driver for the Cleveland Police Patrolmen's Association. The idea of putting himself among cops intrigued Ronnie. He applied and landed the job.

Ronnie's main duty turned out to be less glamorous than he expected: picking up checks for the ads that telephone solicitors sold in a program for the union's annual fund-raiser. But he enjoyed a great fringe benefit: a "courtesy card," blue with an embossed shield, that amounted to a "free pass" to present to a Cleveland police officer when he got pulled over for a minor offense.

Working for the Cleveland cops, right under their gaze, gave Ronnie a perverse sense of satisfaction. He felt they were too incompetent to capture him, despite the chances he took. A couple of times, he had been right under their noses as they rolled up to a rape scene, watching them from his car or a nearby hiding place. Now he was raising money for them.

By the end of the first week, Ronnie learned that Cleveland

cops bought their badges and holsters at a store in a warehouse east of downtown. He drove there and bought a police badge, flare gun, shoulder holster, and handcuffs. No one at the store asked him to prove he was a policeman. The next day before his rounds, Ronnie strapped on the shoulder holster and gun, pinned the badge and handcuffs at his hip, and put on a sports coat. Dressed in his image of a detective, Ronnie found that he commanded respect, especially from attractive young receptionists at some of the law firms he made stops at. One receptionist called him "Officer," which made him feel powerful and respected. He wished his father could see him.

The next day he sent the young woman flowers and asked her out on a date. She said yes.

January–February 1986

ED GRAY

The day after New Year's, Gray and Zeb dropped in on Elmore at his apartment building. Gray said they were investigating a rape and a break-in. Elmore seemed concerned and said he would help.

Gray mentioned the times Lorraine Kaye and Becky Roth were raped and asked Elmore where he was. He replied that he was at work, both times.

"We'd like to take your picture and fingerprints, to see if we can eliminate you as a suspect," Gray said.

Elmore said, "I got no problem with that."

Gray had a hunch Elmore wasn't the rapist and that this was

all probably a waste of time. Elmore was probably just another suspect in a long line of look-alikes whose alibis had been checked out and verified by Bob Matuszny and other detectives.

The next day, Gray talked with Duvall. She said to get his prints and a photo for lineups, and to ask the police doctor to examine Elmore for venereal warts.

Later Gray and Zeb stopped at Elmore's apartment and took prints and photo. "The suspect has something peculiar about his penis," Gray told him. "We can eliminate you by a check of your penis."

After a moment Elmore said, "This is weird. No way. I did everything you asked, but I'm drawing the line here."

Now Gray and Zeb were suspicious. "Well, will you let us look in your car, at least?" Gray asked. "If you're not the rapist, we'd like to eliminate you as soon as we can."

Elmore said okay.

Gray opened a back door and on the seat of the old Ford found a pair of work boots, a black sweater with diamond shapes, and . . . a blue disposable cigarette lighter.

Interesting, Gray thought. The paperboy mentioned the suspect had a blue lighter. With a pen, Gray pushed the lighter into a small evidence envelope. He reached under the front seat and searched the floor in methodical swipes until he touched something flimsy. He pulled out a pair of panty hose. Both legs had been snipped off.

Gray's pulse jumped. Two recent victims had said the rapist wore a nylon stocking over his head! He tried to stay calm. "This your stuff?" he asked Elmore.

"The sweater's mine, the lighter's mine," he replied. "The nylon, I don't know where that came from."

Back at Sex Crimes, Gray and Zeb briefed Duvall. The panty-hose mask clinched it for her.

"We'll just get a court order that compels him to let us check for warts," Duvall said, excited. "We'll see how Mr. Elmore likes that."

A week later, with the court order in hand, Lieutenant Duvall and Detectives Gray and Zeb picked up Wade Elmore and took him to the office of the police department doctor. The doctor took Elmore into an examining room. After a few minutes, he came out and said, "Mr. Elmore has a lesion on the top of his penile shaft."

The detectives smiled.

"How unusual is this, uh, condition?" Gray asked.

"Not very. These lesions are not uncommon. They are easily cured."

"These things just come and go?" Gray asked.

The doctor said, "All the time. Very typical."

Gray realized that they were going about the suspect's ID all wrong. The warts were too common, too unreliable.

Back at Sex Crimes, Duvall was still fired up about Elmore. She felt he most probably was the rapist they were looking for and said it was time to charge him. She wanted the case referred to the prosecutor.

Gray was worried. He felt the case on Elmore was weak. The real rapist, most likely, was still out there somewhere. "I can't refer. He's not the guy."

"I order you to have him referred."

"You can't order me to refer if I think he's not right," Gray said sharply. "You fill out the booking slip then."

Now Duvall's face matched her hair color. A booking slip that was not signed by the deckhand was a giveaway: The detective didn't believe in the case. If the case fell apart, her reputation would be at risk.

She mentioned a seasoned homicide detective she respected. "I'll have him talk to Elmore," she said.

Gray exploded. This was a slap in the face. "What the hell does he know about this case? You won't use me, you won't use Matuszny. Why don't you just take me off the case."

After a minute, Duvall said, "Okay, have Bob come in." She stomped off and later tried to calm down over a drink with Arnie Hovan, a Sex Crimes detective who was her good friend.

"I can't believe he wouldn't charge him," she said at the bar, still shaky from the blowup.

"Lucie, what are you complaining about?" Hovan said. "He's

a good detective. He's just doing what he believes is right. In fact, I think he is right."

She managed a laugh. "Great, a mutiny."

Late in the afternoon Ed Gray telephoned Matuszny at the Second District. "We're holding this guy for the West Side rapes and we're about to refer him."

"You don't sound happy about it," Bob said.

"I think he's the wrong guy."

"So don't refer."

"Lucie wants it."

Matuszny understood the dilemma Gray faced. He was getting pressure from his supervisor to have the suspect charged.

"Can you take a look at this Elmore for us?" Gray asked.

Later that afternoon, Matuszny warmed up the unmarked car and drove over salt-covered streets to visit Elmore in a tiny interview room outside the jail unit in the Justice Center, a poorly designed twenty-one-floor complex that included the county jail, four dozen courtrooms, and the slowest elevator in downtown Cleveland. Immediately he knew Elmore was the wrong man. He was too big and dim-witted, hardly the devious stalker who had eluded capture for more than two years. Afterward, Bob told Gray and Zeb, "I really don't think it's the guy."

Gray agreed and said he was still going to have to refer Elmore to the prosecutor—"Lucie will go nuts otherwise"—but that he would explain to him privately what was going on.

The next day, Elmore was referred to the city prosecutor for rape charges. After getting a fill-in from Gray, the prosecutor quickly made a call: insufficient evidence to charge. Elmore was released.

RONNIE

Early one morning in February 1986, Ronnie unlocked the door to Connie's apartment with his key. He had been up all night, stalking, and was exhausted. It was tough living a double life, lying to Connie, keeping her in line with lies and threats. He felt pressure building at the front of his head. A pounding migraine was coming on.

Anticipating his girlfriend's anger, Ronnie prepared a cover story about where he had been all night, then changed tactics. He decided to rekindle an argument they had gotten into the day before, a bitter fight about children. He wanted to keep her off-balance.

It seemed perverse, but because of the beatings and abuse he suffered as a kid, Ronnie loved the notion of having children. Kids would make him appear normal, an all-American family man. Kids would camouflage his repugnant secret. So last night, once again, he told Connie he wanted a son and a daughter, just like his parents had had. But Connie held out, saying she wasn't ready for anything as serious as marriage and family. This deflated a favorite fantasy and enraged him.

Now, this morning, he shut the door loud enough for her to hear and walked down the hall, his high-top tennis shoes scuffing the carpet. Ronnie psyched himself up: It's all *her* fault. It's all her fault because she doesn't want to have my babies.

He found her in the bedroom and attacked. "I can't believe

110

what you said. I love children. I want us to have a baby someday."

Connie was nearly ready for work, but running late. She looked elegant in her business suit and silk blouse. "We aren't even married," she said quickly. "And all we do is fight." She immediately regretted saying anything. It would irritate Ronnie and slow down her escape to the office.

He grabbed her arms.

"Let go!" she said. She knew what was coming and tried to run to the bathroom, where she could lock the door. She backed down the hall, struggling to pull free. With a free hand, Ronnie slapped her across the face. She started to cry, then yelled, "Get the hell out of my apartment! Get out! I hate you, you bastard!"

Rage hit Ronnie like a thunderclap. He hated being called a bastard. His parents had tried to hide the fact that he had been born before they got married, but he had picked up hints over the years, and it shamed him.

Using his weight, he shoved Connie into the bathroom. She skidded backward across the floor, her high heels flipping from under her, and crashed into the slightly cracked toilet tank, knocking it from the wall. It smashed on the floor, and water flooded the room, spraying Connie's clothes. Pain shot up her back.

Suddenly mortified, Ronnie pushed into the smallish bathroom and tried to turn off the supply line to the toilet. He stood silent as Connie ran out, changed, and left for work, her back throbbing and her face swollen.

He felt sick, embarrassed at his outburst. To soothe his feeling of self-hatred, he turned, reflexively, to self-pity, and blamed Connie for his violence. I was trying to be a family man, he convinced himself. But she turned me down. This is her fault.

A few hours later, Connie answered the phone at work. In the background she heard a love song by the band Air Supply playing on her stereo, then his voice. "I know I've hurt you, and I just called to say good-bye," Ronnie said softly. "Good-bye, Connie."

"Good-bye," she said. She slammed down the phone, then

looked around to see if anyone in her office had noticed. She hoped the call meant Ronnie was moving out.

A policeman from North Olmsted slowly walked down the hallway outside Connie's apartment. A call had come in about a man who said he was depressed and claimed to have swallowed a handful of codeine pills.

Outside apartment 312, the policeman heard music, then knocked on the door. No answer. He tried the knob, found it unlocked, and walked in. It was about 4:30 P.M., February 11, 1986.

Ronnie sat at a table with a butcher knife arranged next to a bottle of pills. He looked groggy. An empty pill bottle lay on the floor. The label said, "Tylenol with codeine, 30 mg."

"How many did you take?" the officer asked.

"I don't know . . . ten," Ronnie said. "I just want to die," he moaned, and closed his eyes.

"Can you stand up?"

"No. I want to die."

"C'mon, life can't be that bad."

"I got no job, my girlfriend left me, and she won't have my baby," Ronnie said.

The policeman called for an ambulance, then called in Ronnie's name and social security number to the dispatcher for a records check, as procedure required. Soon he heard back that the suicidal young man had an outstanding warrant in nearby Brook Park. He had not shown up in court for a traffic offense.

"See if they want us to hold him at the hospital until one of their officers arrives," he instructed the dispatcher.

The Brook Park police responded, saying they did not want to arrest Shelton now. Brook Park had a tiny jail and limited resources. The last thing it wanted was a suicidal prisoner charged with only a petty crime.

It was near the end of her workday when Connie took a call from a nurse at Fairview General Hospital. "Your boyfriend tried to commit suicide," the nurse said. "Do you want to talk to him?"

While Connie waited for Ronnie to get on the line, she felt tremendous guilt, believing that somehow it was her fault that her unstable boyfriend was in the hospital. She knew he was a manipulative bastard, but knowing that didn't help her control her confused feelings. She had grown up in an overprotective home, speaking Italian to her Old World mom and dad, learning early and repeatedly that men were not to be trusted, that they wanted sex and then would disrespect her once she was no longer a virgin. But her parents also planned for Connie to marry. She wondered, Does my fiancé instantly turn trustworthy at the altar? How are his base instincts held in check once we're married? She was confused by her parents' old-fashioned concept of men.

Now, finally, at age twenty-six, she was trapped in her first serious relationship with a man whose emotional rages and romantic reconciliations—sobbing, hugging her knees, begging for forgiveness—seemed to spring from the pages of the pulp romance novels she devoured each week. Connie hated herself for staying with Ronnie, but she couldn't force herself to cut him off. He's so needy, she felt. If she could just let him down easy, maybe he'd take the hint and walk away.

Ronnie finally got on the hospital telephone and told her he'd tried to kill himself because he loved her. "I need you," he said. "Will you come see me?" Connie found herself saying yes.

When he saw Connie walk in the hospital room, Ronnie turned his head to the wall. He waited, wanting to hear, "I'm sorry. I love you."

At this moment, he seemed utterly pathetic to her, lower than she had ever seen him. Still, she was afraid to end their relationship. In the past when he'd sensed her pulling away, Ronnie had threatened to drag her parents into their disputes, because he knew this terrified her. She had never told them about the emotional and physical beatings she suffered. If she had, it would only have made them angry and disappointed in her for being so foolish and weak. She loved her parents and was prepared to suffer tremendous pain before she'd ever hurt them.

Finally she told him, "I'm sorry about this. I'll help you get back on your feet."

A moment later Ronnie's parents swept into the hospital room. Quickly, Ronnie shut his eyes and turned away, feigning sleep. He wanted to hear what they had to say.

Ronnie's dad whispered, "He's faking. He's not asleep." Then in a louder voice, "Ronnie, we want you at home. You live with us so we can keep track of you."

Ronnie opened his eyes and saw his mother's sad, concerned face. He smiled weakly.

The next morning, coincidentally, the first full-color composite sketch of the West Side Rapist was released to newspapers and television stations. Ed Gray and the Sex Crimes detectives were hoping to keep the case alive by releasing a new composite photo and offering a $2,000 reward. Cash usually flushed out tips, leads, and jailhouse snitches. Most calls were junk, but among the dross was often something of value. It was remarkable, Gray thought, how many cases were cracked by snitches or once-apathetic neighbors who would finally get up off their haunches in hopes of getting paid for information.

That evening, the composite sketch of the West Side Rapist was prominently displayed on the four local television newscasts. The next day, the composite was printed in more than half a million copies of the *Plain Dealer*.

The next night, Ronnie was fully recovered from his botched suicide and shooting pool with a pal at Harlow's, a nightclub. They played eye-contact games with a couple of young women who watched them from nearby barstools.

"Hey, Shelton," his friend said at one point. "I know who you really are."

"What do you mean?" Ronnie asked.

"You're the West Side Rapist," he said.

Shelton missed his shot and looked up, trying to stay calm. He struggled to keep his voice nonchalant. "What are you talking about?"

"I know you are that West Side Rapist," he said. "You know, the one on TV." Then he laughed.

Ronnie joined in quickly, relieved. His pal was teasing. It was his idea of a joke.

Then Ronnie felt the young women looking at him again. He didn't want to find out if the looks were of desire or suspicion. "Hey, there's nothing happening here," Ronnie said. "Let's go someplace else."

BECKY ROTH

In the weeks after Ronnie raped her in her bathroom, Becky Roth could not force herself to strip off her clothes to take a shower. She hated being naked, and the thought of stepping inside the bathroom terrified her. She talked about it to her mom, who agreed to help her. First, Becky's father, a wealthy businessman, installed a shower in a small second bathroom. For the next few months, her mother drove over each morning and stood outside the bathroom door while Becky showered in a swimsuit.

Moments into a shower, Becky called out, "Are you there?"

"Yes, it's okay," her mom replied.

A minute later: "You there?"

"Yes."

During their marriage, Becky's husband, a rough-hewn construction worker, had masked his own problems by drinking. His possessiveness was a problem too. Each time she took the tiniest step toward independence, he dug in his heels. After she was raped, he seemed to step up his drinking.

115

Their life together had sunk into misery. After the rape, Becky found herself withdrawing from him and from everyone else. She knew what she was doing but could not help it. She did not want to go out. She jumped at every sound, and she absolutely refused to step into the bathroom where she had been raped, not even to clean it.

One evening, she listened passively as her husband complained about how lousy her cooking and her lovemaking had become after the rape. He made it sound as if he was the victim, Becky thought. She kept quiet during these tirades because saying anything seemed to provoke him.

Suddenly, he threw her purse into the bathroom where she had been raped. "Go get it," he ordered.

"What are you doing?" she said, frightened.

"Get it."

"I can't, I can't."

"Get with the real world!" he insisted. "You got to get over this!"

"I can't go in there," she said, crying.

He pulled her to the bathroom and Becky dropped to the floor, limp as a sack. "No, no!" she screamed.

He tried to push her inside, but she fought him with surprising fury. He gave up and she ran to the living room. He followed, yelling, "Get over it! Get over it!"

He trailed her from room to room, yelling, and she ended up on the kitchen floor, huddled into a ball, her hands over her ears. But she still heard his screams, and wanted to die. Death seemed so peaceful.

After that fight, Becky felt as if she had remained in the position she took on the kitchen floor. She retreated inside herself and avoided her husband. She did not leave their house, other than for work and necessary errands. She lavished affection on the guard dog she bought to feel safer. She never wanted to make love to her husband again.

RONNIE

Despite the perks of his job with the Cleveland police union, Ronnie quickly began doing shoddy work. It was late winter, and his nightly prowling for victims took its toll; in the morning he showed up at work exhausted and red-eyed, with the unmistakable look of someone who had been up all night. The office manager couldn't figure out Ronnie's problem: He was well-spoken, neatly dressed, and didn't smell of booze; why was he so frazzled?

On his collection route, Ronnie frequently didn't complete his pickups. He often went back to sleep or got distracted by a pretty woman and followed her to her apartment or home, making sure to note her address so he could come back at night. Meanwhile, the telephone salesmen were furious when Ronnie returned without checks for sales they had closed, which killed their commissions.

Before he could be fired, Ronnie quit. He had other ways to make money. One night soon afterward, he carefully shaved, showered, and splashed on a heavy cologne. He was excited about the night he'd arranged. This would be different, something he hadn't done in a while.

He slipped on a G-string and then pulled a pair of bikini underpants over it. He took a blue police uniform off a hanger and put on the pants and shirt. He strapped on the thick black belt and holster. He clipped on a navy-blue police tie and positioned a tie tack in the middle. He liked the touch with the tie tack. It was a tiny silver pig.

He positioned a blue police hat over his longish hair and snapped a flare gun in the holster. There, he was ready, Ronnie felt. One macho-looking dude.

He got in his car and drove to a West Side address. It was about ten at night when he got out of his car and heard music and women laughing. He walked to the front door and saw a living room full of young women, drinking and dancing, having a lively party.

Ronnie rang the doorbell and was let in. Right away he saw another male stripper, wearing ripped jeans, a muscle T-shirt, tool belt, and construction hat. He was finishing a drink.

"What are you doing here?" Ronnie demanded.

"I had a gig. They wanted me to dance."

"I was supposed to dance," Ronnie said.

"They changed their minds. They wanted me and couldn't get ahold of you to cancel. So I did it."

Ronnie looked around the bachelorette party. The women, including the bride, were already loose from the drinks and from the other stripper's act. He was furious; all this preparation for nothing. The hostess came over and he started to complain. She said she'd see what she could do, and took up a collection. She came back with about $50, and Ronnie said, okay, he'd dance.

Ronnie worked the room, making eye contact, smiling, dancing quickly at first, grinding his crotch and pumping his hips, an exaggerated pantomime of sex. He loved dancing for private parties. Sometimes he was solicited and ended up in a bedroom before the party was over.

He didn't feel like a sex object to these women, but rather a powerful god. He was turning them on, making them want him. He controlled them. Just as he controlled his rape victims. Just as he controlled girlfriends, his sister, and every other female in his life—except for his mother.

Ronnie had heard his mom say many times that she loved him, but her whippings had been far worse and unpredictable than his father's. She lost control and went too far; many times, using an electrical cord, she crosshatched his back with thick, bloody welts. One time Rodney Shelton saw them and made his wife apologize to Ronnie. A day or two later, at a summer baseball game in the neighborhood, Ronnie stood up to bat and like the other boys stripped off his shirt. Usually he covered his arms and back to hide his marks. This time, perhaps, he was asking for help. He squared at the plate and . . . the game stopped. The boys ran up and gazed at his back. One ran for his mother, who came out and appeared stunned. The next day he was called into the junior high school office and referred to Child Guidance, the school system's social services arm that dealt with family problems.

A Child Guidance counselor asked about the bruises and welts. Ronnie wouldn't talk because he knew that to tell the truth would get his parents in trouble. The counselor smiled and asked more questions, which forced Ronnie to remember things he wanted to forget. He sat in the office chair, tears rolling down his face, wanting to run out. The man pointed to a large blowup clown with a heavy, rounded base.

"Hit the clown," the man said.

"What?" Ronnie was confused.

"You're angry at your father. Take it out on the clown. Go ahead, beat it up. You might feel better."

Ronnie felt stupid. He didn't want to hit the clown, but the counselor kept pushing. To please him, Ronnie slugged it, and the goofy face rocked back and forth, back and forth.

Now at the bachelorette party the women were loving Ronnie's act. They hooted and clapped as he pulled off each piece of clothing, especially after the second song, when he stripped to bikini underpants. Two songs later he was in his G-string, smiling, rocking his crotch in their faces, coyly pirouetting, slowing when a woman had a folded dollar bill to slip inside his waist string. Other women were bolder, taking turns pushing money inside the tiny triangle of material stretched over his crotch. They fondled his genitals for a moment before he swirled away, flirting with his eyes and lips.

When he finished his act, Ronnie dripped sweat, flushed with excitement. He felt like a real man.

119

BETTY OCILKA

Two years had passed since she was raped, and Betty Ocilka wanted answers from the police. She knew the Second District detectives by name because she ran into them on her mail route at C&J Donut, the tiny coffee shop across from the police station. What's going on with my case? she would ask, and the answer was always: No news; we're still working on it.

" 'We're working on it, we're working on it,' " she said to a friend, mimicking their responses. "They're working on it, shit."

Each day as she trundled through her mail route, she thought of her attacker. She had gotten over the terror and sleeplessness and her inability to concentrate on what people were saying to her in ordinary conversation. But she still had to live with her rage, and it ripped her like a saw.

Betty's mail route wove near the scenes of four of the West Side rapes, and brought her into contact with scores of men each day. When she walked her route, her eyes were like security cameras—constantly alert, swiveling, checking out each man who crossed her path.

"The cops won't find him, I will," she told friends. "I'm gonna find the son of a bitch that did this to me."

Her anger got her out of bed and kept her going. The only other thing that mattered to her was her young son. She would burn in hell before she let anything happen to him.

The weather warmed up for the day and Betty took her son

and his cousin to Edgewater Park on Lake Erie. In the early afternoon, on the way back to the West Side, they stopped at the McDonald's at the corner of Fulton Road and Memphis Avenue. Even today, a day off with the kids, she found herself comparing each male face to what she remembered seeing in the early dawn two years ago: a slender, strong-jawed young man, sort of a common look, dark skin, with no exaggerated features other than his feathered hair.

Betty had run across several men who resembled the shadowy man who raped her that morning and had called the detectives each time. Now at McDonald's she spotted a man who she felt *certain* was her attacker. The only problem was he was wearing a security guard uniform and patrolling the place.

Without alarming the two boys, Betty got up and went outside to call the police. Soon, a police dispatcher was relaying her call over the airwaves. About a mile away, in the Second District detective bureau, Bob Matuszny heard the call, radioed in that he would take it, grabbed his partner, and sped to McDonald's.

Bob knew he wasn't supposed to be working the case. What the hell, he felt. By the time the call got relayed downtown to the Sex Crimes Unit, it could take a day or two before someone came out on this suspicious-person call. The creep could be long gone by then.

He saw Betty Ocilka at a table and walked over. "He looks like the guy?" Bob asked.

"I wouldn't have called otherwise," she said, testily.

Matuszny took the security guard outside and said, "You've been identified by an eyewitness as a suspect in a rape case. We would like to ask you a few questions."

The guard soaked in the information. "This is crazy!" he exclaimed. "I never raped nobody."

"You don't have to help us if you don't want to," Bob said. "But then we'll just investigate you more."

The guard agreed to come back to the Second District and talk. Bob radioed in that he was detaining a rape suspect.

Meanwhile, Lieutenant Duvall was told that a suspect in the

West Side rape case had been picked up for investigation, only it wasn't one of the Sex Crimes detectives who grabbed the suspect. It was Matuszny, which infuriated her.

At the Second District, Bob decided that the security guard did strongly resemble the composite sketch of the suspect. But the guard had an alibi for his early-morning whereabouts. Bob took him into the men's room and asked him to pull down his pants.

"You're clean," Bob said. "C'mon, I'll drive you back."

The next day, Bob listened as Lieutenant Duvall blistered him: You defied orders and continued to work the West Side rape case. If you want to continue in this, you better have the chief of police on your side. Otherwise, you're asking for trouble.

"It pissed me off," Matuszny said later on. "What were we supposed to do, let the guy disappear? It would have taken Sex Crimes two days to get over there."

That was it, Bob decided, he wasn't going to let himself be dragged before the police disciplinary board for insubordination. He wanted more than anything to nail the West Side Rapist. He had spent hundreds of hours tracking him. He had knocked his brains out trying to figure him out. He had worked overtime without pay. He'd sat in all-night stakeouts. Now he had to wash his hands of the case, and it hurt him deeply.

Fine, he tried to tell himself; Sex Crimes can have it all to themselves. But there's no way they'll catch that guy with her in charge. Not unless they get lucky.

RONNIE

Ronnie passed a red Pontiac Fiero stranded in morning rush hour on southbound I-71, just south of Strongsville. He was headed to his parents' place in Brunswick Hills for sleep and a shave. The woman inside was young, pretty, and Ronnie pulled over on the shoulder. He shifted into reverse and, transmission whining, backed up past the roaring traffic.

She looked scared. All the doors were locked but she opened her window an inch and said she had run out of gas.

He laughed. He knew fear when he saw it. To ease her fright, he slid his driver's license in the window to let her know his name and maybe feel safer. She gave him a few dollars and kept his license while he went for gas. When he came back, she showered him with thanks.

Several days later he got a letter at his parents' address with a $5 bill.

Dear Ronnie:

I just wanted to thank you for helping me the other day. If you hadn't stopped, I don't know what I'd have done. If more men were like you, we'd all be a lot safer. Here's a little something for your trouble. If I had more, I'd give you more. Thank you, Ronnie!

Tricia

Ronnie folded the bill in his pocket. He wished she had included a return address. She was cute and he would like to have dated her. Then he reread the note and began to cry.

Ronnie felt good when he protected women—his sister, his girlfriends, women in nightclubs he rescued from unruly dates. Most of these young, pretty blue-collar women found his protectiveness touching. He told them to lock their doors and he checked the backseats of their cars at night and the window locks in their apartments. He knew all too well how easy it was for someone to break in and hurt them.

He offered to help fix their cars or move furniture or go shopping with them at the malls. Sometimes he blamed his helpfulness for bringing him trouble. Especially the time in 1978 in Brunswick Hills when he was sixteen.

He had spent hours watching their next-door neighbor, Ramie Ann Reilly,* an attractive twenty-nine-year-old woman with long brown hair and a good figure. Ramie Ann loved gardening and treated her flowerbeds and three-acre lawn like an only child. Ronnie always ran over to her house if she was cutting the grass or when she came home with groceries and volunteered to help. He didn't feel like a boy around her because she talked to him as if he were an adult, which thrilled him. The first time Ronnie saw her in a halter top washing her car he thought she was the most exciting woman in the world.

Ronnie was jealous of her husband. He was short, soft in the waist, not particularly handsome, and Ronnie felt he didn't deserve someone as nice as Ramie Ann. When they weren't home, Ronnie broke in and rooted through Ramie Ann's clothes hamper to touch her slips and panties and bras and rub them against his peach-fuzz face. He saw an adult magazine on an end table and figured the Reillys were swingers. He imagined violent sex with her and masturbated.

It was about seven in the morning, June 21, 1978, a year after the Sheltons moved to Brunswick Hills. Ronnie heard Ramie Ann's husband leave for work. He crept to her house with his father's handgun.

---

*Not her real name.

He tapped on her front door and she answered it in her robe. "I'd like to have sex with you," he blurted out. He dug his hand into the pocket of his jeans and pulled out some crumpled bills. "I have money."

"You gotta be kidding," Ramie Ann said. "Get the hell out of here!"

Ronnie was locked in his fantasy. He pulled out the gun and pointed it at her. She froze for a second, then dashed to the sliding door to try to let in her dogs. Ronnie grabbed her by her long hair, jerked her to a stop, and hit her with the gun butt.

She fell facedown, screaming, and he pinned her to the carpet, her face mashed into the blue pile. A hammer lay nearby. Her husband, Pat, had been remodeling and had left his tools out. Ramie Ann squirmed and reached for the hammer. Ronnie snatched it instead and hit her in the head. Blood poured from a gash in her scalp, flooding into her ears and across her face.

Ramie Ann pretended to have a heart attack and asked for a glass of water. When he turned for an instant, she ducked and sprinted for the front door. Ronnie yelled, Stop, then fired at her twice, plugging the front-door frame.

Face and hands slicked with blood, Ramie Ann Reilly ran shrieking across her beautiful wide yard.

Nine days later Ronnie pleaded guilty to attempted rape in Medina County juvenile court and was sentenced to the Training Center for Youth, a medium-security institution in Columbus for juvenile sex offenders and other delinquents whose crimes were linked to psychological problems.

Ronnie felt like an oddity at the school, and its demographics bore this out. Only one of fifteen prisoners was incarcerated there for having committed a violent crime, and of those only one in four had lived with both parents in the same home. When asked about it years later, he said he did not remember getting any therapy.

On March 30, 1979, after eight months of incarceration, he

was discharged to his parents and enrolled in eleventh grade at Brunswick High School.

Whenever he was outside chopping wood or cutting the grass, he looked for Ramie Ann. He still felt like helping her with yard work. Only now a five-foot board-on-board fence divided the huge yards, and he had to make do with his fantasies.

PART THREE

A Crack
in the Ice

February–March 1986

Lucie Duvall

Lucie Duvall was wading through troubled waters. Her friend and protector, Cleveland Police Chief Bill Hanton, had just retired, and she was not close to any of the rumored top contenders for the job.

Then disaster struck. On February 23, 1986, the *Plain Dealer* bannered a story across the top of page 1: "Problems Handcuff Police Sex Crimes Unit, Say Critics." Based on quotes from anonymous detectives and from a Cleveland city councilman who had helped to form the unit, the story painted a dismaying portrait of Duvall's team.

> A major concern is that four detectives left the unit within its first four months, including one considered a top sex crimes investigator. Only one of those who quit has been replaced.
>
> The unit is understaffed and too overwhelmed with work to respond properly to complaints, police sources who requested anonymity said. They said many of the staff lacked the background and training to conduct sex crimes investigations.
>
> Police sources also said the unit's chief, Lt. Lucie J. Duvall, had a rigid management style that left little room for compromise and was a major reason some personnel left the unit.
>
> "I had hopes of it being the best in the nation, but I don't think it's effective," said a policeman. ". . . I have people calling me saying they can't get anyone from the unit to respond to their complaints. And I get cops from the unit asking me how to proceed in their investigations. The background skill is missing."

Lucie felt blindsided by a carefully choreographed character assassination plot. With the new police chief to be named in a

129

week, the article put intense political pressure on him to reassign her to another job.

Battling sex crimes was the toughest, most frustrating assignment Lucie Duvall had faced in fourteen years as a cop. It was far trickier than the wham-bam sting operations she ran as head of the downtown vice unit, sweeping up hookers and johns on Prospect Avenue. In Sex Crimes, detectives were saddled with reluctant witnesses, victims who disappeared, often-unreliable testimony of little children, perishable physical evidence, and emotional burnout. And the crimes occurred relentlessly—two, three, four new rapes a day. In the Homicide Unit, where detectives were the cock of the walk, the unit got two or three new killings a week. They solved half of them within twenty-four hours, usually when a family member confessed or an eyewitness came forward.

Lucie never would have imagined that she'd end up in a job where a typical day might entail interviewing a five-year-old boy about how he contracted gonorrhea of the anus. She had grown up in rural northeastern Pennsylvania, a sheltered redheaded tomgirl who liked to jump off garage roofs using an umbrella as a parachute.

She moved to Cleveland with her first husband, a high school sweetheart, and after their divorce took the Cleveland police exam on a dare. She scored high. It was 1973, and the Cleveland Police Department was reeling from a federal district judge's order to open up its ranks to women. At her physical, Lucie failed the vision test, but the doctor passed her anyway, saying his actions wouldn't matter since he believed she was too tiny to be allowed on the force. (At twenty-eight, Lucie was five-foot-three and weighed only 100 pounds.) When she broke in on the job, patrolling the roughest sections of Cleveland's East Side, she turned out to be sturdy enough to weather the work, as well as the sexist jokes and condescension that were the norm in the 1970s.

A week after the damaging news story, Cleveland's mayor, George Voinovich, named Howard Rudolph, a stern workaholic lieutenant with a straight-arrow reputation, as the new chief.

Rudolph currently headed all police investigative units, including Sex Crimes.

Lucie was worried. She and Rudolph were opposites who had never developed a warm working relationship. Rudolph was stiff, all business, and he unwound by jogging around the tiny track in the police gymnasium or playing a round of golf. She preferred dinner with friends or a movie to escape the rigors of the job. For a while, she took acting lessons. There was nothing she could do but wait and see if the *Plain Dealer* article sank her.

In his first days on the job, Rudolph promised the citizens more police in the neighborhoods and faster response time to calls for help. Everyone on the force knew what that meant: pushing blue uniforms from headquarters to the six districts. Rudolph announced 110 transfers among the police brass. Forty-two lieutenants were affected. Lieutenant Lucie Duvall was not one of them. She had survived, for now.

RONNIE

Spring finally brightened the urban landscape and gently pushed people outdoors to their yards and sidewalks. Ronnie appreciated the warmer weather. He could prowl at night without leaving footprints in the snow. Also, young women were more apt to have their windows opened or unlocked. And they wore shorts and skimpier tops.

After his suicide try, Ronnie kept on his best behavior for a while. Feeling sorry for him, Connie decided to help him get on his feet, then leave him. Meanwhile she insisted that Ronnie get the recurring venereal wart at the end of his penis removed. She made an appointment for him to see a doctor in Parma and told Ronnie she'd pay for the procedure.

In his office, the doctor promised Ronnie the removal wouldn't hurt. He chilled the wart with liquid nitrogen and then cauterized it with what looked like an electric soldering iron. Ronnie yelped in pain.

"It hurt like hell," Ronnie told Connie later. "I hope you're happy." He milked the operation for every drop of sympathy he could squeeze from her. Secretly, he was tremendously happy that he was clean: The warts hurt his playboy image among his girlfriends.

He didn't realize it—Cleveland detectives carefully withheld this clue from the press—but he had also just eliminated a physical idiosyncrasy that made it much easier for rape victims and police to identify him.

The police continued their chase, and Ronnie could feel them a few steps behind him. He had watched detectives drive over to Elsetta Avenue, where he'd raped Becky Roth in the shower. He recognized the big maroon Ford and the methodical walk of detectives as they banged on doors up and down Elsetta Avenue, looking for witnesses. They'll never catch me, he thought.

In the weeks after the attack, he became obsessed with Becky, the timid young woman whom he had forced to say "I love you" while raping. He wondered what it would be like to meet her in a nightclub or a restaurant and then get to know her. Maybe he'd even date her, all without letting her know he was the guy who raped her.

That would be wild, he thought.

April–May 1986

BECKY ROTH

By April, Becky's life was a twisted wreck. She drank heavily, her husband abused her, and her work with handicapped kids dragged her spirits even lower. In a burst of optimism, she persuaded her husband to accompany her to a marriage counselor. But it turned out to be a waste of energy. He didn't take it seriously, and Becky could not warm up to the counselor, a mannish woman with the finesse of a drill sergeant. They never went back.

Becky became so depressed and lethargic that her doctor prescribed antidepressants and anxiety relievers. For weeks, she floated through her life, zoned out on the pills, not knowing what was taking place at work or at home.

One night, when the weight of her troubles seemed to be smothering her, she lifted her body off the couch, gagged down a handful of pills, and fell asleep. Hours later, she opened her eyes, feeling nauseated, her head pounding. She started to cry, thinking, God, I'm so fucked up I can't even kill myself without making a mess of it.

Later, she remembered a nurse at the emergency room who told her about the Cleveland Rape Crisis Center. Becky called and asked for help. A volunteer on the phone reassured Becky that her feelings were normal. It also sounded like her attacker was the West Side Rapist, Becky was told. Another of his victims had just gone through rape crisis training. Maybe you should talk to her, the volunteer suggested. She gave Becky a phone number and a name: Marian Butler.

The two women met outside a Friendly's restaurant near the Parmatown Mall & Plaza, then walked in together. They ordered coffee, then both fired up the first of a long chain of cigarettes.

"Talk to me, Becky," Marian said. "What's your story?"

Becky hesitated. It was so painful to dredge up.

"Look, I'll tell you my story," Marian said after a moment. "Then you tell me yours, okay?"

Marian recounted the attack while Becky shivered at the familiar details. At the same time, Becky was comforted to know she wasn't alone, that someone else had suffered what she had and could understand her.

When it was Becky's turn to talk, she said she was afraid that the rapist was going to return and kill her. After all, that was what he said he would do if she called the police, and she sure as hell had called the police.

"Let him come back and try me," Marian said. "I'll be ready for him this time." She pointed to her purse. "I've got something in here—I don't go anywhere without it—and I'll kill him. I will."

"Oh God, I don't want him anywhere near me," Becky said softly.

"I dare him to come back," Marian said. "That would make my day."

Becky was impressed with Marian's bravery, but it also made her uncomfortable. She felt that she should fight back with the same anger and strength. Becky wanted to tell this to her new friend, but kept it to herself.

MIKE RHOADES

Ronnie had fallen into a familiar routine during his months with
Connie. He slept all day, had dinner at home with her, then after
she fell asleep he hit the nightclubs looking for new conquests to
bed. Then, in the early morning, he stalked, mostly outside
apartment buildings that rimmed the shopping centers and strip
malls of North Olmsted, only blocks from Connie's apartment.

One man was disrupting his routine—probation officer Michael Rhoades. He was making him work off his Colorado
probation on a grand theft conviction. Rhoades was intent on
making him follow the rules, and Ronnie hated it.

On April 4, 1986, they had an appointment. Rhoades sat in his
tiny office in the State Office Tower in Akron that day, dreading
the meeting. A savvy employee of the Ohio Department of
Rehabilitation and Correction, Rhoades carried a heavy
caseload, overseeing eighty-five felons who were back in society,
supposedly trying to stay straight. Of that number, about five
were problem cases, and the biggest headache of those five was
waiting to be called into his office.

Rhoades was simply sick of Shelton. He found that most
convicts on probation did whatever they could to obey him, for
whatever reasons: out of sincere efforts to change their circumstances or simply to outslick him and not have to go back to
prison. Rhoades wasn't an easy guy to con. He liked to make
unannounced visits at the homes of his charges. Just drop in,

135

look around the house, see if they were chopping up drugs or sleeping when they said they were working, or whatever.

Ronnie constantly broke appointments, so several times Rhoades went to Brunswick Hills to locate him. Ronnie's mother was little help, always making excuses for him. When Rhoades finally did get Ronnie to come to his office, he had an excuse for every missed appointment and why he hadn't looked for a job. Nothing was ever his own fault. Secretly, Ronnie was afraid his parole officer might connect him with the composite sketch of the West Side Rapist, and he stayed away.

Before buzzing Shelton into his office, Rhoades quickly reviewed the latest entries in the file. More headaches. According to one note, Shelton had beat up his girlfriend and then, depressed, swallowed a load of pills and called for help.

Rhoades sighed. The problem was Shelton had violated his probation agreement seven ways to sundown: He didn't have a job, refused to send restitution to Colorado authorities, drifted from address to address, and now, according to Rhoades's latest notes, had borrowed money to buy a van. Ronnie was not allowed to sign a banknote without clearing it with him.

Reviewing the rest of the file, the probation officer noticed that Ronnie had been convicted of assault the month before, the result of a bar brawl. This was a fairly serious probation violation, and now Rhoades had to make a decision: jail Shelton for probation violations or give him another chance. Rhoades strapped on his service revolver and told the receptionist to send in Mr. Shelton.

Rhoades arrested Ronnie as he walked into his office.

"I thought your job was to help me," Ronnie whined.

"I'm here to help someone who'll work with me."

"You guys are two-faced. You don't care about me—you just want to put me in jail."

"Yeah, well that's our job, Shelton," Rhoades replied. "We walk the line. If you make an effort, I'll help you and back you up with services. If not, you're gone."

Now Rhoades had breathing room to decide what, ultimately, to do with Shelton. After some thought, he decided that he needed jail time; nothing else seemed to make a dent in his hostile, uncooperative attitude. So Rhoades sent a letter to Colorado authorities and informed them that Ronnie Shelton had broken the terms of their probation and asked them to extradict him to their prisons.

Several days later, Colorado authorities called him and in effect said: Keep him in Ohio. We've got half the restitution, about $3,000. We're not going to revoke his probation. He's your problem.

Rhoades hung up the phone, disappointed. He decided to let Shelton sit in Medina County Jail for a couple of weeks and see if it changed his attitude. Two weeks later, Rhoades visited Ronnie in jail and found him contrite. Ronnie insisted that he wanted help, that he'd learned his lesson. "I'll keep my appointments," he said. "I'll live at home. I promise."

Rhoades wanted to believe him, but his gut told him Shelton was headed for more trouble. Back in his office the next day, Rhoades struggled to make a decision, then dictated a memo to his supervisor:

Now that Mr. Shelton is in jail, subject is promising to live up to the conditions of probation. Writer would recommend that subject be given one last chance to demonstrate a cooperative attitude under probation supervision.

Rhoades initialed the memo. He hoped he wasn't making a huge mistake.

JANIS WREN*

Ronnie had been watching the two young women for some time. It was late May and a few nights earlier, as he crouched outside their first-floor window at Jamestown Apartments in North Olmsted, the older of the two spotted him and screamed. He fled, but that did not stop him from coming back the next night.

He liked both of them. He figured them to be sisters and in their early twenties. They were good-looking, and to his eye they both probably worked out in a gym. The younger one had long chestnut hair and a bouncy laugh that carried outside.

He thought their apartment was a mess. Dirty dishes and clothes everywhere.

One morning just before dawn, he came back and found the younger one lying on a couch in red shorts and a tank top, asleep in front of a TV test pattern. This is nice, he thought. He determined that the other woman was not home, and at 4:45 A.M. Ronnie cut the screen and crept in.

A few hours later, Janis Wren was escorted into the North Olmsted police station by a rape crisis volunteer to talk to Detective Frank Viola.

Janis was scared. She was going to have to tell yet another stranger how she had been raped. She tried to fortify herself, thinking, I really have to do this; someone has to catch him.

---

*Not her real name.

Detective Frank Viola introduced himself, asked if she needed something to drink, and slowly started questioning.

"He had a knife," Janis explained. "He said, 'Don't look at me! Do what I say and you won't get hurt.'" He'd had her red negligee wrapped around his head, but she'd seen one eye and part of the rest of his face.

"He told me he didn't want to leave evidence," she said. "He said to swallow it. I tried to spit it out and he told me if I didn't swallow it, he would kill me. So I did."

As she described the rape, Viola typed quickly. He asked her to draw a picture of the rapist's knife. Janis was relieved at how comfortable she felt with the detective.

After the interview with Janis Wren, Viola returned to police headquarters and gravely told his chief about the case. "It's the West Side Rapist."

Two years earlier, he and detectives from North Olmsted and other West Side suburbs had met with Detective Bob Matuszny about a serial rapist who was crossing city boundaries to rack up a sickening string of rapes. Now each element of Janis Wren's rape seemed to fit the modus operandi Matuszny had described.

Viola also told his boss that the creep was getting sophisticated: He was making his victims swallow the physical evidence. The only good news was that a partial fingerprint had been successfully lifted from a windowsill in the victim's apartment. That was a start.

After the rape, Janis needed emotional support and security, so she stayed at her parents' house. Two days later, Hands Across America, the nationwide chain of people, was scheduled to link up at noon. The route across the country went through Cleveland's western suburbs and right past Janis's parents' home.

Flags were flying at nearly every house. The street was blocked off, and kids on bikes and at lemonade stands filled the street. It was an inspiring sight, as thousands of people, as far as you could see, linked arms on cue. A high school band struck up the national anthem and voices lifted to the skies. The national anthem had been one of Janis's favorite songs when she was a cheerleader and when she competed in volleyball and gymnastics, and she always sang out lustily, not caring that her friends thought she was being uncool.

But now, linked in the human chain of hundreds of thousands of people across the nation, in what was supposed to be a joyous, uplifting moment, she started to sob. Soon she couldn't control herself.

"It was the saddest thing," Janis would later recall. "Everybody is cheering and I'm crying. Everyone is looking and pointing at me. Nobody knew I had just been raped. I was just so sad. I really knew at that point that I was a different person. I didn't think I was going to get over it. It was like losing your very best friend. Only it was *me* that was lost, the real Janis."

A few weeks later, Janis got dressed for a party at her parents' house. She dreaded it. Every time she arrived at a family event, her relatives began an annoying buzz of whispers about her well-being. They had watched her sad transformation. Before the rape, Janis went club hopping six nights a week. She worked out for an hour or two a day. She went on late-night bike rides when she wanted to be alone, enjoying the cool night air streaming across her face.

Now, Janis rarely left the house. The bar scene terrified her; she was convinced her attacker had spotted her at a nightclub, then stalked her to her apartment. In fact, a week before the rape, she and her sister had seen a Peeping Tom outside their window and reported him to the North Olmsted cops, but they didn't catch him. Janis felt the peeper had been the rapist, some screwed-up, bar-crawling creep she had unwittingly attracted with her good looks.

Within weeks after the rape, Janis was well on her way to adding pounds onto her trim, 110-pound frame, having almost deliberately decided to make herself ugly. No guy will ever look at me twice, she decided. She punished herself, giving up biking and exercise and stuffing herself with junk food. She was so unhinged by the rape that this destructive strategy seemed like a smart thing to do.

Now, as she drove over to her parents' house for the family party, she found herself just a few blocks from Vineyard Beach. As a girl she had walked to the tiny park and painted pictures while sitting on the rocks at the base of the bluffs overlooking Lake Erie, where the blue-green water seemed to stretch forever. This memory sent her spirits crashing down. She wished for her carefree cheerleading days again. But that seemed impossible now. Overnight she had been turned into someone she didn't know.

The party did little to lift her mood. Later her stepmother took her aside. "Here's a number for that clinic I told you about. It's in Lorain. It's supposed to be good."

"Not this again," Janis said.

"Go, go. You'll feel better."

"Leave me alone about this!" Then she softened. "Please, okay? Stop."

They'll never catch him anyway, she thought. She really couldn't identify the monster. So what's the use?

June 1986

ED GRAY

Shortly after the rape of Janis Wren, Detective Ed Gray read about it in the newspaper. Has to be our guy, he decided.

This new rape was the first in five months that could be linked to the West Side Rapist. Gray telephoned the North Olmsted police, hoping to turn up fingerprints or an eyewitness, anything that could help in the investigation. After getting the details, Gray now was certain that the West Side Rapist was operating in North Olmsted, which was terribly frustrating for him and his partner. The crime had occurred outside their jurisdiction; they couldn't go in and work the case.

Gray had brought Detective Zbydniewski along pretty well in the eight months since the unit was created. She worked hard and showed particular skill in interviewing kids who had been sexually abused. Zeb got down on the floor and used toys and games to slowly pull out the awful details from the little ones. She was a great asset to the unit.

Gray prayed that he and Zeb would catch the West Side Rapist soon. He was tired of working in Sex Crimes, didn't much care for his lieutenant's style, and planned to soon ask for a transfer. It would be sweet to have this serial pervert locked up before he left.

In mid-1986, it was nearing the one-year anniversary of the Sex Crimes Unit. Anticipating an annual review, Duvall felt tremendous pressure to capture the West Side Rapist. She felt her career depended on it, especially since the new police chief had now gotten personally involved in the investigation. Believing that the West Side Rapist had been arrested in Cleveland before on other charges, Chief Howard Rudolph ordered a fingerprint technician to sort by hand through the files to seek a match to the print recovered from Janis Wren's windowsill.

On top of everything else, rapes were still climbing in Cleveland. A recent *Plain Dealer* article had been headlined: "Major Crime Down 10 Percent Here/City Bucks U.S. Trend—Except in Rape."

Just great, Duvall thought. Murders, arson, break-ins—everything goes down but rape. She didn't need the morning newspaper to enlighten her about that however—Sex Crimes kept its own depressing statistics.

Duvall told herself that she and her detectives needed a boost of some kind. They needed to catch the goddamn West Side Rapist.

RONNIE

Ronnie slipped out of Connie's apartment into a cool summer night.

A little over a mile away at the North Olmsted police station, the uniformed officers on the third shift were told to patrol apartment buildings—with headlights off—and look for a man peering into ground-floor apartment windows. As a result of the rape of Janis Wren a few days earlier, the patrolmen were instructed to pay particular attention to the Jamestown Apartments.

They knew that the Jamestown rape fit the pattern established by the West Side Rapist. This new crime was a big deal—North Olmsted police received fewer than a dozen rape reports a year—and they didn't need a pep talk at roll call to get fired up.

Ronnie slipped in along the shadows at the back of the Jamestown Apartments to locate one of the targets he enjoyed spying on, an attractive woman whose husband, a grocer, left early each morning to buy produce from a nearby farmers' market.

Until this morning, Ronnie had been content to watch her shower and dress. This time, he decided to go inside. He waited until the grocer left, then crept to the back patio door.

But the husband had forgotten something and, a minute later, returned to his apartment. In the predawn darkness, he saw a man dressed in black prying open his patio door.

143

"Hey, what the hell are you doing!"

Ronnie ran, heading for the woods that separated Connie's apartment complex from the Jamestown. He had a four-minute sprint back to his girlfriend's apartment.

The grocer ran inside and telephoned the police. His call was immediately dispatched to a patrolman who was gliding his black-and-white, lights out, along the north end of the sprawling Jamestown complex. He spun the car around the buildings and scanned for a man running on foot.

Within a minute, five other North Olmsted patrol cars flooded the area. Excited about the prospect of catching a serial rapist, the police combed the side streets and the perimeter of the James-town, ready to apprehend anyone walking, running, climbing into a car, or driving.

For an hour police combed the area; then they called it off. Whoever the intruder was, he wasn't out there now.

Once again, Ronnie had slipped through.

CONNIE BELLINI

By now Connie had had it with Ronnie. She bought him clothes, she made him dinner . . . but nothing could keep him home with her late at night. Without asking, he took her bank card and withdrew cash from the automatic teller machines. Who knew what he spent it on. He came home after dawn with excuses. His standby was that he had been out with the guys, then stopped for a long, leisurely predawn breakfast at one of the twenty-four-hour diners along Brookpark Road. Nothing Connie tried seemed to tame him. When he said he'd stay home if they could watch movies on a VCR, she went out and bought one. He stayed home for two consecutive nights, then started renting porn movies and asked her to watch them with him. She tried, but the movies disgusted her.

She moved out for a month and lived with her sister, a trial separation to see if she and Ronnie missed each other enough to try to patch up the relationship. They did. However, when she came back, she found her apartment a mess, littered with video-rental slips signed by different women. When she complained, Ronnie slapped her.

Then came an encounter that snapped the spine of their relationship. Connie had spent the day with her parents in Parma and came home to the apartment in the dark. Ronnie slipped in behind her, smiling, silent. She hadn't seen him in days, and noticed a rash of beet-red hickeys on his neck.

"You're disgusting," she said. He started to kiss her and she pushed him away.

She went to bed, shutting the bedroom door, which did not lock. Ronnie came in and got on top of her. She tried to push him off, but he overpowered her. He tore off her nightgown, then raped her. "Go ahead, call the police. They won't do anything," he said as he climbed off.

Connie sobbed on her bed, shell-shocked. He's right, she told herself. There is no way to prosecute him. Who would listen to me?

Her mood turned desperate, and she fantasized about killing him. Many times, he had shown her the indentation in his head where a surgeon had cut out a piece of his skull to remove a blood clot that had collected there after his fall from a garage roof in 1983. Throughout their relationship, he had used the defect as a way to attract her sympathy, whining about the need for a protective plate. But he had never gotten around to having it done; that would take planning and money, and would remove his excuse for why he couldn't apply for a whole range of jobs.

Now Connie was glad he had not undergone the corrective surgery. She fantasized about snatching up a telephone handset, swinging it like a hammer, and cracking him with all her strength—right on that spot! The blow might kill him. That would get him out of my life, she thought. He'd never threaten me or my family again.

Connie made up her mind and called her brother-in-law and asked him to help her move. She reserved a small U-Haul truck, then called Ronnie's father to let him know what she was doing. She asked if he'd come and stand guard during the move. If Ronnie showed up, she knew he would fight with the movers. His father was the only one who could keep him at bay.

Midway through the move, Ronnie burst in. He demanded that Connie stop. Then he saw his father, arms folded, leaning against a wall, his eyes menacingly tight from a migraine. Ronnie looked as if he wanted to punch his father, but instead pulled Connie into a corner. "Why did you get my father in the middle of this?" he demanded. She spun away.

Later, he caught Connie in the bathroom, knelt and wrapped his arms around her knees and, sobbing, pleaded with her to stay. She started crying, too, but pulled away and kept on with the move.

Afterward, Ronnie figured she'd come back to him, as she had before. If she didn't, he sure as hell wasn't going to let her drop him. He'd make certain of that.

CARLA KOLE

On a warm summer night in 1986, a cheering, chanting crowd of casually dressed women marched the normally empty streets of downtown Cleveland. They represented a movement, "Women Take Back the Night," and they were angrily protesting the disturbing rise of rapes in the city. They had marched in previous years, and their message had been the same: Society did not take crimes against women seriously.

They poured down Euclid Avenue through the heart of the deserted business district, carrying signs that said, "Try the Rapist, Not the Victim!" and "Violent Pornography Is Not Freedom of the Press, It Is Misogyny." Several television cameramen beamed bright lights and backpedaled at the front line of the marchers.

One of the women activists leading the march stopped and explained to a reporter, "It's a rare woman who hasn't changed her plans or even altered her lifestyle to avoid possible violence." But, she added, women should not have to restrict their lives to avoid being raped. They are entitled to the same freedom of movement as men. The solution to rape lies in eradicating family violence, poverty, and pornography—the social conditions that cause men to erupt into violence, she said. Women must take back the night!

Several minutes later, the pack of demonstrators slowly came to a halt at the Justice Center, where dozens of accused rapists awaited trial. One of the women, a self-defense instructor, told

147

the others, "The idea of passivity is nonsense. Rape is going to be violent no matter what. The question is whether or not you respond." There were cheers and clapping.

Soon the speeches ended, and the marchers turned around and walked en masse through the dark, back up Euclid Avenue to their locked cars and vans, then headed home.

One of the march supporters, Carla Kole, drove to her West Side neighborhood, West Park, only one block from where Ronnie had raped Becky Roth. Carla was short, with shiny brown hair that fell to her waist, and, like Becky, she lived with a husband who often left for work before she did. Carla worked for the Witness/Victim Service, a section of the county court system, counseling crime victims and providing emotional support for witnesses or victims who testified in criminal trials. She saw firsthand how rape shattered many of her clients, most of whom required intensive therapy and boundless support from husbands, family, and friends. Many rape victims, on their road to surviving the attack, ended up getting divorced or spun out into depression, eating disorders, agoraphobia, or other maladies. Carla knew only too well why some experts called rape "unfinished murder." That was rape's effect on victims: They were spiritually murdered; they felt as if their lives were over. Except that, in fact, they were still alive.

Carla worked daily with Cleveland police detectives and normally wasn't paralyzed by the fear of crime. But despite her tenacity, Carla found herself spooked by the West Side Rapist. This criminal struck her as different. He was out there and kept raping and no one seemed to be able to catch him. She and her husband had started talking about moving from the neighborhood.

Unlike Carla Kole, most people in the middle-class West Park neighborhood didn't have the freedom to tear up roots and move. As a precaution, they kept windows locked, even in the summer. Others bought guns or dogs. Even David McGuirk, the councilman, was scared. "I used to dread late-night phone calls," he would later admit. "I had calls from women in their seventies and eighties, just scared to death. I had inside information from the police that there was a pattern to the attacks, that they were mostly attractive younger women who were victims. I tried to figure out a way to reassure these senior citizens that they were not targets. But really, nothing worked.

"The whole community was on pins and needles. At my house, at night—no matter how hot it got—we closed and locked all the downstairs windows. I replaced the storm door. It had to be locked during the day, all day. We were extra careful about where our kids went.

"I knew one of the victims. Her rape deeply affected me personally. It really shook me up. These were my first years on city council and it was the most horrible thing. There was a big jump in crime watch meetings. People were forming klatches on all the blocks to watch out for each other. Every time there was a rape it became more apparent that the police couldn't do everything. It seemed like this guy was a phantom, impossible to detect. Everyone was watching for him. I had the chief of police, cops, firemen in my ward. There are two hundred active and retired firefighter families here, too. They were looking. It was amazing. The guy blended into the woodwork.

"I'll tell you one thing: The West Side Rapist made people realize how easy it was to be robbed and violated. You used to go up and down the streets and see garage doors open and no car in the garage. People were lax. A robbery over here was a big deal. He changed all that."

After months of soul-searching, Carla Kole and her husband decided to move far from West Park. But as Carla would soon find out, buying a house in a faraway suburb didn't free her from the West Side Rapist. In fact, in three years he would take up nearly all of her waking hours.

RONNIE

Ronnie had another brush with Brook Park police on June 29, 1986. They had detained him during a fight at a club on Brookpark Road and run his name through the warrant computer, and found he was wanted for not showing up months earlier to be sentenced after he was found guilty of assault during a bar fight.

In the past few years, Ronnie had had good luck in ignoring court summonses for minor crimes and traffic offenses. Usually he got picked up, spent a night in jail, made bond, and was given a suspended sentence and a fine.

This time it was different. Brook Park police handcuffed him and locked him in the tiny jail.

Ronnie didn't like their attitude. Guys with guns who think they can tell me what to do, macho guys like my dad, he told himself.

He didn't realize he was a bundle of contradictions. He hated cops yet wanted to be one; indeed, he had masqueraded as a police officer. Ronnie hated his father yet wanted to be just like him, and even tried to enlist in the navy, where his father had served. And when Rodney Shelton coached Little League, Ronnie tried his best to impress his dad—even making the All-Stars as a catcher one year—and felt like a hero to the other boys when his father argued with the other coaches.

For seven days Ronnie stayed locked in the Brook Park jail. His parents refused to bail him out this time. Then a judge released him, fined him $500, and put him on probation.

Walking out of the courtroom, Ronnie smiled and felt light-headed. He had stepped into court, faced an arresting officer and a judge, served a week inside a suburban justice system, and walked out free. He couldn't believe his good fortune. The Brook Park cops had not connected him to the rapes—even though a composite sketch of the West Side Rapist probably was taped to a station house wall somewhere.

August 1986

LUCIE DUVALL

The headline on page 1 of the August 23, 1986, *Plain Dealer* hit Lucie Duvall like a nightstick to the temple: "West Side Rapes Suspect Nabbed." She was furious. "Why don't we know about this?" she said. She looked at the story again.

A man believed to be the "West Side Rapist," sought by Cleveland and suburban police for three years for about 35 rapes on the city's West Side and southwest suburbs, has been arrested near Little Rock, Ark., on a federal fugitive warrant.

He was identified as Emilio Gabriel, 27, who reportedly used several aliases. Law enforcement officials said before Gabriel left here he had lived at four West Side addresses, all in the area of the rapes. His last two jobs here—laborer at a business on Brook-park Road near the airport and employee of a pizza shop near W. 150th St. and Lorain Avenue—were in the same area as some of the rapes.

He left Cleveland after a police composite sketch appeared in the

Plain Dealer in May along with an article on the West Side Rapist, said Lt. Chester M. Zembala of the Cuyahoga County Sheriff's Department. Ultimately, the composite likeness also led to Gabriel's arrest in Arkansas.

A Cuyahoga County grand jury had indicted Gabriel twice last year—in January for rape, kidnapping and aggravated robbery, and in November for robbery with specifications. He was arrested, but jumped bail and an arrest order was issued for him in January.

Zembala noticed the similarity between the composite and police pictures of Gabriel taken last year in connection with the two indictments. He alerted Second District police and the hunt for Gabriel was on. . . .

The news story rocked the Sex Crimes Unit. Gray, Zeb, and the others were dumbfounded. Lucie came out of her office and asked, "Why were we cut out of this and not notified?"

No one had an answer.

"How the hell does Zembala know if he's the West Side Rapist? Go talk to him."

"Zembala or this Gabriel?" Gray asked.

"Both."

Turf battles were not new to Gray. Some cops would do anything to horn in on the arrest of a high-profile criminal. At higher levels, entire units and agencies competed, hoarding information, engaging in petty jealousies. The bad guys benefited, bouncing from jurisdiction to jurisdiction, stringing crimes together like rosary beads, eluding arrest.

The Justice Department had realized this years ago when it formed the Strike Force Against Organized Crime, made up of agents from the FBI, Treasury, IRS, and DEA, who battled the Mob together. By the 1980s, metropolitan police forces across the country had borrowed the concept and created task forces to target sophisticated criminals. That was what Bob Matuszny had in mind in 1984 when he'd met with detectives in the suburbs where the serial rapist appeared to have struck. Now, two years later, cooperation had broken down.

Gray and another detective hustled down to the county jail

and waited for Gabriel in an interview room. When he shuffled in with a slight limp, Gray got excited. The man closely resembled the victims' descriptions of their attacker: olive skin, longish, wavy brown hair, small build, medium height. But the detective had doubts the second Gabriel spoke: He had a Latino accent.

Gray obtained a copy of Gabriel's lengthy rap sheet and asked that his fingerprints be sent upstairs to the Scientific Unit for comparison to prints lifted from the scenes of rapes already linked to the West Side Rapist.

Gray walked him through the Cleveland rapes, and Gabriel had an alibi for most of them. He was either out of town or immobilized with his foot in a cast. Gray doubted he had the right guy. As far as Gray knew, none of the victims had said anything about the rapist clumping through their apartments with his foot in a cast. He checked a little further and found that Gabriel's medical records supported his claim about a broken foot.

Gray called Matuszny, swore him to secrecy, and told him what he had. Bob quickly concurred: Gabriel was not the West Side Rapist.

"Goddammit, he was clearly not the guy!" Gray would later complain. "Not even close. What was Zembala thinking? He released this crap about Gabriel without even checking with us."

Gray called Sex Crimes and said, "Forget about Gabriel. We're ruling him out. He couldn't have done them."

Duvall was furious. Since Gabriel was not the right suspect, his arrest could torpedo the entire investigation when they finally did arrest the right rapist. She could just see some smiling defense attorney at trial: "Well, Detective, it says right here in the newspaper that the police thought Mr. Emilio Gabriel was the West Side Rapist. And now you're saying it's my client. You were wrong once; how can the jury be sure you're not wrong this time?"

Later Ronnie happened to pick up the *Plain Dealer* and read the front-page story about the arrest of the West Side Rapist. He laughed. What a joke.

Ronnie thought about cutting out letters from newspaper headlines and gluing them into words to fashion an untraceable, anonymous communication to the cops to tell them he was still out there.

He wondered why he felt like doing something so stupid. Then he realized: He didn't want them to give up the chase. He didn't want to get caught either. He just wanted to let them know he was still out there, and that he really wasn't going to stop himself. He felt he couldn't.

That fall, Detective Frank Viola in North Olmsted flushed a few suspects, but they were quickly cleared.

Gray and Zeb worked the case between new assignments, but fresh leads were scarce. The rapist seemed to be lying low or else had moved away. Or maybe his victims weren't making reports. Gray dreamed of cracking the case and leaving the unit on a high note.

Bob Matuszny monitored his old case from the Second District. Whenever he ran into Gray outside a grand jury room or Zeb in the police weight room, he got news of the case's dead-end status.

And Duvall, feeling political heat, kept wondering where the hell this mastermind was.

November 1986

RONNIE

In November, Ronnie found himself in suburban Strongsville, where he had a new girlfriend. He took the opportunity to stalk the new territory and quickly honed in on a first-floor unit at the Coventry Tower Apartments rented by a beautiful twenty-one-year-old woman.

On his first morning hiding in the shrubs outside her bedroom window, he watched her strip off her nightie, shower, then carefully dress for work. The next morning, he tapped on her window while she was nearly nude and she moved closer to the window to investigate. Her innocent, inadvertent exposure blasted Ronnie to sexual heights. On the third morning, he wanted something new: for her to see him—with his cock out. He tapped on the window. Only this time she left the room.

Minutes later, a Strongsville policeman arrested him outside the apartments. Ronnie calmly explained that he was looking for a lost dog. The officer didn't buy it.

At the police station, Ronnie brought out the courtesy card from his police union job and asked for a break.

This is not a "Get Out of Jail Free" card, the policeman told him. Later Ronnie was fined $250 for voyeurism, a misdemeanor, and sent on his way.

In the months after their breakup, Ronnie hounded Connie by calling her at work, following her in the car, and hanging around the stop where she caught the downtown bus. He refused to give her up. And in a strange way, she found herself gratified that she could inflict lovesickness in a man.

Two days before Christmas, he telephoned Connie and begged to see her one final time to wish her Merry Christmas; then he would leave her alone forever. He sounded so pitiful, she was lonely, and they had had such intensely romantic moments. She agreed to see him just this once.

An hour later, Ronnie pulled up in his car. Its ragged backseat was strewn with clothes and trash, so they switched to Connie's small red sports car. He pulled into traffic, smiled nervously, and said nothing. In an instant, Connie felt uncomfortable and regretted her decision to see him.

Suddenly, he snatched her left wrist with one hand and pulled out a pair of shiny handcuffs. "You're a fucking fool!" In a flash he cuffed Connie's wrist to the gearshift between the bucket seats.

"What are you doing! Take this off!" Connie screamed. She pulled hard, jangling the handcuffs, unable to yank the steel bracelet over the gearshift knob.

"You don't want me, so nobody else can have you," he said.

Oh my God, he's going to kill me! she thought.

He drove recklessly west, toward Bay Village, the upscale bedroom community stretched along bluffs overlooking Lake Erie. "We're going to Huntington Beach," Ronnie said. "We're going off the cliff." He was sobbing.

All she could think of was dying. She visualized the car speeding off the cliffs, crashing eighty feet down on the boulder-strewn shoreline. She wished she had told her mom and dad how much she loved them.

"Oh God, I've got problems you'd never understand," he said. He drove for several minutes, sobbing, as Connie begged him not to kill her. Suddenly, he turned the car away from the beach. "Connie, I need help. I've got to get help."

She realized he was totally strung out.

Connie had seen him snort cocaine a few times, but he knew she hated it and he hid it from her.

Ronnie drove around, eventually ending up at Metropolitan

General Hospital, Cleveland's public teaching hospital with its widely respected Cleveland Psychiatric Institute.

Ronnie knew he was submerging himself in an environment where his secrets might be disclosed, but at the moment he was too agitated to really worry about being uncovered as the West Side Rapist.

After Ronnie was screened and admitted, the intake nurse took Connie aside and gave her the telephone number of a local shelter for battered women. "You gotta watch it," the nurse told Connie. "You never know what can happen. A friend of mine, her husband shot her in the face."

Connie stiffened and stared at her.

"Yeah," the nurse went on, laughing darkly. "He does that to my friend, then *he* ends up in *here* and I have to take care of him."

Forewarned, Connie drove off, hoping they'd never let Ronnie out.

A psychiatrist came in and questioned Ronnie, who ran through a litany of complaints. "I got a temper. I get it from my dad. I know it's a problem. I beat up my girlfriend, and I know she loves me. Then I tried to kill myself."

"Why do you think you wanted to do that?" the doctor asked.

"I guess I wanted to die and come back and watch my parents and see if they were sorry," he said. "I live at home. There is no love at our house. I hate living there. I yell at my mother a lot." He turned away. "I know I'm sick."

The doctor kept questioning, and later filed a report.

Patient is a neatly groomed white male who was cooperative and not overtly bizarre in speech or behavior. He appears to minimize and rationalize his various problems and at the same time is somewhat dramatic in presenting them. He appears to be manipulative and is somewhat general and vague about his specific details. No delusions, hallucinations or overt psychotic symptoms elicited. Patient has a longstanding history of substance abuse as well as repeated social problems such as frequent and impulsive brawling, beating his girlfriend in the past, repeated misdemeanor violations and probations for assault.

Patient states that he never had a problem with alcohol. However he has used speed as well as cocaine in excessive amounts. He denies any other problems with substance abuse at this time. Patient has had no prior psychiatric hospitalizations and/or treatment. . . . He appeared to be explosive and had a short frustration tolerance.

After several days, Ronnie became restless and pressed the staff for his release, saying he would get treatment on the outside. By then, the psych unit's test data were completed. Ronnie was diagnosed as having "a strong personality disorder (antisocial) that would be difficult to treat at best. Prognosis: Guarded in view of past history of substance abuse and personality disorder. Disposition: Discharged to self."

February–March 1987

RONNIE

With Connie out of his life, Ronnie felt his moorings pull loose. Far from her disapproving eye, he snorted coke and speed. He turned more violent in nightclubs. There he would stand rooted, dressed in the latest clothes, looking like a diminutive Chippendale dancer, eyes clouded, lost in fantasy. If another man accidentally jostled him or said something he interpreted as an offense, Ronnie erupted, throwing punches, biting, pulling hair. He couldn't focus on any task for long, other than his relentless search for glimpses of unsuspecting women getting dressed before dawn.

In February 1987 he drifted to the east side of Cleveland, far from Connie, to places like Mayfield Heights, a middle-class bedroom suburb that adjoined some of the wealthiest communities in Ohio. There at the Plymouth Apartments he found a woman who fit his specifications—young, pretty, dwelling on the first floor. Dressed in a dark ski mask and a winter jacket, Ronnie stood outside her apartment window on February 27. He was jittery with excitement and held his position for hours, watching, waiting for a glimpse of skin, feeling that he knew her.

A neighbor spotted him and called the police. When a patrolman arrived, Ronnie told him he was looking for his dog. The cop arrested him for criminal trespass but did not connect him and his minor sex crime to the ongoing case of the West Side Rapist. Ronnie was fined and released.

Twice in three months an opportunity to nab him had been squandered.

Ronnie could never understand why the police let him off after picking him up as a Peeping Tom. Didn't they know that was how serial rapists selected their victims? In another life, he felt, he could be a consultant to the police and tell them exactly how to catch rapists: Look for anybody picked up or questioned as a voyeur, trespasser, suspicious person—any funny behavior. The rapist would be in that group. He knew it.

After paying a fine, Ronnie decided to stay out of Mayfield Heights. He began prowling again on the West Side, using as his base of operations the bungalow on Cable Avenue owned by his friend Danny Todd.

At the time, Danny was in love with a petite young woman he would marry a few months later. Her name was Josie George, and her aunt was a powerful Democratic U.S. congresswoman, Mary Rose Oakar. Josie's grandparents had come from Lebanon and her large extended family now owned and ran successful restaurants, nightclubs, and small businesses throughout the city.

Josie immediately clashed with Ronnie. "His eyes were scary," she would say later, after her divorce from Danny. "I told Danny, I don't want him near me. I never let him in the house. I said, 'Get away from me.' He tried to hit on me. He was afraid to try anything because of my family.

"He'd sleep until one or two in the afternoon and then go work out. Then at eight o'clock, he and Danny would primp and get ready to go out. They used to dress faddish, to be cool, to get the girls. They wore those high-waisted Italian pants or skintight jogging pants with the leopard-skin pattern. They would wear the muscle T-shirts, with maybe a leather jacket over it and real expensive leather boots with different accessories on them. They were typical male-stripper kind of guys—lots of gold, lots of jewelry, earrings. At the bars, some guys would tease Ronnie, saying he looked faggy, and Ronnie would get all upset, and say, 'I'm going to kill him.'

"Ronnie always had a girl around. Always. The only one he had a real relationship with was Connie. But then, he was dating a girlfriend of mine while he was going out with Connie.

"You never knew what was going to trigger Ronnie to fly off the handle. He did it quite a few times in front of me in Danny's yard. They used to sell stolen property that Ronnie came in with. They sold drugs—marijuana. So they had a lot of traffic to the house. Those kinds of people. There was this guy with long blond hair. He called Ronnie a fruit. He flew off the handle. Danny was amused by all this. He had found a friend in Ronnie. I think Danny thought Ronnie had the courage and strength he didn't have. Ronnie had the guts to approach any girl, even though Danny had the looks but was still a little shy about his approach. With his outgoing personality, Ronnie was what Danny wished he could be. Ronnie had no fear. He would say or do anything. Nobody could control him. Ronnie was out of control.

"After a few months, I knew my marriage was gone and I wasn't happy at all. Part of it was Ronnie's influence on Danny."

Ronnie continued to unravel. On March 30, 1987, he got into another bar brawl, at Flash Gordon's, a nightclub in the West Park neighborhood. One week later, while driving on I-71, he pulled out his handgun and pointed it at a twenty-two-year-old woman driving a car in another lane. She pulled off the highway and reported him to police, and he was arrested for aggravated menacing by a police officer from Middleburg Heights, a West Side suburb bisected by the freeway. But once again, a chance to snare him slipped away when police didn't connect his face with the composite sketch that already had been widely distributed to Middleburg Heights, where two rapes were already linked to the West Side Rapist. Ronnie made the small bond and walked out.

Soon he began to take even bigger risks.

April 1987

RONNIE

It was a weekday morning. A Catholic grade school girl dressed in a tartan-plaid uniform skirt held her face inches from the window glass and stared in at Ronnie. Unshaven and reeking of old cigarette smoke, he was sleeping in his Mercury Lynx. Soon other children gathered around the car at the edge of the parking lot playground.

Minutes later, a tapping on the window woke him up. He was stiff and tired but sat up fast, ashen-faced. Two Cleveland cops! He thought of his gun under the seat and remembered parking behind the church, exhausted, just before dawn. He hadn't realized the church lot doubled as its school's playground.

One of the dark blue uniforms asked Ronnie for his driver's license and told him to wait in his car. They were checking him for outstanding arrest warrants, Ronnie figured. But what else? He would just have to wait and see. . . .

Ronnie could barely remember the last time he had been

inside a church. He used to go to church nearly every week as a kid when his mother was going through one of her religious kicks. He and Maria went to services with her at Holiness churches around Cleveland, and during the summers they attended Christian camp.

His mother was forever bringing people home from service. That's how Mary and Michael Gooding came to live at War Avenue for almost an entire school year. Katy Shelton had befriended their mother at a Billy Graham revival meeting and when Marcella Gooding was hospitalized for a nervous breakdown, Katy agreed to take in Mary and Michael from the county children's welfare home.

Ronnie had hated twelve-year-old Mary Gooding and her ten-year-old brother from the moment county welfare placed them at the War Avenue house, paying a monthly stipend for their care. He was intensely jealous that his mother lavished attention on the newcomers. Within weeks, whenever his parents weren't around, Ronnie tormented Mary Gooding. "Suck my toes," he would say, and when she refused, he would pummel Michael in the face with drumsticks, which made Mary give in.

Later on, Ronnie would come home with an older pal and command eleven-year-old Maria to stand guard at the door leading to the attic. The two teenaged boys would then drag Mary up there and force her to strip. Ronnie hated her, but at the same time was fascinated with her pubescent body. Once Ronnie pushed an arm snapped from a doll's body inside Mary's vagina. Another time he undressed, pushed her down on his parents' bed, and took off her clothes. He tried to force sex with her, but she fought. He then slapped her, but Mary struggled until he gave up. When Maria walked in and asked, "What are you two doing?" Ronnie commanded Mary to remake the bed exactly as it had been.

When Mary Gooding complained to her caseworker about Ronnie's attacks, the caseworker didn't believe her. Then Mary complained to Katy Shelton, but she told the girl she was lying. Shortly thereafter, Mary tried to run away.

* * *

Sitting in a black-and-white zone car in the church lot, the two Cleveland cops got a hit when the dispatch unit checked on the name Ronnie Shelton. He was wanted on a warrant in Brook Park: failure to appear at court.

They arrested Ronnie, cuffed him, and took him to the First District lockup. That day Brook Park police picked him up and moved him to their tiny jail. Later, Ronnie made bond and was released.

July 1987

BETTY OCILKA

In the three years after she was raped, Betty Ocilka struggled to keep her life on an even keel: She delivered mail on her West Side route, she reared her son, she didn't drink, and eventually she began dating a policeman from the Second District.

On July 10, the morning sun had just started pouring in her kitchen, where she sat in her nightgown drinking coffee, when she sensed something: a rustle, a puff of air, a barely perceptible flicker . . . something. She looked around.

The thick brown curtains across the kitchen window were pulled closed and hung nearly to the sill. Normally, the sun formed a thin, bright band of light along the bottom of the curtains. But this morning, a shadow the width of a man's head broke the line of light and moved slightly, side to side.

Betty froze for an instant, then forced herself to casually walk to the sink, as if she were reaching to refill her coffee mug. She opened a drawer and felt for her .38-caliber Smith & Wesson revolver.

Since the rape, she had kept the handgun on her nightstand when she went to sleep. Each morning, she moved it to a drawer next to the kitchen sink, then made coffee, ironed her postal carrier uniform, and got ready for work.

Now she found the gun, gripped it in her right hand, and cocked it while she swept open the curtain with her left hand. She saw a man, screamed, and fired. The gun kicked, the window shattered, and she heard footsteps running away. Betty hoped she hadn't frightened her young son.

The instant he heard the scream, Ronnie ducked under the window. He felt glass fly, then sprinted away in the soft morning sun, flooded with fear and excitement.

Ronnie caught his breath, gunfire still ringing in his ears. Gotta cut this out, he thought. I almost caught it in the face.

Now he'd have to scratch her off his list of good-looking women to watch getting dressed for work. He was truly disappointed. She had shown him she had guts, and he admired her.

Ocilka telephoned the Second District police station, less than a mile away. An officer in a zone car arrived to find her babbling about almost getting raped again. She explained what had happened, then said, "I should have used two hands. I know better than that. I would have shot him if I had two hands on the grip."

"Don't blame yourself," the patrolman said. "Look, he'd be dead and you might have to go to court."

"I don't care if I went to jail. At least he'd be off the streets."

Later, the shooting was referred to Detective Bob Matuszny, who jumped on the information. It had been ages since he'd had news of the West Side Rapist, and he desperately missed being involved in the case. In the early months of the investigation, the chase had been thrilling. In fact, it had been the rape of Betty Ocilka that had convinced him a serial rapist was operating in the Second District.

Bob was always happy to have an excuse to poke into the case again. But he doubted that the shadowy figure Betty had fired at through the curtains was the man who had raped her. It was too weird. She had called before, more than once, claiming to have run across the guy who raped her. Bob had started to doubt her credibility. He felt she was suffering from an understandable case of nerves. Probably nobody had been at the window.

He called Ed Gray at the Sex Crimes Unit and told him about Betty Ocilka. She's losing it—screaming, firing handguns through curtains. It's almost impossible to believe the same rapist was outside her window, Bob said.

Gray said he had to agree.

LUCIE DUVALL

Lieutenant Lucie Duvall listened as Gray offhandedly mentioned that one of the rape victims had shot at someone out her kitchen window. It seemed to Lucie another insignificant fact to pile on to the mountain of paperwork, pressure, and weird occurrences that made up the case of the West Side Rapist. She felt that any minute the whole crazy mess might come tumbling down, crushing her.

Later that week, Gray told her he wanted a transfer out of the unit. This knocked her back a few steps. He didn't say so explicitly, but she knew he just didn't care for her, which irked her. She felt he did not show her the respect he would a male supervisor.

But she put that aside. After all, he was one of the most experienced detectives in the unit, he had trained Zeb well, and Sex Crimes needed him. She knew the word throughout the districts and the cop bars and union hall was that she couldn't hang on to experienced investigators, that they chafed under her heavy hand and wanted out. She needed him to stay.

At times like this, Duvall wished she were working for her old boss. The new police chief, Howard Rudolph, happened to live on Rocky River Drive in West Park, a prime zone for the West Side Rapist. And in the past weeks, rumors had floated back to her that Sex Crimes had better catch him or Rudolph was going to disband the unit.

"I'm dancing as fast as I can," she told colleagues who passed on the rumors. Then she laughed darkly. "Of all the neighborhoods in the city, the creep picks the chief's to rape in. My God, it's a lieutenant's nightmare."

Unlike some police officers, Lucie had political support from some of the judges, city council members, and social service administrators, and didn't truly believe the rumors about the disbanding of Sex Crimes. But she couldn't be sure.

She turned down Gray's request as smoothly as she could. "I want you to stay," she told him. "We need you here."

But he would not be swayed.

RONNIE

In the middle of the night that summer, Ronnie slipped out of Danny Todd's well-fortified house on Cable Avenue and taped a temporary thirty-day license plate on his car, a plate lifted from his latest girlfriend.

An hour or so later, while slowly patrolling a residential street not far from the Second District police station, he saw a woman's body outlined against a curtain. Her motions showed she was undressing. Ronnie quickly pulled the car over; he couldn't find a parking spot along the street's low, rounded curb, so he pulled up over it and parked on a treelawn. He hurried to her window, high with anticipation.

For several minutes he stood there, peering through a crack in the curtains, masturbating, intoxicated by the woman's inadvertent display. A neighbor noticed the car up on the grass, then saw a thin, darkly dressed man, his forearm pumping. She wrote down the license number and called the Cleveland police, who dispatched a zone car to the scene.

Parking on the lawn was a reckless move for a man being hunted by police departments throughout the county, but Ronnie thought only of the woman undressing. He might have to drive and hunt for two or three nights to find such a satisfying target.

By the time the police zone car arrived, Ronnie had zipped up and left.

Two days later, Second District Detective James Facemire and another detective stopped at Danny Todd's house in the early evening and banged on the door. Danny eyed them nervously as they asked for Ronnie.

"Not here," Danny said.

Facemire, a slim, sad-faced detective with a bald crown and basset hound eyes, gave him his business card and said, "Tell him to come in and see us or we'll be back and pick him up."

Ronnie didn't show up and Danny had a date with Josie, so he left Ronnie a note:

Ron
Went to the consert with Josie. Be back later. Oh Ron you are in big trouble. Two Dick Tracy's was hear for you. You have to call them Mon. They seen your car and they went in your car.

Dan

The note scared the hell out of Ronnie. He had had a ton of close calls with the cops, but this one was serious. A detective, looking specifically for him, had driven across the city to

Danny's house. Later Ronnie dialed the Second District detective bureau's number and told Facemire he'd stop in voluntarily.

It was Monday, and Ronnie made plans. If he was going to get arrested, he didn't want his motorcycle impounded, so he asked Danny to drive him there. Then Ronnie showered and shaved, taking extra time because he cut off his mustache. He put on slacks and an expensive sweater. He wanted to look clean-cut.

Within minutes, he and Danny were humming over the Harvard-Denison Bridge, nearly three hundred feet above the Flats. Danny noticed Ronnie's clean-shaven upper lip but said nothing.

This is it, Ronnie thought. They've finally got me. They'll lock me up forever. My family will be humiliated. All my girlfriends will know. I can't do it.

He looked over at Danny and was about to ask him to stop the van on the far side of the bridge. Ronnie imagined vaulting the low steel railing and falling, falling, falling. . . . He'd be dead—what would it feel like?—but at least he wouldn't be locked in a cage. He could not stand the idea of being captured. It was time to end this. . . .

He felt sick and hopeless, like he did as a boy when he saw his parents fight. He would hear the shouts and run in and attack his father, crying and screaming, "Dad, don't hit her!"

He remembered his mom coming after his dad with a knife. Dad had her by the wrists, her arms separated and aloft, and he turned to his son. "See, I'm not the one who is doing all this, Ronnie. It is your mother. She is the one."

As Danny continued to drive his van over the bridge, Ronnie jiggled his leg nervously, saying nothing. In a minute they were across the bridge and parked in the Second District parking lot.

At the station, Facemire brought Shelton and Todd upstairs through two heavy locked steel doors into a squad room with several high windows no bigger than briefcases. There they were joined by another detective.

Ronnie forced himself to act cool. "What's this all about?" he asked.

Ronnie had had the misfortune of peeping on a West Side

block that had been struck repeatedly by a canny, successful burglar. In combing the neighborhood for leads, Facemire had learned about a car parked on a treelawn the night of a burglary. Perhaps the car could be linked to the burglar. Facemire also had another lead: Fresh blood was found on a broken windowpane at the home of a recent break-in victim. The suspect most likely would have a cut on his hand.

Facemire had traced the license plates, then visited Ronnie's new girlfriend, who said it hadn't been her car on the lawn. Based on the description, she said the car had to belong to a guy she dated, Ronnie Shelton. She was going to break up with him soon; he was jealous and had a scary temper. She gave Facemire Ronnie's address on Cable Avenue, where she told the detective he lived with his pal Danny.

In the squad room, Facemire told him, "Turn around, I want to see you from the back."

Ronnie felt like he had been snorting speed for a month. He was twisted piano-wire tight.

"Okay, let me see your hands," Facemire said.

Ronnie was supremely alert, soaking up every sound, every nuance. Time crawled. They've got me. This . . . is . . . it. He showed his hands, watching the detective's eyes.

"What do you think?" Facemire asked the other detective.

The man shook his head, nope.

Facemire looked at Ronnie, then at his hands again. "You can leave," he said, and Ronnie floated out of the police station. They had had him and let him go. Ronnie couldn't believe it.

In the van, Danny asked, "What d'ya think all that was about?"

"Hell if I know," he replied.

November 1987

HOWARD RUDOLPH

Starting in mid-November, not far from Chief Howard Rudolph's brick Tudor home, the West Side Rapist struck three times in a row. Rudolph knew one of the victims, a woman who walked past his house early every morning to attend Mass at the Monastery of the Poor Clares, a cloistered convent in the neighborhood. Rudolph, an early riser, had noticed her for years, though he didn't know her name or ever speak to her.

When he learned of the attack on her, Rudolph, a churchgoer, was shaken. From his days as a detective, he knew that for most victims, being raped was like getting murdered, only they were still alive to feel its aftermath. Psychologically, few of them seemed to fully recover.

What kind of a beast would do this? he wondered.

Rudolph could feel the fear in the neighborhood and again started to closely monitor the investigation. With the chief looking over her shoulder, Lieutenant Duvall put more pressure on her detectives. Everyone was getting tense and impatient.

The chief felt even worse when he learned a few days later that the Mass-goer now refused to cooperate with detectives and had moved from the city.

It was Howard Rudolph's opinion that the quality of much of the evidence collected at crime scenes was lousy. Five years earlier, detectives in the Scientific Investigations Unit had been disbanded and sent out to the six neighborhood districts, a political move intended to make the department's dwindling

170

police force appear greater, a numbers game. Because SIU was disbanded, detectives on general duty had to do their own forensic work: fingerprinting, searching for trace evidence, photographing victims, scraping blood or skin from underneath fingernails—whatever was required. Some, like Matuszny, conducted their investigations carefully. Others were not so scrupulous.

Rudolph knew this, and believed that many crimes went unsolved because fingerprints were not properly lifted or evidence was mishandled, out of sloppiness or incompetence. A semen-stained nightgown might be tied into a plastic bag and put on a shelf in an evidence storeroom; within days it was a worthless memento. Proper procedure called for storing the nightgown in a brown paper sack that let in air and didn't destroy blood, saliva, and semen samples.

Though forensics wasn't his personal strong suit, Rudolph firmly believed in solving crimes through science. In November, in the midst of the neighborhood rapes, he issued an order: All scientific evidence was to be collected by a beefed-up Scientific Investigations Unit at police headquarters. He selected Vic Kovacic, perhaps the most ingenious police scientist in the state, to head the new unit. Ed Gray put in for a transfer to SIU, and it was approved.

Because of a tight city budget, every police unit except narcotics was being cut by attrition or transfers. In Sex Crimes, Lucie Duvall was unable to replace Gray.

RONNIE

It was midmorning, November 18, when twenty-two-year-old Michelle Baldwin,* a tall, voluptuous, husky-voiced woman, left her first-floor apartment door ajar while she quickly dumped a load of clothes into a washer in the laundry room a few steps away. When she returned to the apartment, Ronnie grabbed her from behind and put a knife to her throat.

He said he was being chased by police and needed money. Then he added, "Everyone around here thinks I'm a fag. Now I'm going to prove I'm not." Then he raped her orally and vaginally as she sobbed. He pulled out to ejaculate on her stomach, then promised to kill her if she called the cops. He wiped her stomach dry with a tissue, not wanting to leave evidence, and left.

Two weeks before Christmas, twenty-seven-year-old Keri Hansen* let herself into her fiancé's house in the heart of West Park, only two blocks from Police Chief Rudolph's home.

Keri had just gotten off work, and it was dark. She knew about the nearby rapes everyone was talking about and she carefully relocked the door behind her. Her fiancé wouldn't be home for an hour, around 7 P.M., so she sat on the family room floor and wrapped gifts.

---

*Not their real names.

Suddenly, Ronnie sprang out and grabbed her hair and clamped a hand on her mouth. Keri shoved his hand away and screamed for help while she fought back with the scissors she'd been using.

Ronnie punched her in the face and tore the scissors from her hand. Clenching them in his fist, he banged her across the face again and again. "Shut up and you won't get hurt!" he told her as he pointed the scissors at her throat and asked for her money. She said she had $2 in her purse.

"I know that. Where's the money in the house?"

"I don't know. I don't live here."

"When's your boyfriend get home?"

She thought for a moment. "Now. Soon. Between six and six-thirty." Her watch said 6:20 P.M.

He yanked her up by her hair. "I want to leave. Don't look at me."

He dragged her through the kitchen and down a three-step landing to the back door. He didn't want his fingerprints on the doorknob. "Open it!"

She struggled with the rarely used door, but couldn't get it open. This pushed Ronnie over the edge. He forced her to take off her sweater and jeans and snipped off her bra with the scissors, which he then pointed in her face.

Looking down, he saw a sanitary pad. You bitch! he thought, and changed plans. He fondled her breasts, then raped her orally. "If you call the police," he said, "you won't have a Christmas."

As he ran off, he felt sick about beating Keri Hansen. He had just shed one of his long-standing taboos—beating a victim. Which one was he going to break next?

The next day, Chief Rudolph heard about the rape in his neighborhood and immediately called Sex Crimes for details. He listened impatiently as Lieutenant Duvall filled him in.

"I want full and immediate attention on this," he ordered. "We have got to catch this guy."

Duvall could not believe the pressure on this case.

February–March 1988

RONNIE

Whenever he came across the *Plain Dealer* in a restaurant or at his parents' home, Ronnie carefully looked through its pages for news. Had a recent victim called police? Was it safe for him to continue peeping at a certain address? He needed to know whether he should change his routine.

In early February, Ronnie was sitting on the couch in his parents' living room, watching the news with his father, when he snapped to attention. The newscaster said police believed that the feared serial rapist on Cleveland's West Side was now raping women only in the small West Park neighborhood.

My life is so weird, Ronnie thought. Watching a story about me with my dad and pretending nothing is going on.

Of his most recent victims, two or three who had the courage to call the police did live in West Park. But he had also recently raped as far north as Edgewater Drive, a block from Lake Erie, and on the East Side near Danny Todd's house. That the Cleveland cops thought he was now centering on West Park was due to coincidence, not a plan.

Oh, so now I'm the West Park Rapist, Ronnie thought. Well, if that's what they think, then that's where I'll be.

In deciding to stalk victims only in West Park, Ronnie was making it easier for police to capture him. He was searching for women in an area roughly twelve square miles, from West 140th Street west to the Rocky River valley, from Puritas Avenue north to the Lakewood border at Interstate 90.

174

He already had several targets picked out in the area. One was a young woman on Emery Avenue whom he had watched get dressed more than a dozen times. One morning Ronnie actually broke in while she showered, rearranged the drapes and doors, then climbed back outside. Enjoying an unobstructed view, he watched her step out of the shower and dress. She never noticed a thing.

Ronnie felt like a gambler on a roll, scared and exhilarated.

LUCIE DUVALL

By March 1988, the press was diligent in its coverage of the West Side Rapist. Every time he struck, the local news media broadcast the crime, and the residents of West Park, infected with fear drummed up by the TV coverage, lashed out at the police.

Chief Howard Rudolph realized he had a political problem on his hands. He met with neighborhood crime watch groups and assured them everything possible was being done. This was his neighborhood, too, and he understood their feelings, Rudolph told them. Soon, someone was going to see the rapist, or catch him, or police would nail him in a routine traffic stop.

Despite his reassurances, the residents of West Park did not calm down.

Each time the rapist struck, Sex Crimes felt heat rolling down from the chief's office on the ninth floor. Phone calls poured in from the TV stations and the press. What's the latest? Any leads? How close are you to catching this criminal?

Duvall was getting frustrated. Even though it had been Zeb's case since Ed Gray transferred, Duvall assigned other detectives to help out by canvassing streets around a crime scene. This was boring, time-consuming grunt work that usually turned up little of value. But it had to be done. A neighbor might have seen something—a car, a license plate, a face.

Duvall could feel morale in Sex Crimes sinking—and not just because of the West Side Rapist. Her detectives drove beat-up unmarked cars, she had little overtime pay to spread around, and the staff was dwindling. Minor problems became the most exasperating. At the end of a shift, she expected detectives to turn in typed case reports for the day. Of the nearly dozen typewriters in the office, only two worked. So of course, everybody got jammed up at quitting time, and there was general irritation with those who took too long at the typewriter. The situation encouraged detectives to shorten their reports— not an ideal way to conduct investigations.

Something had to give.

RONNIE

It was warm for a few consecutive days in early March, and Cleveland's slush and crusted snow melted, leaving lawns and sidewalks a blank canvas. Then the temperature fell to just below freezing, and moist, fluffy snowflakes drifted down on a nearly windless night, piling on lawns and tree branches like a thick swaddling of cotton. In West Park, streetlights bounced off an all-white tableau.

There, in the midst of this sentimental Christmas card scene, walked Ronnie. He worried about leaving tracks in the snow. On the sidewalk just north of the taverns and nightclubs along Lorain Avenue at West 150th Street, he became captivated by a set of footprints. They were only a few minutes old, and from their crisp shape he was certain a woman wearing high-heeled boots had made them. He tried to imagine what she looked like: her face, her hair, her breasts.

He followed the tracks for several blocks. My lucky day, he thought. The tracks led to the front door of a . . . first-floor apartment. He settled back to watch. Several hours later the woman, Nancy Shift,* saw Ronnie outside the apartment. He was masturbating. She called the police.

Ronnie moved off and hid nearby. He watched as two plainclothes detectives from the First District rolled up in an unmarked maroon Ford sedan. They're taking this seriously, he realized. They must think it's me.

They found pry marks on the woman's front door and cordoned off the apartment doors with bright yellow crime-scene tape until an SIU detective came to photograph the doors and dust for fingerprints.

Hours later, Ronnie crept back and closely inspected the police work. They had even circled his pry marks on the door. You don't scare me, he thought. We'll see how good you are.

Nancy Shift became his obsession.

The next day he knocked on her door and asked directions to the manager's apartment. Nancy Shift looked out at him warily, never taking the chain off the door. "I don't know," she said quickly, and closed the door.

Ronnie let what he had just done sink in: He had stared at his target, letting her see his face, his clothes. And he didn't care! He felt himself buried by an avalanche of exhilarating, supercharged joy. He knew he would be back.

A few days later, Nancy Shift had an argument with her boyfriend, Michael. He didn't want to come over and stay the

---

*Not her real name.

night because he had an early appointment at work the next morning. Nancy really wanted companionship, so she walked a block to a corner bar. Nancy knew the woman who tended bar and decided to cry on her shoulder.

She had picked a bad night to leave her apartment empty. Ronnie was hiding in the shrubs and watched her walk off. He crept to her door and, not worried about making a noise, pried open the doorjamb with a screwdriver and jimmied the lock. Inside, he unlocked a side window. He sneaked back out, pounding the jamb back in place, and waited in the shrubs.

Five beers later Nancy Shift had run out of complaints about her life and her boyfriend. She walked unsteadily home.

Through her bedroom window, Ronnie watched Nancy pull on a nightgown and fall asleep. He put a foundation brick against the house, stepped up, silently opened the side window he had unlocked earlier, and boosted himself inside. He crept to the bedroom in the dark and climbed on her bed.

"Michael, is that you, baby? C'mere, hold me, Michael."

Ronnie got on top of her, but it wasn't exciting. She was not terrified. He flashed his black-handled blade. "Michael, Michael. What's all this about Michael?"

Suddenly Nancy froze. "You're not Michael."

"Don't look at me and you won't get hurt," Ronnie said. She cried quietly as he cut open her nightgown and raped her.

Later he hurried off, thinking, This is great. Creep into the cops' lair, take what you want, shove it back in their faces.

He wondered what he could do to top this night.

Summer 1988

TIM MCGINTY

Assistant county prosecutor Tim McGinty was jogging through West Park in the early evening, enjoying a good sweat. He had wrestled in college as a heavyweight even though he was only five-foot-nine and barely over two hundred pounds. Now he battled his weight. He'd quit drinking, and the only buzz he got these days was a runner's high. Unless you counted the nervous kick of adrenaline he felt when wading into a high-pitched courtroom battle.

His courtroom style resembled a tournament match: Charge in, twist your opponent by the arm, throat, crotch, or whatever works, and slam him to the mat. Defense lawyers hated seeing McGinty walk into the courtroom—chest first, chin out, his thick lips and dark eyebrows fixed into a look that seemed to say, Wanna punch my face? His tactic was not to outsmart but to infuriate, lowering the proceedings to the level of a street fight.

Today he routed his run by Cleveland Police Chief Howard Rudolph's home on Rocky River Drive. If Rudolph was out front, Tim always made a point of stopping to chat. Prosecutors could develop better cases if they had a good relationship with the police chief. They had become friends when Rudolph ran the Homicide Unit and Tim clocked long hours during his first year in his office's "major trials" division. Tonight, however, Rudolph was elsewhere, and after a couple of miles Tim headed home.

McGinty's wife, Ellen, brought up the dog again, a purebred golden Labrador retriever. "Let's get it," she said. "I'd feel

179

safer." She had every reason to want protection. The West Side Rapist had been striking closer and closer to their neighborhood. Up and down West 160th Street, in the two- and three-bedroom brick colonials, their neighbors bought guns and dogs and double-checked window locks. Tim had a gun, but Ellen had never learned to fire it. A dog suited her best. It seemed to Ellen, a nurse, that the West Side Rapist was all her coworkers at nearby Lakewood Hospital talked about.

"Yeah, but three hundred bucks," Tim said. "Why not a mutt from the pound? It'll bark just as loud."

"It's a beautiful dog. The kids have fallen in love with it."

"And who's going to take care of it? You know who it'll be."

Tim felt he carried enough burdens. He had worked his way up to the "A Team" at the county prosecutor's office, the major trials division. Working long hours as the lead prosecutor on murder and political corruption cases left him little free time. The last thing he wanted to do at night, after everyone was settled in bed, was to take a dog outside and give it the opportunity to fertilize the neatly trimmed treelawns of West Park. He'd much rather sink into a book—he was working through Martin Gilbert's massive Churchill biography—until his eyes got tired and he drifted off.

"The kids will help take care of it," Ellen said.

"Sure they will," he replied. Kathleen was eight, Patrick five. "I'll end up taking care of the damn dog. I know it."

"No you won't," Ellen said. "We'll all help."

He shook his head and sighed but said nothing, which meant he gave in. Tim didn't really mind a dog, though he would have preferred a cheaper pet. He just wanted to blow off some steam, stir things up, play the martyr. A simple "Fine with me" would not do. He couldn't keep his mouth shut about anything.

RODNEY SHELTON

Over the past few years, Rodney Shelton had had his fill of his son's smart-ass behavior. Ronnie didn't work and sponged off the family. He drained them financially by constantly getting arrested for traffic tickets, misdemeanor assaults, or voyeurism, then demanding bail bond money. Rodney didn't want to pay, but his wife insisted, and Rodney had to live with her. It was easier to pay than to argue. Sometimes Rodney felt pangs of guilt over how roughly they had punished Ronnie, but whippings were all Rodney knew, and his son had deserved them. He had done what he thought best.

Today, his son had no excuse for his behavior, Rodney felt. Ronnie had sassed his mother and tried to draw Maria's boyfriend, a bodybuilder and Cleveland fireman, into a fight. He'd used foul language, right in the kitchen, in front of women and outsiders. He was out of line, and Rodney let his son know it.

"If you're so moralistic, how come you slept with Mom when she was sixteen and got her pregnant?"

"Get out of this house," Rodney Shelton shouted.

"Make me."

Rodney balled a fist and shook it. "If it wasn't for that accident, why, I'd—"

"You always say that," Ronnie yelled.

"You're lucky you got that hole in your head or—" Rodney clenched his fist.

"Fuck you!"

Rodney reached for Ronnie's hair to pull him out of the house, and Ronnie erupted. Palm open, he smashed his father's face, then dove into him, driving him to the floor.

Maria and her mother ran in, screaming. One of them called the Medina County Sheriff's Department while Rodney tried to pin Ronnie's arms. Insane with rage, he pulled free and smashed his father in the face.

Rodney Shelton, a hundred pounds heavier, was surprised by Ronnie's counterattack. His son had never tried to hit him before. In a moment, Maria's muscle-bound boyfriend pinned Ronnie facedown on the floor and sat on his back until the police showed up.

"Do you want him arrested?" an officer asked.

"Just get him the hell out," Rodney said.

They escorted Ronnie outside. He kicked his motorcycle to life and sped off, at once proud and sick that he had finally, after a lifetime of dreaming about it, punched his father.

Ronnie raced north on the interstate, feeling jittery and on edge. Twenty minutes later, he zoomed down the ramp for the West 150th Street exit and headed into West Park.

After several hours, he found a young woman to watch in an apartment on Rocky River Drive. From what he could tell she was tall, blond, and beautiful. She was asleep on the living room couch in panties and a bra. Open windows gave little relief from the summer heat and she had no air-conditioning. He climbed inside, grabbed a corkscrew off a counter, and moved closer until the floor creaked. She woke up, and instantly Ronnie pushed the corkscrew to her neck. "Don't look at me, or I'll kill you."

He rummaged through her purse and found her bank card and driver's license. Her name was Teresa O'Brien.* Great face, Ronnie thought. He pocketed the bank card. Then he found a police card in a black leather case. "What the fuck is this?"

"My father gave me that. It's a courtesy card."

He flipped it over to see who had issued it to her. "Detective Jake O'Brien." Her father's a Cleveland cop, Ronnie thought. But

---

*Not her real name.

at this point he had no choice; he'd have to force her through his routine. . . .

Afterward he said, "Your father is going to want to kill me. So if you call the police, I'll know. I've been watching you. I'll come back and kill you." He put her in the bathroom and demanded her bank card password and her phone number. He told her he would call, hang up, and then she could come out of the bathroom.

Minutes later, Ronnie sat on his motorcycle at a gas station across the street and dialed her number from a phone booth. He wanted to tell her that he liked her, that he was sorry, that she was beautiful, but hung up after one ring.

As he watched, the zone cars screeched to her apartment. They had arrived incredibly quickly. They must know her dad's a cop, Ronnie thought. Gotta get out of here.

He headed for an instant-cash machine at a branch of Society National Bank on Lorain Avenue, a few minutes away. If he was lucky, he'd be able to withdraw the maximum, $200. He put on a pair of huge sunglasses to hide his face and tapped in his latest victim's formerly secret code.

The next day, detectives checked with Teresa O'Brien's bank and found out that someone had used her bank card at five in the morning. A security camera had been operating at the time.

Now, after the West Side Rapist had been investigated by a dozen police departments and the FBI for half a decade, this crude surveillance camera had provided the case's biggest breakthrough yet: a picture of him using a stolen bank card.

But police had something of a problem. The photo was a close-up, dark and blurred. Half of the suspect's face was hidden by white-rimmed sunglasses. Visible was a jean jacket collar, the outlines of his lower face, his mouth pinched on a smoldering cigarette, long, wavy hair framing his face, and little else.

Even so, this new evidence gave a tremendous boost to the Sex Crimes detectives. At last they could say, Here's the guy! This is what he looks like! We know who we're looking for.

Now all they had to do was find him.

TIM McGINTY

Cleveland Police Chief Howard Rudolph telephoned Tim McGinty and requested him to come to his ninth-floor office at police headquarters in the Justice Center. Rudolph was a respected police commander who put work ahead of his personal life. His big corner office matched his personality: spartan, precisely organized, unwarmed by personal memorabilia. Unlike some, he didn't display photos of himself with prominent politicians or celebrities.

He had doubts about Lieutenant Duvall and the case. He felt she had become intoxicated by the mostly adulatory press coverage she received as the city's highest-ranking female officer and head of a high-profile unit. Further, with her strong-willed management style, she had chapped the egos of several veteran detectives whom Rudolph respected. Even so, he did not reassign her. She clearly had expertise now in investigating child porn, child abuse, and other Sex Crimes.

When Tim came in, Rudolph's mouth was set sternly. "All this television coverage about the rapist—in our neighborhood," Rudolph said. He shook his head, disgusted. What little hair he had left was silver and trimmed to putting-green length. Wire-rim glasses softened what was otherwise a severe face.

"I think the case could be handled better," the chief said. "Would you take a look at it?"

McGinty thought for a moment. He had a tremendous person-

184

al stake in seeing the case to a conclusion. After all, the criminal was terrorizing *his* neighborhood, frightening *his* family. It definitely was a plum assignment.

But he already had a heavy trial load and worked one or both weekend days. Ellen had been after him to spend more time with the kids. Moreover, taking this case would spark jealousy among the 110 assistant Cuyahoga County prosecutors. Many of them griped that McGinty sponged up all the good cases, that he was a shameless media hound.

"Sure, Howard. I'd love to get involved." If his colleagues were jealous, Tim decided, they could just go fuck themselves.

After clearing it with his boss, Tim started reviewing the case files linked to the West Side Rapist.

CLOSING IN

Lieutenant Duvall bustled into the Sex Crimes office. Everybody knew why she was smiling—the bank photo of the West Side Rapist using Teresa O'Brien's stolen bank card.

"You wanna go CrimeStoppers on it?" one of the guys asked.

"Of course," she said, giggling.

Duvall sent the grainy, dark photo of the West Side Rapist to CrimeStoppers, the county agency that paid cash rewards for crime tips that led to arrests.

CrimeStoppers distributed the photo and requests for information to the media. The newsrooms at Cleveland's four TV stations practically exploded with the news—a photograph of the long-hunted serial rapist caught in a criminal act. The stations played the story prominently on their evening newscasts and gave the CrimeStoppers hot-line number.

That night, in the middle of the eleven o'clock broadcast, an older woman called the confidential hot-line number that had been displayed moments earlier on her TV screen. She said she knew the man in the photo. He worked in the railroad yard for LTV Steel. He even had a pair of the distinctive white-rimmed sunglasses seen in the bank surveillance photo. His name, she said excitedly, was Steve Monroe.

The next day, Duvall jumped into the Monroe investigation herself. Using utility records, she found Monroe's addresses over the past year. The last two were close to the West Park crime locations. She found out he worked as a brakeman for LTV Steel, close to the rape cluster in the Fourth.

Right away she called the chief. "I think this is our guy. We're going for a search warrant."

"Fine," he said. "Use McGinty."

Duvall didn't like McGinty, but she had to admit that he could be counted on to enthusiastically write a search warrant at any hour and then track down a judge to sign it. She called him. "I think we've got the right guy. He has the glasses and he has lived in the areas where the rapes are," she said.

"Great," McGinty said. "Sure, I'll get a search warrant."

At ten-thirty that night, Sex Crimes detectives slipped up on Monroe's West Side apartment, showed his wife a warrant, and tromped inside. After a few minutes of searching, they hit what they thought was pay dirt: a pair of white-rimmed ski goggles that matched exactly those worn by the shadowy figure whose face was photographed as he'd used Teresa O'Brien's stolen bank card.

Steve Monroe got home from work shortly after 11 P.M., and police immediately handcuffed him and shoved him onto the floor of an unmarked car. "Hey, what is this about!" Monroe screamed.

"We have your picture, stealing from Society Bank."

"Yeah? Then I'm going to own Society Bank."

The next day, Lieutenant Duvall called McGinty and told him about the sunglasses.

"Great," he said.

"Monroe denies everything so far," she said. "He'll be in interrogation later on and we'll see how he handles it."

"I'll be there," McGinty said.

Later, in a police interview room, Duvall and McGinty confronted Monroe with the bank photo.

"No way is that me," Monroe said. He pointed out minor discrepancies. With just the right mix of anger and indignation, he denied he was a rapist. For a suspect facing a mountain of serious criminal charges, Monroe's performance was striking, McGinty thought. He was either the wrong man or the coolest, most self-controlled criminal he'd ever seen.

Later Lucie said she wanted him charged. But McGinty insisted on a lineup identification first.

"None of the victims got a good look at him," she said, reddening. "If they can't formally ID him, it will kill us at trial."

"If they can't ID him, then we don't have shit anyway."

"We've got the glasses."

"There might be five thousand of those glasses in Cleveland."

Duvall insisted—no lineup.

McGinty leaned in. "Yeah, well let's call the chief and see what *he* wants."

Rudolph said to conduct a lineup.

Duvall, McGinty, and Rudolph waited behind one-way glass for Teresa O'Brien. In a minute, she strode in, tall, honey-blond, comfortable around cops. A split second later she said, "He's not there."

"Whoa, whoa, wait a minute. Take your time. Make sure," Duvall said.

Rudolph and McGinty locked eyes, and each knew what the other was thinking: We don't have the guy.

It was the Cleveland Police Department's policy, based on U.S. Supreme Court rulings, to hold a suspect up to forty-eight hours without filing a charge. If there wasn't enough cause for prosecutors to indict him, then he had to be set free. If detectives found more evidence, the suspect could be rearrested and charged.

After Rudolph left, McGinty told Duvall, "You've got twenty-four hours to come up with something or we cut him loose."

She was furious. She felt McGinty treated her like trash. Plus, she'd be damned if she was going to let the serial rapist her unit had hunted for three years just walk out of the Justice Center.

Later, she called McGinty. "I want to search his locker at LTV."

Good idea, McGinty said. He quickly crafted a search warrant and got a judge to sign it.

At the steel mill, Duvall found Monroe's locker. It was nearly empty, and there was nothing incriminating. Still, she was convinced Monroe was the West Side Rapist. She called McGinty again and said she wanted him charged.

He refused. "After the next rape, get over to him real quick and check his alibis," he said. "See if it's him. If this guy is charged now, you'll queer it when we get the real guy."

Duvall decided to go around McGinty. She went to the Cleveland city prosecutor, a good friend who mostly handled misdemeanor crimes but could charge for felonies. Duvall explained that nearly two days had gone by since Monroe's arrest and she wanted a way to hold the suspect. Could he be charged with using a stolen bank card, at least?

The city prosecutor complied.

Within hours, a Sex Crimes detective who didn't like Lieutenant Duvall called McGinty and told him about her maneuver. McGinty called the chief and told him what Duvall had done. A meeting among the three of them was set up.

"What the fuck is going on?" McGinty yelled. "Where's the evidence?"

"That's him in the picture, using her card," she said.

"There isn't a single juror anywhere who would find him guilty," McGinty said.

It was getting ugly and Rudolph waved his hand. "Release him," he said. "Kibosh it."

After Duvall left the meeting, Rudolph told McGinty, "Get Vic Kovacic involved. He's been following it for a while."

August 1988

RADA STOVICH

Rada Stovich was stunned. The photograph appearing on her television screen during the evening news looked remarkably like her ex-boyfriend Ronnie Shelton.

She listened closely as the TV anchorman, his tone gravely serious, said that a security camera at an automatic teller machine had photographed the suspected West Side Rapist using a bank card stolen from a woman he had just raped, and that anyone with information should call CrimeStoppers. Tips would be kept confidential. A $2,000 reward was being offered.

Rada wondered what to do. She knew it was Ronnie.

She and Ronnie had dated five years earlier, off and on, for a few months, and he'd even taken her to his parents' home for dinner. She still ran into him in nightclubs and had briefly lived in an apartment with his sister. One night she saw him explode in rage at a nightclub and beat someone up. "Someday," she'd told a girlfriend, "Ronnie is going to kill somebody."

A day or two after the newscast, Rada gathered her nerve and called CrimeStoppers. She told the man who answered that the photo of the West Side Rapist looked like someone she knew.

"They've already arrested the man," she was told. "We've got the suspect in custody right now." He was referring to Steve Monroe.

"Don't you want anything from me?" Rada asked.

"No, we have him in custody, ma'am."

Rada was surprised at CrimeStopper's response but didn't think anything more of it—until a few months later.

VIC KOVACIC

On August 26, two days after the arrest of Steve Monroe, Lucie Duvall wasn't ready to cut him loose. She felt he was too good a suspect to just dump back on the street. She had an idea—DNA matching. DNA was a new area of forensics and had been used in a criminal trial for the first time the year before. Her idea was to get samples of hair and blood from Monroe before she had to release him, then have his DNA analyzed. Hair, blood, and spit possessed unique molecular identifiers, a cellular fingerprint. The next time the rapist struck, the DNA structure of his sperm—if he left any—could be compared to that of Monroe's. A match would lock up the investigation and lock up Monroe.

Monroe cooperated. "Anything to get me out of here."

An hour after tufts of hair and roots were yanked painfully from his groin and armpit, Monroe was released from the overcrowded Cuyahoga County jail.

Lieutenant Duvall decided to keep an eye on him. She had her detectives ask the banks in West Park to install surveillance cameras at all cash machines, if they hadn't already. Sooner or later, she felt, Sex Crimes was going to nail Monroe.

Shortly thereafter, Tim McGinty met with Vic Kovacic, head of the Scientific Investigations Unit. If Duvall wasn't going to cooperate with him, McGinty knew he needed allies at the detective level. Vic Kovacic was vital.

"Howard wants us to work together on the West Side rape case," McGinty said.

"Fine with me," Kovacic said. He pointed to a map of Greater Cleveland on his wall. Red pushpins formed three loose clusters, around West Park, the Cleveland Zoo, and lower Broadway, just east of the steel mills.

"You sneaky Slovenian, you've been tracking this all along," McGinty said.

"I sure have. One of our serologists lives right there," Kovacic said, pointing to the rape cluster near the Cleveland Zoo. "And one of our detectives, his daughter was raped there." He pointed to West Park.

"Yeah, O'Brien. I know all about that one. Lucie thought she had the perpetrator and I made her cut him loose. She doesn't know what the hell she's doing." He filled him in on his clash with Duvall.

In twenty-five years on the job, Kovacic had risen to the rank of inspector, and he knew how to be diplomatic when necessary. "We're going to catch this guy," he promised Tim. "He's going to make a mistake, and we'll be there."

"Yeah, when?"

"We've got his picture," Vic said. "We'll have him off the streets by the holidays."

RONNIE

Ronnie saw his face on the TV news and nearly got sick. A bank security camera had caught him using a stolen bank card.

Shit, those sunglasses don't hide enough of my face, he told himself. Next time I use some bitch's bank card, I'll have to figure out something else.

He had other ways to make money besides the bank cards. He had befriended a midlevel cocaine distributor, a well-connected Cleveland woman, and made deliveries for her. With a gun tucked in his waist and hidden under a leather jacket, he roared around town on his motorcycle, a cocaine cowboy.

Ronnie got paid in cash or drugs. As a fringe benefit, he also had a standing deal that his supplier would sell him high-purity "eight balls"—three and a half grams of cocaine—at $150 each. The going rate for an eight ball was $225 to $300. Ronnie diluted his eight balls with an expensive look-alike cocaine "cut" sold at head shops. Then, using a pocket-sized Calibron precision scale, he packaged his "product" in $10 or $20 vials and sold them at the nightclubs. He made back his $150 investment in a few hours and snorted the rest.

Later that night, Ronnie stopped at the Charterhouse, a motel with a small restaurant on Brookpark Road. For a week or two he had been seeing Rebecca Buehner, a topless dancer. Only twenty-one, Becky was making good money dancing at the Crazy Horse Saloon, and she was burning through her nightly

192

cash stash with abandon, living in hotels along the strip, tooting drugs and dating recklessly. They were a good match—two attractive young people with sexual behavior that was far from normal. Tonight, they argued over her money. She said Ronnie had ripped her off. As the shouting escalated, motel tenants called police.

Brook Park police broke up the fight, then called in their names for a computer records check. Ronnie was wanted in North Olmsted, where he had missed a court date on a charge of disturbing the peace. North Olmsted was hazardous territory for him. It was where he had raped Janis Wren and, later, been arrested for voyeurism. Detectives there might be familiar with the composite sketches of him, he thought.

Ronnie was calm and polite to the North Olmsted police. After another night in jail, he was given a low bond and a court date for his misdemeanor trial, and released. Another near miss.

At odd moments, such as now, sitting alone at Danny Todd's bungalow on Cable Avenue, Ronnie wished he could change his life. The rapes, the brutality, the near misses with police, his gut-wrenching swoops from sexual intoxication to violent self-loathing—he had to do something about his mixed-up life. He could not keep this up forever.

Ronnie picked up one of his handguns, a .38-caliber. It wasn't his favorite. He preferred the sleek, black squared-off 9-millimeter semiautomatic he had stolen. But the .38 was a revolver—its cylinder could spin—and that's why he toyed with it now.

He opened the cylinder and dumped out the bullets. He picked up one, a single shiny piece of death, and slipped it back into its chamber.

He spun the cylinder. Russian roulette, just like in the movies. He was scared.

Do I have the guts to kill myself? he wondered. What's the use? They're going to catch me: then what? How can I face Mom?

He turned the gun around and put the barrel in his mouth.

I can't stop, but I really don't want to stop either.

He pushed back the hammer and tensed his thumb on the trigger.

They'll never know who it was.

Click.

Ronnie put the gun down, sweating. He felt like telling Danny right away. He was amazed at his bravery. What a fucking rush.

September–October 1988

Lucie Duvall

Perplexed, Lucie Duvall slipped her telephone into its cradle. Steve Monroe had just made his fourth call of the day to her, offering to help her "catch this monster." He'd even coughed up the name of a neighbor who he said looked just like him and was probably the West Side Rapist.

Duvall couldn't figure out Monroe. If he had been wrongfully arrested last week, as he claimed, then why wasn't he reacting in a more typical fashion—lashing out at her, calling her a motherfucker, threatening a lawsuit? She still believed he was the rapist.

More than anything Duvall wanted to get the West Side Rapist off the streets, but she felt she faced a flood of opposition. It was like trying to sprint under water: slow and exhausting, and you didn't get very far.

For one thing, she didn't have an overtime budget, so it was impossible to assign detectives on an off-day if something important came up. And the unit had only two cars; the brass got new cars each year, while Sex Crimes had to stand in line with all the other units to get a piece of junk to drive on a detail.

Worst of all, the Sex Crimes staff had been cut in half by

attrition. This month, September, Duvall had been torpedoed by one of the chief's allies, the city council president, George Forbes. The most powerful man in Cleveland, the council president had asked for one of the Sex Crimes detectives to be assigned as his personal driver. The chief had said fine. Duvall now fielded only eight detectives.

Chief Rudolph, she felt, was punishing her personally by ignoring her unit. She'd practically had to organize a charity fund-raiser to scratch up the $300 needed for a DNA test of Monroe's blood and hair at a private Maryland laboratory that could do chromosome analysis. Morale was sinking.

Weeks later, a front-page story in the October 16, 1988, *Plain Dealer* hit West Park like a bombshell:

Sex Crimes Unit Shrinks
Rape Rate Rises as Detective Staff Nearly Halved
The frequency of rape, child molestation and other Sex Crimes has risen sharply in Cleveland, coinciding with deep cuts in the strength of the Police Department's Sex Crimes Unit. . . .

The article pointed out that the unit was down to eight, with the council president having taken one detective as his driver. "It's a crime to be making these cuts," a Rape Crisis Center administrator was quoted as saying. "This is ridiculous. Does Mr. Forbes have recurring nightmares and need years of counseling because he doesn't have a chauffeur? Well, my clients do experience those things." The administrator added that she had noticed the effects of the staff cuts the summer before, when rape victims began complaining to the center that sex crimes detectives were taking up to a week to interview them.

It was a lousy way to conduct investigations, and Lucie Duvall knew it. She had talked off the record to the newspaper reporter and hoped his article would shake things up.

She was right. The citizens of West Park responded to the article with furor. In barbershops, Laundromats, and corner taverns, they could talk of little but these cutbacks in the middle of a neighborhood nightmare. The West Park Community Council demanded a meeting with police, and several days later Duvall agreed to send a detective to explain what was going on. The community council sent out hundreds of "Neighborhood Alert" fliers that warned of the rapes and announced the meeting.

The night of the meeting, all three local TV stations sent camera crews, and 150 people packed the meeting room. Duvall's detective had his hands full. When he said the staffing cuts would not be reversed immediately, the crowd hissed. He went on gamely, urging everyone to serve as extra eyes and ears of the police: Note anything unusual, write down license plate numbers, watch each other's houses in the early morning, lock all windows and doors all the time, and recheck window locks at night. If you see pry marks anywhere, call the police.

The meeting seemed to make the neighborhood more tense.

November 1988

MAGGIE DALEY*

A flood of publicity in the Fall of 1988 made it tougher for Ronnie to find rape targets. Women were more careful, in particular older women, those with long ties to West Park. There was still a large pool of vulnerable women: young, single, high school–educated women living in their first apartments who didn't read the newspaper or watch TV news, and socialized outside the neighborhood. Some of them still went about their lives largely unaware of the West Side Rapist.

---

*Not her real name.

196

Ronnie had no intention of selecting a different raping zone just because detectives had narrowed their scrutiny to the few square miles of West Park. It had become a frightening, tantalizing game: Outfox the cops.

One night just after Halloween, Ronnie prowled along Puritas Avenue, a busy mixed-use thoroughfare that cut West Park in two. On Puritas, modest houses were spaced between apartment buildings and commercial strips anchored by doughnut shops, pizza places, and convenience food stores. Ronnie blended right in, just another stranger cutting through the area.

At the back of an apartment building where a favorite target lived, Ronnie settled into his voyeur's crouch and waited for titillation, his face inches from the bottom of Maggie Daley's window.

On this night Maggie Daley came home on schedule, about 3:15 A.M. The daughter of a Cleveland police captain, she tended bar at a tavern near the Baldwin-Wallace College campus. Maggie undressed and slumped into bed. The next thing she remembered was a noise waking her up. She slipped out to the living room in her nightgown to investigate. She pulled up the blinds and found herself staring at a man dressed in a denim jacket and unbuckled jeans. He was kneeling, peering up at her, masturbating furiously.

The screen had been removed! She dropped the blinds and ran to the bedroom and called the police. They got to her address fast, but Ronnie slipped right by them on the sidewalk with a wave and a hello.

After filling out the police report, she called her father, who knew right away that the disturbance fit the modus operandi of the West Park Rapist. He came right over.

Captain Daley was a fitness buff who wasn't afraid to use deadly force if he had to. Now he began driving by his daughter's apartment in the early mornings, ready with handcuffs and a gun.

Over the next few nights, Ronnie noticed the unmarked cop cars coming and going past Maggie Daley's apartment. Then, on November 26, after a night of barhopping, reeking of cigarettes, Ronnie made his move. He stashed his car down the street and slipped along the back of her apartment building, out of sight of patrolling cop cars. As he moved along the building he noticed a window without curtains. He looked in. The apartment was empty. Ronnie jimmied open the window and hurried back to his car. He grabbed a gym bag of fresh clothes, a towel, and toiletries, then strolled back and climbed into the empty apartment.

In the dark, he slowly showered, shaved, and blow-dried his hair, his precourtship ritual. He had liked what he had seen of Maggie Daley over the past weeks. Now he wanted to make a good impression. He felt she deserved someone clean, fresh. He pulled on dark clothes and waited.

At closing time at the Front Street Tavern in suburban Berea, Maggie Daley cleaned up, then had breakfast with a friend at an all-night diner. She picked up a few groceries at Carl's Superstore and came home. It was five in the morning, and nothing seemed unusual. She stripped off her clothes and got in bed. . . .

She snapped out of deep sleep. Someone was sitting on her, pinning her arms!

"Maggie," the man said softly. "Why did you call the police on me the last time I was here?"

She felt a knife at her cheek and was too terrified to answer.

"I saw the detective car in front of your place; I know what they look like," he said.

She wished her father were here. He would save her. Please don't kill me, please don't kill me, please don't kill me, she thought.

"I'm not going to hurt you if you do what I say." He pulled back the blankets and got on top of her.

She turned her head for a second and saw a horrifying face, mashed by a tight nylon stocking with a crude hole cut out for his mouth.

"Don't look at me!" he threatened.

He pulled out and ejaculated on her stomach. He daintily cleaned her stomach with a blanket, then grabbed her purse and took her money and a bank card, demanding her secret code.

"A-eleven-A-D-A," she said, her voice cracking. She was more scared than ever. Now that he had everything he needed, she knew he was going to kill her.

She saw him at the foot of her bed, looking at videos on a shelf. He laughed at one title, *The Good, the Bad, and the Horny,* and slipped it into his jacket. He threatened to kill her if she called the police, and left.

After a few minutes, she grabbed a pair of scissors from a drawer and ran to the living room to get her telephone. She pulled it back into the bedroom, trailing the long extension cable, and slammed the door. The phone was dead—he must have cut the line.

She burst into tears, then got dressed and, clenching the scissors, ran to her car. She drove recklessly to the First District police station, where her father worked. It was Saturday, his day off.

When he got the news, Maggie's father was devastated. His daughter had been raped, right under the nose of the police. He was a police officer, and he had failed to save his daughter. He did not want Maggie to have to explain the rape over and over to uniformed cops and then to detectives and scientific unit technicians. He wanted one qualified detective to handle it. Sex crimes was busy, so Daley asked for a detective from his own First District, Barbara Parker. She was an expert rape investigator, and one of Duvall's original fifteen sex crimes detectives. But she and Lucie had clashed and within six weeks Parker had asked for a transfer.

Barbara Parker gently took the young woman through an account of the crime. When Maggie mentioned that the rapist had stolen her Ameritrust bank card, Parker got excited.

Right after he raped Maggie Daley, Ronnie drove about a mile and a half to a Third Federal Bank in the heart of West Park. He parked his old car along the curb and headed to the machine. He looked around to make certain no one was watching.

This is too easy, Ronnie thought. He walked to the money machine.

* * *

Later that day, Sex Crimes detectives called the bank and learned that Maggie Daley's money card had been used several minutes after her rape. The surveillance camera had been on, and the film was turned over to Duvall's detectives.

The bank's camera snapped images every three seconds. In the first shot, detectives could see the grayish outline of a man with long hair, holding a newspaper in his hand. Behind him was the right rear quarter panel of his car.

In the next shot, he was holding a newspaper in front of his face. The third shot was of his hand placing the paper over the camera window. The next several snapshots were black. The newspaper had done the trick. The last photo in the series showed a man with his back to the camera, almost back at his car.

And that was it. You couldn't make out his face or a license plate. Sex Crimes detectives were crestfallen. Another setback.

VIC KOVACIC

A day later, Vic Kovacic got copies of the grainy time-sequence photos of the West Side Rapist. He realized they were no help in determining the suspect's looks, but he could see the car's right rear quarter panel. Vic wondered if his lab could do something to determine what kind of car the rapist drove.

Kovacic asked one of his civilian technicians to see if he could enhance the photographs using the department's VSC-1, a video spectral comparer, a desktop computer that analyzed forgeries, photographs, and other physical evidence.

The image was so blurry and gray that not much could be done with it. The tech scanned the photo of the car into the computer, then enlarged and enhanced the car's rear quarter panel. He asked the computer to filter out middle tones of gray. Suddenly, the image of the car became sharper, all blacks and whites. The sharper image, when blown up, revealed clues. Based on the outline and using reference books, they decided the mystery car was a dark-colored 1975 or 1976 Monte Carlo. The car was distinct; it had a pushed-in rear bumper, a rusted wheel well, a missing piece of trim, and a six-inch tear in its vinyl top.

Kovacic was elated—this was breakthrough information. He gathered his staff. "We're going to catch this guy, and we're going to catch him soon," Kovacic said. "I want all of you who live on the West Side to be looking for cars that match. If you're coming in on the bus, driving, going shopping, whatever you're doing—get a license plate and a location and let me know. Okay? Now let's get to work."

When McGinty heard the news, he ran over right away. "This is great," McGinty said after seeing the photo. "You know, I can't believe he has such a piece-of-shit car."

"He's not some genius. He's a criminal. Garbage," Kovacic said.

"He's been out there so long, I figured he was smart."

"He's been lucky. Tim, we're going to get this guy off the streets by the holidays."

"You said that before," McGinty said, smiling. "Look, it's already past the holidays. Thanksgiving was last week."

Vic laughed. " 'The holidays' means Christmas, McGinty. Even an assistant county prosecutor should be able to figure that out."

Sex Crimes detectives had their own set of photos of Shelton's car, and they also kept an eye out. All across the police department, at the beginning of each shift, supervisors told uniformed cops to watch for the car.

But Kovacic took it one step further. He was an inspector, not a grunt, but he was obsessed with finding the car himself. It had become a personal challenge. Studying his pin map and the crime dates, he had a hunch that the West Side Rapist was living between the rape clusters in West Park and the Cleveland Zoo. That target zone included parts of suburban Brooklyn, near the Cleveland border. On his lunch hours and after work, Kovacic drove through the strip shopping centers and the apartment buildings in the zone he had selected. Everyone on his staff who lived on the West Side looked for the car on their commute or on weekends.

"He's made his mistake," Kovacic told everyone. "Now we just have to figure out who he is."

December 1988

RONNIE

By December 2, Ronnie needed a place to live for a while. He had fallen out with Danny Todd and his parents, and for the moment was between girlfriends. He asked a casual friend, Paul Solnick, if he could crash for a few days at his apartment. Solnick, a go-go dancer, wasn't around much. He told Ronnie okay.

Within the hour, Ronnie moved his clothes, a VCR, and his gun into Solnick's apartment at the Floridian, a three-building complex in Brooklyn, a working-class suburb with excellent police protection just southwest of Cleveland. And he quickly went to work spying on his new neighbors.

Four mornings later, just before dawn, Ronnie was spotted peeping into first-floor apartment windows at the rear of the Floridian, his pants unzipped, looking with satisfaction at a possible victim. Suddenly, a Brooklyn police car with lights and siren off pulled around the corner, and Ronnie was caught.

Back at the station, police found three rings of the Floridian's master keys in Ronnie's pockets. He thought that this was the end; he had finally been captured. The police had to know now. He felt himself coming unhinged.

He could not provide a plausible reason for his having had the keys. The Brooklyn police booked him for voyeurism. Later that day, he was given a court date and released on bond. He was still rattled when he left.

It had been a week or so since Ronnie had talked to his mother, and he called home.

"Your cousin is coming tomorrow," she said. "She has never been to Ohio. I want you to see her."

Ronnie agreed. The last time he had seen his cousin was during a family trip to California more than ten years before. She had to be a pretty young woman by now.

When he finally made it over to Brunswick Hills, he and his mother got into an argument over a trivial matter. He lashed out, swearing.

She moved in close as if to hit him. "Don't use that talk in front of me. I will tell your father when he gets here."

She tried to slap him, and he moved back. Ronnie was sick of her threats. She had treated him like this since he was a child, but he was a man now, and he resented her trying to run his life. All these stupid threats about his father. He'd kick both their asses.

"You better leave me the fuck alone," he said.

"Don't you say *fuck* to me," she said. "Fuck you."

Ronnie had never heard his mother say *fuck* before, and it enraged him. He turned and hit her, his hand open, smashing her across her face. "Stop it!" she screamed.

Yelling obscenities, unleashing years of rage, Ronnie slammed her to the kitchen floor. Her dress was pushed up and her face twisted. She cowered, crying, her arms up, palms open.

Her expression riveted him. It seemed as if time had stopped. Her face was white with terror.

I've seen this face before, he realized. It looks like the faces of the women I rape.

He moved over her, and Katy Shelton cried, "Please, don't! Please, don't!"

Ronnie grabbed his mother by her thick black hair and dragged her across the kitchen floor. He didn't know what he was going to do to her now, and it scared him. He wanted to do more, to hurt her.

"No, no, no," she sobbed.

Something inside held him back. He released her hair, dropping her head to the floor. She scrambled up and ran next door and called the police.

I have to get out of here, Ronnie thought.

His cousin stood paralyzed, shocked by the sudden thunderclap of violence.

She hasn't seen me since we were both kids, Ronnie thought, and this is the way she gets reintroduced to the family. God, this is sick.

He got into his maroon Monte Carlo and drove off as fast as the old clunker would go.

VIC KOVACIC

On December 21, Vic Kovacic drove out to the West Side on his lunch hour. He planned to eat at Aldo's, a new Italian restaurant in Brooklyn that was midway between the two clusters of rape locations on the big Cleveland area map on his office wall. For the past three weeks, he had driven through scores of shopping centers and apartment buildings looking for the dark 1975 or 1976 Monte Carlo. Today he just wanted a good meal and a chance to do some Christmas shopping.

The tiny parking lot at Aldo's was full, so he pulled into the parking lot in front of the Floridian next door and looked for an opening. Suddenly he saw it—a beat-up maroon Monte Carlo. His pulse quickened. He got out and looked at the right rear fender. It was rusted, similar to the one in the bank surveillance photo. Unbelievable. He sketched its broken outline on the back of an envelope, noted the car's license number, and headed to his office to compare.

His crude sketch matched the blurry bank photo. This was the car! Vic wanted to shout, We've got it, we've got it! But first, who owned it? A computer check showed it to be registered to a man named Ronnie Shelton. His driver's license records showed him to be five-foot-eight, 138 pounds, twenty-seven years old. So far, it matched the description of the West Side Rapist. Kovacic ran Shelton's name through the criminal records computer. Up popped several previous arrests, including one for voyeurism. "Bingo," Vic said.

An SIU detective quickly located a fingerprint card for Ronnie from a 1985 arrest in Cleveland for theft. Ronnie's prints were compared to those recovered from the Cleveland rape scenes. In minutes, the detective found a match.

Kovacic was exhilarated. "Yes, we *are* going to get this creep off the street by the holidays." He called Sex Crimes and broke the news.

"We have definitely identified the West Side Rapist as Ronnie Shelton," he said. "Now all we have to do is find him."

PART FOUR

The Ice Breaks

December 1988

ARREST

On December 20, Ronnie got in a fight with his roommate after calling Paul Solnick's girlfriend a slut.

"Get out! Pick up your clothes and go, asshole," Solnick said.

Ronnie pulled out his knife. Solnick, a handsome male dancer, wasn't a fighter, and didn't want his face cut. He called the Brooklyn police.

Infuriated, Ronnie told himself he had to get even with Solnick somehow. It was a point of honor. But first he had to leave before the police got there. "I better not find my stuff outside when I get back here," Ronnie said on his way out.

It didn't matter, since they were being evicted the next day.

The next morning, while Ronnie slept in a Parma motel room with a woman he'd met at a club the night before, the Cleveland police closed in. Lucie Duvall and a detective went to Ronnie's parents' house, a white ranch set far back on a deep lot. The driveway curled behind the house, with the garage door facing away from the street. There was no sign of a ratty Monte Carlo, but they knew it could be out of sight in the garage.

After watching for a few hours, Duvall debated whether to go to the house. Even if Shelton wasn't home, he could find out later from his parents that Cleveland detectives were looking for him and he might flee the state.

She knocked on the door and Rodney Shelton answered.

She showed her badge and asked for his son.

Rodney said he hadn't seen him and didn't know where he was staying.

Back in the office, Duvall learned about the eviction of Shelton's friend at the Floridian. She told Detectives Mark Hastings and Arnold Hovan: "Go out there and sit on the apartment. Do not move. He's going to come back and help his friend move. I know it."

Hovan, battling a fierce cold, said, "What about an undercover?" The unit didn't have a civilian car available.

"I'll get Narcotics to give me one," she said.

About six that evening, Hastings and Hovan drove out to Brooklyn in a gaudy white Cadillac Eldorado, seized from a pimp in a drug bust. They backed the car into an open space at the far end of the apartment building's parking lot. In the dark, they had a clear view of the building's entrance.

Hastings and Hovan, partners since 1985, were a good pair to snatch a suspect. Hastings, about six-foot-three, weighed 270 pounds. Hovan, at six-foot-five, was even broader, more than 300 pounds. They were an intimidating team.

It was a cold night, but they couldn't risk turning on the car. The exhaust and sound of a motor running would give them away.

"Of all the fucking things, to run into a serial fucking rapist," Hovan said.

"Yeah."

"If he's halfway good, then you're in for a fucking lot of work."

"No kidding."

"Turn on the heat, my cold is killing me."

"No way—we'll be made in a minute," Hastings said. "Suffer."

Back at the Justice Center, Tim McGinty and Vic Kovacic waited in their offices for word of the arrest. McGinty, pacing around, got on the phone to Vic. He said he was worried.

"These two guys can handle him," Kovacic said.

"I'd feel better if we had a backup team for a doughnut run," McGinty said. "You know those two: They're probably hungry already and will go out to grab something and the asshole will sneak back and get his car."

"They're not going out for doughnuts on a stakeout," Kovacic said, laughing.

Shortly after 7 P.M., a blue Chevy Nova pulled into the Floridian lot. Shelton sat in the passenger seat, scanning for danger, while a friend drove. He spotted the Eldorado, parked with its rear to the fence, a giveaway. He saw two big, dark forms inside, facing the apartment entrance.

"Pull around the parking lot and go back out," he told his friend. Ronnie figured the two guys in the Eldorado were Solnick's friends, waiting to ambush him for pulling a knife on their buddy.

Back out on Memphis Avenue, Ronnie had his friend stop at a pay phone in front of Aldo's Restaurant. He got out and dialed the Brooklyn police. "This is Ronnie Shelton," he told a dispatcher. "I'm going to pick up my clothes and I think I was supposed to call you guys for an escort so I can get them. There was a fight and I can't get them back."

The dispatcher asked his location, then said, "Okay, someone will be over."

Ronnie and his young pal spun back into the lot. Now Paul Solnick was at the apartment entrance, dumping clothes into a car. "Pull in front, cut it off," Ronnie commanded. The Brooklyn cops were supposed to be coming, but first he was going to smash Paul's pretty face. Ronnie opened the car door and got out. . . .

In the dark, Hastings saw the Nova and said, "Hey, look at this." Then, "That's Shelton getting out of the car."

"No fucking way," Hovan said. He knew how important this arrest was. He wanted to be dead certain they had the right suspect, and the guy he saw wasn't what he was expecting.

"No, it's him," Hastings said.

211

"Mark, don't fuck this up. She'll kill us."

"It's him."

"She'll have our balls for dinner," Hovan said.

"Let's go." Hastings ran out of the Eldorado, pulled his gun, and in a few seconds had it pointed at the driver's head a foot away.

Hovan, with a huge gut and an arthritic back, was moving as quickly as he could around the back of the Eldorado. From the crime reports, he knew Shelton had a gun. As a uniformed cop, Hovan wasn't afraid to use his gun; he had been in two shoot-outs in which suspects were fatally shot. Now, irritated by his cold and the weather, Hovan was ready to smoke Shelton, or whoever it was, if he tried anything cute.

Ronnie got out and froze. He thought he was being executed: two big thugs, dressed in soft clothes, their guns out.

Hovan yelled, "Freeze!"

Ronnie was confused. "Hey, wait a minute," he said. "I called you guys." Then in the background he spotted a Brooklyn police car rolling into the parking lot.

His mind raced: Cleveland cops, shit. My gun my gun I need my gun. Dive for it three feet away, so what if they shoot, be like Richard Gere in *Breathless*. I can't go to jail for rape, my family can't know.

He watched the Brooklyn cop stop his car and take his time getting out.

I'm not afraid, I'm powerful. No hostages, I'm gonna shoot, put the gun to my head and shoot. Shit, it's in my car. Fuck.

"Cleveland police!" Hastings said to Shelton, and Hovan shoved him facedown on the hood of the Nova. As Hastings got out his handcuffs, Arnie Hovan looked up and said, "Jesus, we've got problems."

The Brooklyn cop was out of the car. To him it looked like an assassination, two gangsters with guns in a drug dealer's ear.

Hovan knew what he'd do if he were in the uniform's shoes and two evil-looking jamokes with semiautomatics were looking his way. He'd frigging shoot and take cover.

Hovan screamed, "Police officer! Police officer!" He held out

212

his gold badge and slowly walked toward the Brooklyn cop. The uniformed cop was older, gray-haired, soft.

Is he as scared as I am? Hovan wondered. Oh, man, don't shoot me.

Ronnie felt desperate. Distraction, cops at each other, they're fat, can't chase. Run into the lobby, out back, over the fence, into the woods, they won't shoot. I run, run far away, start over, a stranger.

The Brooklyn cop looked at Hovan's gold badge and then at Ronnie. Hastings finished cuffing him. "What are you boys doing over here?" he asked.

Hovan said, "We're with Sex Crimes."

"Oh, what do you think you got there?"

"A rapist. Ronnie Shelton. We have an arrest warrant."

"Oh, you're gonna have to turn him over to me."

"What!"

"You turn him over to me."

"Pal, he's my arrest," Hovan said. "I got a warrant. You ain't getting him from me."

"Listen, I got specific orders that if Shelton's arrested, I call the Second District and turn him over."

"You did see my badge?" Hovan said. "He's mine!"

"You're in my city," the old cop said.

"I don't care if I'm in Chicago," Hovan shot back. "You ain't the fuck getting him."

The uniformed cop stood his ground. "I got to call the station. I'll see what the chief says about this." He got on the radio in his squad car.

Hastings and Hovan put Ronnie in the backseat and read him his rights. "Hey, where's your car, Ronnie?"

"At my parents' in Brunswick Hills."

They knew he was lying. Lucie had just been there. Hastings got out and walked to the terrified driver of the Nova. "Where's your buddy's car?" Hastings said softly.

"At my mom's house on West Sixty-eighth Street." He gave the detective the address.

"Okay, you can go," Hastings said.

They drove to West 68th Street and quickly spotted Shelton's car. Dark maroon, torn top, missing chrome, mag wheels in the rear, the same license tags that Vic Kovacic had noted. They got out and looked inside. Tools, auto parts, stereo gear. "Jeez, it looks like he's running a regular True Value out of this thing," Hovan said.

"That or a Goodwill, all those clothes," Hastings said.

They piled everything from Shelton's car into the trunk of the Eldorado for processing: clothes, traffic tickets, two sets of Ohio license plates, sunglasses, a couple of cameras, women's jewelry and a watch, a black switchblade, an air drill, two pairs of binoculars, a VCR.

Hastings called Lieutenant Duvall at home on a portable police radio they had brought along on the bust. "We got him. Everything went okay."

"Oh, that's great." She was ecstatic. "What did you find in his car?"

Hastings gave her a rundown.

"Good. Great work, guys. Thanks."

Hovan settled his bulk back in the front seat. It was a ten-minute drive back to the Justice Center to book Shelton, and he decided to ride him a little.

"Want a cigarette?" he asked. "Marlboros, right?"

Ronnie said no thanks.

"Look, you're a good-looking guy. You gotta have a lot of girlfriends. Why would you want to rape a broad?"

Ronnie looked at him but kept his lips locked. He had been arrested more than a dozen times. He knew better than to say something stupid.

"You know what," Hovan said after a moment. "You're a fucking asshole. You destroyed a lot of broads' minds. Well, we got you. We got you good."

From the front seat, Hovan saw that Ronnie was shivering. And it wasn't from the cold.

Ronnie had to strip off his clothes in the jail and put on a paper jumpsuit. They left two other pairs of pajamas in his cell.

Ronnie felt sorry for himself, but also relieved that it was all over. He cried for a while, felt better, and tried to go to sleep.

The inmate in the next cell woke him up. "They talkin' 'bout you." It was near the midnight shift change.

Ronnie heard the voices of the new jailers. It sounded like a question: "O'Brien get here yet?" As it turned out, Jake O'Brien, the SIU fingerprint man, was assigned to the jail now. He printed all new prisoners.

"No, not yet," came the reply.

"Shit's gonna hit the fan when he gets here."

In one moment Ronnie made the connection with the man's name. One of his most recent rape victims was the pretty woman on Rocky River Drive, sleeping on a couch in her bra and panties. Her name was O'Brien, and he remembered from going through her purse that she had a blue police courtesy card signed by her father the cop. Now, he thought, it's all over. O'Brien is going to come in and beat the shit out of me for raping his daughter. Ronnie didn't blame him. He'd do the same thing.

As quietly as he could, Ronnie tore the long zipper out of his paper jumpsuit. He needed a couple more. He stripped two more zippers from the other paper suits in the cell and tied them together. He made a slipknot and, pulling himself up, tied the other end to the top cell bar and tightened it around his neck.

He gently dropped his weight. But the makeshift noose couldn't hold him. Later, when he was discovered, the jailer transferred Ronnie to the suicide watch. O'Brien never came.

Back at the Sex Crimes Unit, Detective Zbydniewski decided to take a crack at Shelton. Zeb didn't want to interview him alone. She wanted a backup in case he confessed.

In the jail, Zeb was surprised at Shelton's size. A weight lifter and holder of the national Police Olympics medal for the javelin throw, she had at least twenty-five pounds of muscle on him. Most of the men she worked with were bigger than average, and some, like Bob Matuszny, whom she saw lifting weights all the time, were huge. Shelton looked like a pencil-neck, someone she could take down in two seconds. No wonder he had to surprise his victims with a knife in the dark.

She started with innocuous questions to get him used to talking: place of birth, parents' names, his job history.

Ronnie was smooth. He denied raping anyone but hinted that he may have taken a few credit cards in his career. He also hinted at a drug problem, hoping for sympathy.

"Were you ever abused as a child?" the detective asked during a lull. Silence.

Ronnie's eyes teared up and he looked pitifully at the detectives. No, no, he said. His parents used to beat him, but nothing to do with sex.

Zeb felt he was unsettled now, vulnerable. She flipped out the photos of Ronnie on hidden camera, taken at the automatic teller machine just after he had raped Maggie Daley. His eyes widened and the color drained from his face.

"That's it," he said. "I'm not saying any more."

The next morning, McGinty went to the Sex Crimes Unit to fire up the troops. He had been told about the interrogation of Shelton, and wanted more. He wanted the detectives to go back in and hammer on Ronnie. His philosophy was to pressure a suspect with questions, again and again, before he got smart and asked for a lawyer. Every little admission, any scrap of information—girlfriends, jobs, associates—could end up being helpful.

So far Ronnie hadn't asked for his lawyer, but he would soon, McGinty felt. All the major scumbags did.

"He doesn't have a lawyer yet, so go back in," McGinty told the Sex Crimes detectives. "And get out and talk to anybody associated with him—his male dancer buddies, all the women whose phone numbers were scrawled on the matchbooks in his car . . . everybody. Lock them into their story," McGinty insisted. "Before they get lawyers and start changing things or clamming up. Okay, let's go."

Later, he wondered just what lucky defense lawyer was going to land this case.

Jerry Milano

It was Christmas morning, a sunny day, as Jerry Milano raced his Lincoln Continental west on the empty freeway to the Justice Center. He had never met a client on Christmas before. If one had ever asked for such a meeting, he would have yelled at him in his raspy, unmistakable voice, "Are you out of your fucking mind? G'bye!" and slammed down the phone.

Today he and his wife were supposed to be at the home of their son Jay, his law partner, for their usual Christmas morning ritual. Jay's two young children opened presents and then the whole family—including both sets of grandparents—sat down to a ham dinner, paying tribute to the Irish heritage of Jerry's wife.

But Jerry had to miss the fun this morning. He had an unusual client he hoped to impress, a serial rapist, a man accused of raping women on the West Side. It was the hottest criminal case in town, and ever since Shelton's arrest, Cleveland's criminal defense lawyers, a close-knit group, wondered where the case would land.

Maria Shelton had called Milano the day before and asked if he could help her brother. Milano reassured her that he could do a very fine job for him. He mentioned that he had tried hundreds of cases, defending every sort of criminal, from Hell's Angels to made members of the Mafia, on charges ranging from drug trafficking to aggravated murder.

"I haven't lost a rape case yet," he said. He didn't mention that he had only had four such cases in his thirty-three-year career.

217

He explained his fee, and she later gave him a $5,000 check as a retainer. (A week later Milano learned the check had bounced and had to demand another.)

Milano walked briskly into the county jail's visiting area. Some of the holiday-shift jailers recognized him. His nails manicured and polished, Milano looked every inch the prosperous lawyer in his expensive casual clothes. He was short, a bit soft in the middle, with a bald dome rising above a narrow semicircle of close-clipped black hair. His dark, deep-set, cunning eyes seemed to hone in on each person he encountered, as if he were trying to read their minds.

The jailers brought Shelton into the interview room. Milano was surprised. He's such a good-looking young kid, Milano thought; why the hell does he have to go out and rape? Right away, he knew he had to have this case.

Milano introduced himself and offered Ronnie a cigarette, and quickly learned that his prospective client smoked as incessantly as he did. Whiskey and cigarettes gave Milano's voice deep brass tones, so that he boomed like a tuba in the courtroom.

"Mr. Milano, I didn't do what they said I did," Ronnie said. Beneath the sincere surface of his voice, Milano could hear a whine.

Yeah, right, Milano thought. They all say they're innocent, at first. We'll get to the fucking truth soon enough.

Right now, he just wanted the kid to like him. He wanted Shelton's family to hire him and secure his fee. And after the holidays, at lunch in the Lincoln Inn, down the alley from the Justice Center, he could let the other criminal defense lawyers know that he, Milano, had caught this case. They'd be jealous as hell.

"If you really didn't rape these women, then I'll prove that in court," Milano told Ronnie. "You'll be a free man."

Ronnie asked a few questions and Milano saw that he had charmed the kid. "I'll be back to see you after I find out what the cops have," Milano said. He pushed over his cigarette pack. "Here, keep 'em."

LUCIE DUVALL

In the first days after Shelton's arrest, SIU matched his finger-prints to latent fingerprints lifted from four of the rape scenes. Four cases solved, wham, just like that.

Despite the good news, McGinty and Duvall were not getting along. Duvall wanted to wrap up the Shelton case and move on. She and the Sex Crimes Unit were saddled with at least a dozen new cases a week. She felt the unit had plenty of work without wasting time reinvestigating every case that could possibly be linked to Shelton.

But McGinty blocked her way. He wanted Matuszny and his new partner, Jim Facemire, to reexamine every rape case that could possibly fit Shelton's modus operandi. That could mean bringing in dozens of rape victims to try to identify Shelton in police lineups by his appearance or his voice.

Duvall met with McGinty, and she told him firmly, "I don't want all these lineups. It's a waste. Milano said he would plead him out. Shelton'll get just as many years as if he was convicted at trial."

"I don't care what Milano says," McGinty shot back.

"He'll be up for parole in fifteen no matter what you do," she said. "Look, as part of a deal, he could explain to us why he did it. The FBI could study him. It would help catch future serial rapists."

"I don't care why he did it," McGinty said. "At the end of this, he's going to hate us and won't talk to anybody. If he doesn't threaten my life by the end of all this, I'll be disappointed."

"The victims don't want to go through all this again," Duvall said. "It's painful."

"How many victims did you talk to?"

Duvall mentioned Maggie Daley. She had been withdrawn, barely able to speak above a whisper at the lineup a few days earlier. She had picked out Shelton, but she didn't make an impressive witness. She was devastated.

"We're not going through lineups," she said finally. "We won't be there."

"Your people want to be there, Lucie," McGinty said. "Why don't you ask your own people for a change."

Chief Rudolph was away on Christmas vacation, and the standoff between Duvall and McGinty stretched on for another week. Meanwhile, McGinty briefed Vic Kovacic on the disagreement and lined up his support.

On her side, Duvall lined up the commander of the specialized units, which included Kovacic's SIU.

After the chief returned, a meeting was scheduled to hash out the Shelton case. Kovacic and Duvall met with him in his office.

Duvall explained that McGinty wanted to reinvestigate every unsolved rape on the West Side in an attempt to pile more indictments on Shelton. The case was already a lock, she said. There were fingerprint matches in four of the cases and a bunch of rape victims who wanted to get on with their lives. Why drag them through the hell of testifying? Plus, her unit didn't have the resources to spend on the case. It was swamped already. "We've solved this case," she said. "Let's go on to solve other cases."

It was an effective presentation. Now it was Kovacic's turn. "We don't want overkill," he started out, "but the prosecutor wants to go forward with all the cases we can link to this rapist. Shelton shouldn't get a free ride on the other cases just because they don't have fingerprints. I think each victim deserves her day in court or to know that we did the best we possibly could with her case."

After a moment, Rudolph said, "I was so happy when we

caught this guy I said I'd send Vic to Hawaii. But of course, we don't have the money for that. Now, here is my thinking. To put five or six cases on this guy is not sufficient. You put everything on him that you've got. He's always got a chance—maybe not much of one—to get off easy. If you put the totality of the crime spree on him, he might never get out. We give every victim a shot. Understand?"

Duvall looked flushed. It was a painful rebuke, especially coming from the chief, and she could just imagine McGinty gloating. She had lost this round.

January 1989

BOB MATUSZNY

McGinty decided the best way to get a few dozen victims linked to Shelton was to have Bob Matuszny assigned to the investigation again. He called the detective at the Second District and explained what he was trying to accomplish.

"Tim knew I'd do the job for him," Matuszny would say later. "We had done a couple of cases together, some high-profile shootings. He trusted me, and I knew he'd do a hell of a job. I felt at ease knowing he'd run the investigation. He'd take our information and make a good case out of it. He worked. He'd locate witnesses and talk to them. So I said, yeah, see what you can do."

Soon McGinty asked the chief to reassign Matuszny to the case. Bob had already poured his guts into the investigation, McGinty explained. He's on good terms with half the rape victims already.

Rudolph said fine, but Matuszny would have to keep up with his cases in the Second District as well.

McGinty called Matuszny and told him the chief had okayed the reassignment. "I've got some overtime authorization, but not enough to cover all the hours you're going to have to put in," McGinty said. "You still interested?"

"Sure, why not," Matuszny said. Secretly he was thrilled to get back on the case. It had haunted him for the past three years. While the West Side Rapist had kept ruining women's lives and eluding the cops, Bob had watched with a sour stomach, picking up bits and pieces of information about the case through the police grapevine. He had always worked long hours when he snagged a big investigation, but the hunt for the West Side Rapist had been different. It had gotten under his skin. It felt like he had handled spun glass without gloves: Touch it and you itched forever. For two years he had fine-combed every inch of the West Side, trying to figure out this rat bastard of a rapist. Who he was. Where he'd strike. Then Duvall bounced him from the case—his case. It still frosted him. When he ran into detectives from SIU or the Fourth District and they asked how the case was going, he had to admit he wasn't working it; Sex Crimes had it. It was frustrating.

The next day Matuszny and James Facemire walked to McGinty's office for a meeting.

They didn't know that days earlier McGinty had asked Lieutenant Duvall to have her detectives obtain a photo of Shelton's genitals. She'd replied that he needed a court order or permission from Jerry Milano.

"Court order, bullshit," McGinty had told her. "Then we'll have to explain why we want it, don't you understand? We'll have to tell the defense exactly what we don't have. Lucie, this is just like a tattoo exam. He *has* to submit."

"Shelton won't agree to one."

"I don't care," McGinty had said. "Tell him we're going to whip him until he drops his drawers."

When Matuszny and Facemire came in, McGinty smiled. "We need a photo of little Ronnie boy's prick. Some of the victims say his prick was smooth, others say it had warts or something. We need to know what's going on."

"Why don't you, uh, handle it, Tim," Matuszny said, deadpan.

"I'm the prosecutor, not a detective. You get paid to do the dirty work, and this is definitely dirty work." McGinty laughed. He and Matuszny were going to get along fine on this one.

"Do we really need it?" Bob asked, knowing the answer.

"Yeah. And I need someone to testify to its markings."

Later, Matuszny and Facemire, with a police photographer, visited Shelton in a holding cell. On request, Shelton dropped his pants. The lensman fired away, but not from an angle that showed anything. Matuszny reached down and lifted up Shelton's penis with a pencil to provide a view from all sides.

"Get it here," he told the photographer.

On the way out of the jail, Matuszny threw his pencil in a trash can.

With McGinty pushing them, the two detectives gathered all the rape reports and follow-up investigations Bob had worked on in the Second District from 1983 to 1985. They added the cases Gray and Zeb had worked after the Sex Crimes Unit started in September 1985.

They also got some help from the FBI's Cleveland office. Agent John Dunn canvassed all the suburban police departments, asking for unsolved rapes that fit Shelton's modus operandi. As a result of this broad sweep, McGinty and the detectives soon were burdened with three dozen rapes that seemed to fit Shelton's pattern.

Now they had to locate all of these rape victims, some from half a decade earlier, and persuade them to come down to the Justice Center as soon as they could and try to pick Shelton out of a police lineup.

As it turned out, many victims had been so devastated by being raped that they had moved from the Cleveland area. It would be impossible to locate them quickly.

February 1989

KAREN HOLZTRAGER

Many of the victims were stunned when Matuszny called to say the man who may have raped them was in jail. It had been more than four years since Karen Holztrager was raped and robbed in a Parma apartment with inoperable, paint-encrusted window latches. Afterward, she and her husband Lee had worked hard to put their lives back together, but she was afraid of everything, which put them under great strain. On one Christmas morning, Karen's three young boys, excited about seeing their presents, ran in to wake her up. When they jumped up on the double bed, she shot up, terrified, screaming, "Never, never do that again!" She calmed down in an instant and apologized, but they were crying and didn't understand.

She and Lee visited a marriage counselor. She forced herself to go to secretarial school to get out of the house, and eight months later she landed a job as an assistant to a business executive. "I was starting to get somewhat of a normal life back," she would say later, "and then all of a sudden we see the newspaper and get a phone call from McGinty's people saying they caught Shelton and to come down to a lineup. It totally threw me into a tailspin."

Soon after the call, Karen had another of her recurring nightmares. The nightmares had started shortly after she was raped and just after an incident one night when she and Lee were coming home in the dark along a semirural highway near their home. The car's headlights had illuminated a deer, down on the blacktop.

Lee had slowed the car to pull around, and at that moment the deer lifted its head and turned into the headlights, its eyes shining like two red coals. It had been smashed by a car and was unable to hobble off the road and die in the comfort of the woods. Karen had been jolted by its pitiful eyes; they'd seemed to drill into her. She'd tried to turn away, but the deer's eyes had said, Help me, and Karen had begun to sob. And then, in an instant, they had passed the animal and were home.

Her nightmares were always the same: the crippled deer lifting its head, gazing with piercing, spooky red eyes that begged, Help me, help me. In her dreams Karen could only look on and cry.

A day or so after the call from the county prosecutor's office, a Parma detective came to her home and drove Karen to the downtown lineup. "Do you think you can identify him?" he asked casually during the drive.

"You put his genitals in the lineup, I'll pick him out right away," Karen said. "That will stay with me for the rest of my life. That and his voice."

A half hour later, she stepped into the sheriff department's narrow viewing room. (Lucie Duvall didn't want them using the Sex Crimes lineup room.) Through one-way glass Karen could see five white men in their twenties.

One of them is the rapist, she thought.

She had read the *Plain Dealer* articles about Shelton's arrest, but the paper hadn't published a mug shot. McGinty had made sure of that. He had called the TV stations and the *Plain Dealer* and asked their news executives to hold off. Showing Shelton's face would contaminate his lineups, he argued, and a defense lawyer would use this fact to confuse a jury and hurt his case. He had been surprised at how cooperative the media were.

The detectives and McGinty and defense lawyer Jay Milano, Jerry's son, were sitting in the room. The "old dago," as Jay called his father, was in court, unavailable; Jay would be helping out today. He was built like his father, only taller, with blond, thinning hair that he kept long in the back. He was his father's closest friend, but his opposite culturally. Jay lived in Waspy Rocky River, was a member of a yachting club, and gave his kids sailing lessons.

The men said hello to Karen, then watched her face as she scanned the five men in the lineup room. She eliminated two suspects immediately because they had blond hair. Another was too tall. That left two.

Karen didn't know that two dozen other rape victims were coming in for lineup identifications. She thought she was the only one who could make the case, and she was frightened. Lee would have taken off from work and come with her if the police had given them more than an hour's notice.

"It's number three or number five," she said.

"Would you listen to them talk?" McGinty asked.

"Sure," Karen said.

Matuszny walked her to the doorway, where she reared back, terrified. "We're going to be in the same room?" she asked.

"Yes. Sorry," McGinty said. The audio speaker in the hidden room was broken, so the voice ID had to be conducted inside the lineup room.

Karen couldn't believe this. She was going to have to stand within six feet of the rapist, the man who had ruined her life.

"You want them to read it facing you or turned away?" McGinty asked.

"Facing the wall," she said, shaking.

In the lineup room, Matuszny handed a piece of paper to number three, Ronnie Shelton. Ronnie gave Matuszny a wise-ass smile. "Face the wall and read this," the detective told him.

Ronnie slowly read, "Don't look at me. I won't hurt you. I need money. Do what I say and you won't get hurt."

The paper was handed to a prisoner standing under the number five, and then he read the words. Everyone stared at Karen. She looked like she was going to run away.

After a moment, she said, "Number five." Matuszny and McGinty looked glum.

As the detective from Parma led her down the hall to the exit, Karen said, "It was number three, wasn't it?"

"Why didn't you say it in there?" he asked.

"I was afraid of him," Karen said.

"We were there. He wouldn't try anything."

"Big deal. What about his friends on the outside? I didn't want to do it in front of him."

"You said five back there. You don't think that now?"

"It's number three," Karen said.

The detective walked her back to McGinty. "She says it's three. She was too afraid to ID in front of him."

"Great, great," McGinty said.

THE SHELTONS

Ronnie's family tried to believe he was innocent but, at least for his father, that wish crumbled quickly. Two weeks after Ronnie's arrest for the rape of Maggie Daley, McGinty walked a multi-count indictment into the county grand jury and asked jurors to return indictments for raping five women—four in West Park and one in nearby Fairview Park. Shelton's fingerprints were found at each crime scene. The grand jury quickly rubber-stamped the case.

This news, trumpeted in the press, rocked Ronnie's friends. His go-go dancing buddies could dismiss one rape case as the result of a jilted lover or a mistaken identification—but not twenty-seven counts of rape, kidnapping, gross sexual imposition, and burglary.

Ronnie's family was devastated by the running news accounts of the case. McGinty, who played certain reporters like a Wurlitzer, made sure every new development was brought to the attention of TV stations and the *Plain Dealer*. "We consider him a serial rapist and will continue to investigate," he told the press, over and over.

In Brunswick Hills, Shelton's parents were dealing with hang-up calls, obscene phone calls, and curiosity seekers who drove slowly by the house. His mother and sister still didn't believe Ronnie had raped anyone. They found this too painful to imagine, and denied that it had happened. Maria argued to friends that Ronnie couldn't be a rapist, because he had lots of girlfriends. He had simply gotten himself in trouble by borrowing girlfriends' credit cards without their permission, she said. Rape? Never!

Defending her brother was a switch for Maria Shelton. In the years up to his arrest, Maria had told friends that she hated her brother, that he smacked her and harassed her dates. Now Maria fought for him with a fury. It was war—the outside world probing the secrets of her family—and in wartime the Sheltons banded together.

She and her mother visited Ronnie faithfully. Maria lived with her parents, but came downtown each day for her job as an office worker at McDonald & Company, the Cleveland-based brokerage and investment banking firm. On visiting days, her mother and father drove into downtown Cleveland after rush hour, picked her up, and parked on West Third Street near the jail entrance to the Justice Center. From eight stories up, the clay-colored Justice Center jail tower looked over the downtown area, with windows facing out from all sides of the building. The jail was packed with prisoners, and on some days its inmate population was nearly twice the number it had been designed to house.

In the area where visitors were screened, the Sheltons waited in line for their names to be called. Most of the visitors were women, smoking cigarettes, with children in hand, on their way to see boyfriends or husbands who had been charged with crimes that carried bail too expensive for their meager resources. Ronnie's bail was set at $250,000 cash.

After their names were called, Maria and her parents locked

their wallets, rings, belts, and purses into one of the lockers lining the visiting entrance. Then they were frisked by a deputy with a handheld metal detector and signed a visitors' ledger. Under the space "Purpose of Visit," Maria wrote, "To pray with him and show him we still love him and are behind him 100 percent."

A large elevator stopped and opened and the previous batch of visitors, their fifteen-minute visit over, exited. The new group, including the Sheltons, was packed in and sent up.

The visiting room was large and bare, with long, narrow Formica-topped tables, set end to end, in a huge square. Folding chairs were set along both sides of the tables. The prisoners shuffled in, dressed in bright orange jumpsuits.

Ronnie had showered and washed and blow-dried his hair. When his father came in, Ronnie asked for a cigarette and lighted it immediately. Ronnie saw tears in his father's eyes and felt a flood of emotion. This made getting caught all worthwhile, Ronnie told himself. To see my father with tears in his eyes. I knew he cared. Too bad I had to get arrested to find that out.

His father said little at his visit; Ronnie's mother and sister did the talking. His mom hugged him, crying and jabbering in broken English. She was praying for him, she said. She begged him to tell her, again, that he didn't do what the police were accusing him of doing.

He turned away. Later Ronnie gave Maria a sketch he'd drawn on ruled notebook paper. In the background was the figure of a judge in robes, mouth open, banging a gavel on the top of the bench. In the foreground of the sketch sat Ronnie at a table with a Bible, wearing uncharacteristic short hair, his hands clasped as if praying.

"To my sister and her church," Ronnie printed on the sketch. "Love you very much. Your brother, Ronnie."

Maria was stunned; she'd had no idea Ronnie could draw.

"Ronnie, we love you so much and we are standing behind you one hundred percent," she said. "God is on our side. Pray daily and we'll defeat the devil."

Like his father, Ronnie didn't believe in the charismatic,

fundamentalist teachings spouted by his sister and mother. But he realized the importance of having a minister as an advocate when you were arrested, and he agreed to talk to the lay ministers from his mother's church who wanted to visit him.

TIM MCGINTY

After the arrest, McGinty and Matuszny began to prepare a counterattack to Shelton's likely defense—not guilty by reason of insanity. They both felt that Shelton would be "getting off easy" with a successful insanity defense. If a jury found him to be insane, Shelton would be locked up at Dayton Forensic Hospital, the state institution for the criminally insane, a much more livable campus setting than Ohio's prisons, especially the brutal Lucasville, the gang-infested "supermax" in southern Ohio.

In theory and law, once at Dayton Forensic, Shelton could be examined by doctors after six months and declared sane and released by the trial judge. It was unlikely, of course, but on average, lawbreakers found not guilty of crimes for reasons of insanity spent only about four years in institutions.

"His only defense was insanity," Matuszny would later say. "I knew that from the day they arrested him. But there was no way he was insane. He had the cunning. There were certain things he did all the time to avoid being arrested. He went out of his way to watch these girls, to stalk, to hide his tracks. He threatened them not to call the police. An insane person isn't going to be that deliberate about it. A guy who goes nuts, he's not going to stop and cover his tracks. You can be goofy, sick in the head, and not be insane."

In January 1989, as part of his investigation, McGinty wrote to all the West Side suburban police departments and asked them to send in any reports that mentioned Ronnie's name. This broad sweep was typical of McGinty. He wanted to know everything about his adversary: old girlfriends, bar fights, traffic violations —any incident that might shed light or unearth damaging information.

This records sweep turned up Ronnie's attempted suicide in North Olmsted at Connie Bellini's apartment in 1986. It also provided two important new witnesses: psychologist Ross Santamaria, who had alerted North Olmsted police to Shelton's suicide attempt, and Ronnie's old girlfriend, Connie Bellini.

When asked, Santamaria told the detectives he believed that Shelton was manipulative, not insane. And yes, he would be willing to testify to that.

McGinty interviewed Connie in the cafeteria of her new employer, BP America, the Fortune 500 company headquartered in a downtown Cleveland skyscraper. As McGinty scribbled notes furiously, she quietly filled him in on Ronnie: his thieving, his violent temper, his arrests for voyeurism and assault, how he had penile warts that she paid to have burned off.

"All *right,*" McGinty said, almost cheering. "We can link those earlier rapes with this." He was excited. She was providing tremendously useful information.

By the end of the lunch hour, Connie had revealed everything: how Ronnie had raped her, beaten her, taken her credit cards, and tried to kill her. She was embarrassed that she had ever dated him. "He could be so charming," she said. "He could get any woman if he really tried."

McGinty stopped taking notes. "He looks kind of like a little fag to me. I don't know what women saw in him."

Connie laughed. "He hated it when someone called him that. He'd go nuts. That would drive him crazy."

McGinty made a mental note of Ronnie's hot button about homosexuals. Maybe he could use it in some way at trial.

"I don't want any of this public," Connie said. "I can't. My parents, they don't know anything about this. My mother is sick. It would kill her."

"But he raped you," McGinty said.

"I know. I really don't want to get involved."

McGinty didn't press her. He had plenty of new leads for Matuszny and Facemire to chase. He'd try to get Connie to file rape charges later.

By now, McGinty and the detectives had pared the three dozen rape cases to twenty-three they felt certain were committed by Shelton. His fingerprints were connected to five. The next step was to see if the saliva, semen, and hair specimens recovered at the rape scenes matched those of Shelton. McGinty asked SIU to reexamine, case by case, all the physical evidence and see if any pointed to Shelton or eliminated him.

The review was disappointing: Some of the rape evidence was worthless, poorly collected by undertrained detectives at the districts. In some cases, hair, blood, and saliva found on the victims matched samples recently plucked or drawn from Shelton. But in other cases, crimes could not be pinned to him because the evidence was uncollected, missing, or contaminated.

Now, McGinty faced a challenge. In nearly a dozen of the cases, the victims were unable to make eyewitness identifications of Shelton at a lineup. Many of these coincided with the cases in which SIU did not have scientific evidence. What could he do with a case in which he only had a Marlboro butt found outside a window and a description by the victim that vaguely fit Shelton? Normally, McGinty would not bring charges in such a weak case. A diligent judge, relying on the law, would dismiss such a case before trial.

McGinty and the detectives and FBI agent John Dunn discussed how to link these weak circumstantial cases to the ones in which Shelton had left fingerprints. Dunn suggested that McGinty get an FBI expert named John E. Douglas to testify about Shelton's "behavioral fingerprint." This was a new concept in forensics that had been developed at the FBI's National Center for the Analysis of Violent Crime. Douglas was one of the

Bureau's leading experts on the behavior of serial killers and rapists. He had interviewed Ted Bundy, Richard Speck, John Wayne Gacy, Charles Manson, and David Berkowitz, probing their twisted personalities for a book he coauthored, *Sexual Homicide*. Douglas and other agents at the center were able to work backward from police reports, crime scene photos, and autopsies to craft uncannily accurate "psychological profiles" of unknown offenders.

If the rape cases were truly similar—if each exhibited Shelton's unique "behavioral fingerprint"—then Douglas could link them all together with his powerful expert testimony, Dunn explained; it wouldn't matter if the prosecution lacked fingerprints, physical evidence, or lineup identifications.

McGinty said he'd take all the help he could get. In private, he was skeptical. The Douglas testimony sounded sort of far out.

March–April 1989

RITA HAYNES

After a couple of unsuccessful visits to Ronnie in county jail that spring, Jerry Milano had to set him straight. "Look," Milano told him, "the evidence is overwhelming that you did these rapes."

Ronnie hesitated.

"Don't bullshit your lawyer," Milano said. "The worst thing is to lie to your own lawyer. I need to know all the cards that the prosecutor might be holding."

After a while Ronnie said, "Okay, I did most of them, but not all of them."

"Okay, we're gonna have you referred to a doctor to see what your state of mind is," Milano said, with uncharacteristic delicacy. "First we'll see what the court psychiatrists say. That's the way it works with the court. Then I'll have my expert—his name is Dr. Emanuel Tanay—talk to you and your family. Be truthful with him."

Later, Milano referred Ronnie to the psychiatric clinic of Cuyahoga County's Common Pleas Court. The court psychiatric clinic's job was to determine if criminal defendants were competent to stand trial. If they were, then psychiatrists conducted tests to see if they were sane. The clinic's reports and conclusions and the materials upon which its doctors made their determinations were shared with both the prosecution and the defense.

The Cuyahoga County court clinic enjoyed a national reputation as one of the best forensic psychiatric training programs in the country. Psychiatrists there were encouraged to come up with their own opinions, which were said to be as fair to defendants as any court clinic's in the country.

Rita Haynes, one of three court clinic social workers, was given the Shelton referral. Her job was to prepare a "social history" of Shelton, typically a fifteen-page single-spaced account of his childhood, education, health, and mental functioning. She telephoned Milano and asked, "Why is he being referred?"

"Any son of a bitch that rapes twenty-three women has got to be nuts," he told her.

Haynes wasn't used to pungent remarks from a lawyer. She told Milano that her first interview with Ronnie Shelton would be on March 28, 1989, three weeks away. She would conduct the first series of interviews with him for a social history, which would then be used by a clinic psychiatrist in his competency and sanity evaluations.

Milano repeated his hope that they would just find the son of a bitch crazy.

A few weeks later, at the end of March, Ronnie Shelton was brought from jail to be interviewed by Rita Haynes. She had a master's degree in social work and had interviewed scores of defendants. Working from a list of questions, she first broke the

234

ice and led Ronnie through a series of questions about himself and his family.

"I feel sad and depressed," he said after a while. "I don't know why I did it. It has caused a lot of pain in my family." He started to cry. "My mother does not know I raped some of these women. She thinks I'm totally innocent and she keeps telling me, 'Ronnie, please tell me that you did not rape anyone.' If she ever learned I was guilty of some of these rapes, it might kill her."

Haynes asked about nightmares.

"Yeah, I get 'em. They started after my first rape. In it I am always getting killed by the police in a shoot-out. They hate me because I'm always getting in trouble. They don't like my hair. They're like my dad: They think it makes me look like I'm a punk."

Haynes asked if he had hallucinations.

"I don't want to be called crazy," Ronnie said. "There are guys in jail that told me to tell you and the doctors that I see spaceships."

Have you heard things? she asked.

"I don't know whether I have or not," he said. "I am not trying to malinger or make you mad, but I don't remember." Then he brought up "the shield."

"When I was doing all this, I thought I was protected by this shield. The police couldn't catch me. No matter what I did. I was, like, invincible. It's hard to explain, but I had this shield, protecting me. That's what I felt."

Haynes asked if he thought people were out to get him.

"People don't like me because of the way I look."

Tell me more about that, Haynes prompted.

"I've always had many different girlfriends, the ones all the guys tried to get, and guys don't like this because I always look nice to the ladies." The prosecutor especially didn't like him, Ronnie went on. "McGinty and the police are trying to railroad me. They're putting every rape from the West Side on me. They're just cleaning the books on me."

Did you commit the rapes? Haynes asked.

Ronnie paused. "I'm guilty of some of the rapes but not all of them. McGinty wants to run for judge and he wants to find me guilty so he has a better chance of winning. I am not guessing this. It is a fact. My attorney—I don't like him either—told me this."

Why don't you like your attorney?

"The Milanos are taking my case because they want the money and the publicity. That's all. They don't care about me. They never tell me anything about the case. Everything I know I have to get from the newspaper or TV. That's wrong. My family is paying a lot of money for this. They want another lawyer."

She asked about his early sexual experiences.

"My first wet dream was when I was fourteen. My friends used to brag about having sex and I used to brag with them, but little did they know I never had sex and I was afraid of it. The first time I had sex was when I was sixteen. It was in a park with the girlfriend of one of my friends. We were walking in a park. She was seventeen. She had just had my friend's baby and was telling me about their problems. Then she kissed me and fondled me and we had sex. I had no idea that she even liked me. I didn't like it because it was outside and two kids walked up during it and I did not see it as fun or exciting. I finally saw what sex was, and I felt dirty. I wanted to take a shower and wipe everything off me."

How do you feel about sex now?

"I enjoy it. I have sex with three to five women a week. One time in a seven-day period, I had sex with seven different girls who were very pretty and very hard to get at the nightclubs. I used to brag about this because I thought it was macho. But I never liked sluts or prostitutes or girls who were easy to get. If a girl walked up and asked me to sleep with her, I'd be totally turned off. I like girls who play hard to get."

Rita Haynes asked how he felt about the rapes.

"The rapes had nothing to do with sex," he said. "One time I just had sex with my girlfriend. I woke up at three or four in the morning, and I had to go out and rape somebody. I was not horny. I just think I was oversexed. When I raped, I used threats, which would excite me and the threats made the women feel that they had no other choice but to do what I said. It was like nothing I had ever felt before! Raping is more exciting because I am already aroused! I can be in bed with one of my girlfriends having sex and I could control when I come. I would wait until she'd come, then I would. I could go for about forty-five minutes having sex and I would hold my climax until I satisfied her. But with a rape, I don't even have to have intercourse; just the excitement would make me come. They could touch me and I would come. I have never had sexual control in a rape. My climax keeps coming and turns into one big one."

Was your general routine before a rape having sex with a girlfriend and then going out in the early morning? Haynes asked.

"Yes. Sometimes I would fight myself. But I couldn't resist. Once I woke up and was out of bed, I was compelled to go on. I'd be in and out of someone's house in five minutes. I always felt bad afterward."

If you were let out of jail right now, would you continue to rape?

Ronnie hesitated. "Yes, I would."

TIM McGINTY

By early April, after conducting more investigations and lineups, prosecutor McGinty and the detectives Matuszny and Facemire felt that seven more of the original three dozen rape cases could be pinned on Ronnie Shelton. On April 3, McGinty presented the seven cases to a Cuyahoga County grand jury, which essentially rubber-stamped the new charges. With the previous twenty-three indicted cases, the victim tally now stood at thirty.

For each victim, Shelton was not only charged with rape but also kidnapping, aggravated burglary, possession of criminal tools, and other crimes. All told, McGinty and the police buried him under a 230-count indictment, the largest in county history.

Reporters swarmed over the thick new indictment. Milano, in answer to questions, said that Ronnie Shelton would use the insanity defense. "He fell off a roof and had brain surgery," the lawyer explained. "This was in 1983, a couple of months before the first alleged rape. Anyway, all these new charges are unwarranted. My client—if he's found guilty—will be eligible for parole in fifteen years no matter how many years he gets sentenced. It's a waste of time."

Questioned later in the day, McGinty shot back that the chance for someone like Shelton to win a parole after fifteen years was an injustice. Ohio law, he said, must be changed.

Milano's plan—to have Shelton plead not guilty by reason of insanity—worried McGinty. He didn't really think a jury would buy it, but he had to be prepared nonetheless. Over the next few days, McGinty brainstormed with Matuszny and his partner. What he needed to do, McGinty explained, was to put a daytime face on Ronnie Shelton, to show that he's far from crazy. Show him to be a cunning, devious, manipulative piece of garbage who charmed women, eluded police, and appeared normal. What they needed, he said, was for Connie Bellini, Shelton's only serious girlfriend, to tell her experiences to a jury.

"I want to show a jury that he's a son of a bitch twenty-four hours a day, not just at six in the morning," McGinty explained at one point. "She is very important to the case. I want to show that he raped her, abused her, gave her VD, took her credit cards. If they go insanity—and Milano has no other way to go—I want to show little Ronnie's manipulative behavior. We can argue that that's how he was able to get whatever doctor he hired to say that he was nuts. Plus we need her to show that he could get laid. She shows that he had normal sexual outlets. That means he raped for thrills. It'll show the rapes were crimes of violence."

It was a fine strategy. Except that Connie Bellini had said she was dead-set against testifying. She had already left McGinty two telephone messages saying she didn't want to charge Shelton with rape, that she wanted nothing to do with his trial.

McGinty set up a lunch appointment with Connie, and suggested the BP cafeteria. He liked the food there because he could get a filling lunch for about $3. She agreed to see him but said she didn't think she'd change her mind.

At an isolated table in the company cafeteria, McGinty gave her a sales pitch. "You're the most important witness. You can put a face on this guy, show him for what he really is."

"I can't," she said.

"All these other women have come forward," he said. "They need you, too."

Connie felt guilty about the other Shelton victims. She didn't want to let them down.

"Look, you'd feel better if you knew you helped put that bastard away," he said.

She laughed at his directness. He seemed to know exactly how she felt. "I'd love to see him rot in jail."

McGinty sensed that he was winning her to his side. "We need you. You're the number one witness. Without you, I can't be sure what will happen. He'll get some expert, say he's insane, do a few years in a nuthouse, and get out."

"I don't know," she wavered.

"You don't think he's insane, do you?"

"No way."

"Let's indict him for his rape of you. The cases might settle and you'll never have to testify."

"I don't want my parents to know," she said. "I can't testify."

"It might settle, but even if it goes to trial, you can change your mind and back out at the last minute. I can pull you right out. You don't have to testify. I promise."

She couldn't think straight.

"No one will know," he said. "The reporters don't use rape victims' names." McGinty looked her in the eye. "Can we count on you?"

"Okay," Connie said finally. "But I can drop it if I change my mind?"

"Absolutely. That's a promise."

After saying good-bye, McGinty practically ran back to his office.

In Quantico, Virginia, FBI supervisory agent John E. Douglas read through stacks of Shelton crime reports sent to him by McGinty. He also reviewed the 1984 psychological profile crafted by an FBI colleague that had been used by Matuszny and the Cleveland police to try to catch the West Side Rapist.

Douglas noticed, just as Matuszny had, the stunning similarities among the rapes: early-morning attacks, first-floor apartments with clear getaways, use of a knife or sharp object found in the apartment. Douglas carefully sifted the reports and victim statements for Ronnie's "ritual behavior," the behavioral idiosyncrasies that went beyond the actions necessary to rape his victims. Douglas felt the West Side Rapist's rituals were extremely unusual. For one, he usually climaxed on the victim's body, often between her breasts. Douglas concluded the rapist resented women and needed to control them.

After completing his review, Douglas sent McGinty a report. Finding: In his expert opinion, all the rapes were committed by the same criminal, and he would gladly testify to that.

Back in Cleveland, McGinty was elated by Douglas's work. The prosecutor now had the glue that could bind all the cases to Shelton.

But there was a problem. So far not a single court in Ohio had allowed expert testimony about a defendant's "behavioral fingerprint." McGinty knew he had a battle ahead.

KATHY BOND

Kathy Bond and her husband, Rex, were watching television news. Their two young children were asleep for the night, Rex had quit drinking, and Kathy's life had settled into a comfortable routine.

The TV newscaster said the West Side Rapist had been indicted in a number of additional rape cases and showed a picture of Ronnie. Kathy pulled up from a slouch.

"God, that looks like him," she said.

"Yeah, him and a hundred other people you thought were the guy," Rex said.

In the years after the rape, Kathy had followed dozens of men in cars whom she thought resembled her attacker. She thought she spotted look-alikes in bars. Maybe Larry McCormick, the first guy she'd tagged, *wasn't* the one, she thought at these times.

"I know, but there's a resemblance," she insisted. "I'm calling that detective, Schaeffer."

She reached the First District and asked for the detective who'd taken her statement in April 1983.

Schaeffer, he's not working the First anymore, someone told her.

Kathy couldn't think of who else to call. She had not heard from the police since 1983. By the next day she'd decided to let the matter go.

Ronnie

On April 10, 1989, the low-paid correctional officers assigned to the seventh floor of the county jail reviewed the day's "specified high-profile information" sheet. It read in part:

> Subject: SHELTON, RONNIE (143298), 7D
>
> An inmate has informed the pod officer during second shift concerning inmate Ronnie Shelton's attempt to confiscate a firearm from a deputy to shoot his way out of the courtroom. Shelton has made statements to the effect that he wants someone to kill him. Therefore he is hoping to exchange fire with deputies and/or court officials for an early death sentence."

The memo said to make logged observations every fifteen minutes of Shelton in his cell.

Dr. Michael Knowlan

That spring Dr. Michael N. Knowlan, a thirty-eight-year-old psychiatrist, was assigned the Shelton sanity evaluation by the Cuyahoga County court clinic.

Many Cleveland defense lawyers assumed that the court clinic, housed in the Justice Center, was a rubber stamp for the county prosecutor. In fact, Knowlan, a forensic fellow at Case Western Reserve University's medical school, who was on leave from the U.S. Naval Hospital in Portsmouth, Virginia, found that not to be the case. The court clinic seemed to be an intellectually freewheeling place, where forensic psychiatry fellows were encouraged to think for themselves.

His criteria for Shelton's sanity were clearly defined. In Ohio the definition of legal insanity was fairly narrow. Two conditions had to be satisfied: (1) The accused didn't think the criminal acts he committed were wrong, and (2) he could not refrain from committing them.

In Ohio, as in virtually all states, defendants can be found "not guilty by reason of insanity." After such a finding at trial, they are committed to a state prison hospital for the criminally insane, treated, and kept there until cured. If they cannot be returned to sanity, they never are released—in theory, at least.

Before the interviews, Knowlan read the Shelton social history and his medical records from emergency rooms and hospitals, including those from his emergency brain surgery in June 1983.

In his first interviews with Ronnie, Dr. Knowlan tried to hone in on a few key areas. Bored after four months in jail, Ronnie seemed cooperative.

Do you find sex more exciting when you force the woman? the psychiatrist asked him.

"The most exciting part was outside, just before I was ready to go in," Ronnie answered. "The highest moment of the whole act is not the sexual climax, it's the drive."

Why not masturbate at those times?

"It had nothing to do with masturbation. A couple of times I had just had sex with a girl. I would sweat. I thought I would go for a drive instead. I wasn't horny. I didn't know what I was going to do. I tried to stop from doing it. Every time I knew it was wrong. But it was exciting. I was someone else. Something changed, even my voice. I'm not myself once I touch her window. It's not me. But I'm coherent to know what's going on. Once I got inside it was like something on TV. Like I was watching myself do these things. As soon as I had an orgasm, I knew what I was doing. I came out. I realized I'm on my own, now I've got to get away from the police."

Did you always rape when you had the impulse to rape? Knowlan asked.

"I had thoughts of raping fifty times a month. But look at the number of rapes. They don't realize the number I could have done and the number I actually did. It was a relief when the sun came up and I hadn't raped or hurt anyone and the police weren't after me. When I fought the impulse I just walked all night or rode the RTA [Regional Transit Authority] to think about it. Sometimes I'd just fantasize and masturbate."

Did you have the opportunity to rape and resist instead?

"Yes. One girl cried and said she was pregnant. She was naked. I masturbated instead. One girl said her baby was in the next room and I didn't. A lot of times I saw girls sleeping while I was in their apartments. I masturbated and left without them knowing it. If a girl kept screaming or fought, I booked. She was free."

In an eight-day period, Knowlan spent seven and a quarter

hours interviewing Shelton, probing his feelings and questioning his actions. The Shelton case presented fascinating issues: Was a man legally insane if he sometimes couldn't stop himself from raping and at the same time also believed he was protected from arrest by an unexplainable "shield"?

Dr. Knowlan noted the records of Ronnie's head injury and, being thorough, referred him to a neuropsychologist. Knowlan wanted to see if Ronnie had sustained brain damage when he'd fractured his skull in a 1983 fall. Knowlan had no way of knowing that this referral would provide Milano with a weapon to attack him at trial months later.

On April 25, the psychiatrist dictated his findings:

"I have diagnosed the defendant as having cocaine abuse, alcohol abuse, and antisocial personality disorder. However, it is my opinion that these diagnoses do not constitute a mental disease or defect. Furthermore, it is my opinion that the defendant knew the wrongfulness of his acts." Among other things, Knowlan noted:

"These acts were not done in response to a psychotic belief that it was the right thing to do.

"The defendant did not have hallucinations suggesting that the crimes were the right thing to do.

"The defendant stated that 'every time' he knew it was 'wrong.'"

Therefore the first leg of the legal standard for sanity—knowing the acts were wrong—was met, in Knowlan's opinion.

Later in the report, Dr. Knowlan wrote:

It is my opinion that the defendant could have refrained from the acts of burglary, robbery, rape, assault, and gross sexual imposition. This is supported by the following evidence:

The defendant reported no delusions that compelled him to commit the crimes.

The defendant was not experiencing hallucinations giving him instructions to commit the crimes.

The defendant stated that he had thoughts of raping about fifty times per month, yet he only committed approximately fifteen rapes. The fact that the defendant had thoughts about raping, but did not act on some occasions, suggests that he had some ability to refrain from committing rapes.

Conclusion: Ronnie Shelton was sane.

JUDGE RICHARD MCMONAGLE

Originally, Ronnie's trial was set for May 4, 1989, by Judge Richard McMonagle, a collegiate-looking forty-seven-year-old with a reputation for running a fair courtroom and keeping his docket up to date. He had been assigned the case in a random draw at Shelton's arraignment a few months earlier. He expected that this case, like 99 percent of his cases, would settle without going to trial.

But the usual progress toward settlement did not unfold. McGinty kept bringing new rape charges against Shelton, prodding the detectives, expanding the quest to the suburbs. He and Milano were not inclined to reach middle ground.

Complicating the negotiations, like an undertow in calm seas, was McMonagle's relationship with the bombastic Milano. Eight years earlier, he and Milano had clashed at a sensational trial in the murder of a twelve-year-old girl. It was a shaky case and Milano, for the first time in his career, was convinced that he had an innocent client. The prosecutor, a longtime nemesis, brought in some preposterous last-minute witnesses, including a jailhouse snitch. Awaiting the verdict that evening, Jerry Milano had numerous drinks in a bar across the street from the Justice Center.

When the jury came back with a guilty verdict, Milano was devastated. McMonagle, who had a vacation planned, sentenced the defendant on the spot—an unusual move, but he had already decided on a life sentence if the defendant was found guilty, no matter what the presentencing report recommended.

Milano lost control during sentencing and accused the judge of making a "show for your television." After McMonagle left the courtroom, Milano told the court stenographer to stay, and he turned to the TV cameras. He was undone by whiskey and frustration and the rare feeling that the wrong man was being locked up. He accused the judge of not having given him time to investigate the surprise witnesses, of having secretly discussed the case with the prosecutor, and of having quickly sentenced his client without the benefit of a presentence report because McMonagle wanted to run for governor and could not pass up all the free publicity from the assembled TV cameras. At the end of his ten-minute tirade, Milano spat, "And with that, fuck this system!"

McMonagle brought him up on contempt charges and Milano was suspended from practicing law in Ohio for one year.

The suspension "ruined me," Milano told whoever would listen. "It put me a million in the hole." Like other flamboyant old-school criminal defense lawyers, Milano dealt in cash and never saved a dollar. He blew tens of thousands of dollars on bets, on high living, and on Milano's, an Italian restaurant run by his wife.

His son, Jay, commented: "My father has a stronger reputation nationally than in Cleveland. He worked on the Wounded Knee case, the Sante Fe prison riots. But he is also America's biggest middle-aged groupie. He's obsessed with stardom. He loves the excitement. I used to travel with him constantly and always carry him home. Las Vegas once a month, front-row seats at Caesars Palace, the full comp at the Hilton, always flashing hundred-dollar bills. He was close to Nicky Hilton's sons. He used to play gin with Larry Holmes whenever he was around. Gin in the suite with Racehorse Haynes whenever he was in town. The suspension drastically changed the way he lived. He became less flamboyant."

A few weeks before the May 4 trial date, a pretrial hearing was held in McMonagle's chambers. Richard McMonagle had a reputation as a judge who settled cases. Fewer than 1 percent of his thousand or more annual courtroom assignments went to trial.

But by the end of this pretrial, none of McMonagle's settlement skills had brought McGinty and Milano closer to agreement. The judge was irked. He was used to getting some movement from one or both parties, or at least a willingness to move. But McGinty seemed determined to try the case. "We'll accept a plea if he pleads to the indictment," McGinty said.

"If I get a little consideration on sentencing," Milano shot back. "Make him probationable before fifteen."

"No way," McGinty said. "This guy is a menace. He has to plead to one aggravated rape for each victim, no probation."

That meant a fifteen-year minimum sentence, with a few years knocked off for good behavior. That was also the maximum penalty Shelton would face if found guilty at trial on all counts. Milano had no incentive to settle.

Milano said fine, he would go to trial, roll the dice, and let his client take his chances.

McGinty said, "We've got more cases coming."

"What!" Milano bellowed. "Are you going for some world record?" He looked at McMonagle. "It's bullshit."

McMonagle was frustrated. He was stuck with an unreasonably stubborn prosecutor who, for reasons unclear at the moment, was insisting on a six- to eight-week trial.

McMonagle asked Milano to leave his chambers so he could talk to McGinty alone. A minute later he said, "Look, Tim, he's going to get out in fifteen no matter what. You take a risk and lose, he'll be out there before that."

"I've got to have an aggravated felony for each victim," McGinty said. "I'm not going to go below that. They'll have to fire me first."

McMonagle was angry. The prosecutor was forcing a trial. The defendant was willing to plead guilty. In the deal Milano had offered, Shelton would spend another six years in prison, at least. The parole board could keep him there up to thirty. A trial was unnecessary.

"You're going to agree with me when this is all over," McGinty said.

"You're nuts," the judge said.

Secretly, McGinty had decided to go to trial with Shelton no matter what—make a splash with a spectacular trial, then use the publicity to lobby the state legislature to remove Ohio's caps on criminal sentences for rapists. Change the law so a serial rapist like Shelton would serve life without parole.

The judge set a new trial date for late summer. He hoped a settlement could be worked out eventually.

June 1989

SUSIE MALINOVSKY*

Ronnie shuffled through the short stack of books his sister had brought him. His trial had been postponed, and he was looking for distraction. It was late June—six months of incarceration in county jail—and other than nightly visits of fifteen minutes from Maria or his mom or one of his old girlfriends, he was going stir-crazy. He couldn't keep his mind on anything, though he had managed to read a skinny paperback bio of Johnny Depp that told the story of the "sexy, shy, supercool star of 21 Jump

---

*Not her real name.

Street, who has the jump on young hearts across America. How sex, drugs, rock-n-roll and scrapes with the law couldn't beat him." Ronnie identified with Depp—handsome, with a droopy earring, baby face, and a way with women. The other books were religious tracts Maria pushed on him. There was nothing else to do in jail, so he thumbed through most of them, even "Don't Waste Your Sorrow," about surviving hardship. Marie signed the thick book, "Jesus loves you!"

Yeah, right, Ronnie thought. Then how come he let all this happen?

The book he spent the most time with was a collection of crossword puzzles and cryptograms. He felt he was improving his mind doing the cryptograms. He studied one: QTA AMHXLCWX WTLVFNXL WFNX CHM QXLV LVCMTXL. Using a pencil, erasing his mistakes as he went along, he deciphered the letters to spell a message: "Big gruesome mistakes make our best stories."

Ronnie's moods swung up and down. Some days he wished he could just admit he was a rapist and disappear into the prison system for life, quit all the legal maneuvering and uncertainty. On other days, he hoped that Jerry Milano and the psychiatric expert could work magic on a jury and he'd be sent to a hospital, where he'd get cured and then released. Day to day, sometimes hour to hour, he careened like a pinball.

Then, at the end of June, he heard from his sister that Susie Malinovsky, a girlfriend from the previous fall, had had a baby daughter, and that he was the father.

Ronnie had spotted Susie last September, walking to her home, only two blocks from where Ronnie was staying at Danny Todd's house on Cable Avenue. Ronnie zoomed up on his motorcycle and introduced himself. She was slim, with long, light brown hair and perfect teeth and skin. The youngest of three sisters, Susie had been reared single-handedly by her mother, an immigrant from Macedonia who worked long nights on a crew that cleaned downtown office towers. With her older daughters married and off on their own, Olga Malinovsky had problems with her pretty, modern, headstrong young daughter, whom she had to leave home on her own five nights a week.

"How old are you?" Ronnie asked her.

Susie laughed. "Never mind."

Realizing she was probably sixteen, Ronnie lied and said he was twenty-two, lopping off five years. Within a month he had charmed and seduced her, and found out she was only fourteen. By then she was hooked on the handsome, macho, romantic young man who was unfailingly polite to her mother and sisters. And she believed him when he told her, after making love, that she was perfect for him and that he wanted her to have his children someday.

He stopped seeing her in November, a month before he was arrested, and in the late spring, after feeling tired and bloated, she visited a doctor, who told her she was six months pregnant. A baby girl with curly red hair was born on June 26, 1989.

Now Ronnie felt he had a reason to try to escape punishment.

When Susie came to visit Ronnie in jail for the first time, she was still spinning. She was fifteen years old, with a daughter who seemed to have come out of nowhere. And the baby's father, a man she had naively thought she loved, was accused of raping dozens of women. She wondered how she could have made such a terrible mistake. She had to talk to Ronnie about why he'd left her.

"I had this burning anger," Susie would later recall. "If he didn't care about me, if that was the case, then why didn't he leave me alone? Why did he lead me on? Or say things like he could be very happy with me and he wanted me to be the mother of his children? I realize it's partly my fault. But there was a part of me that was numb. I didn't know how to get over it. I needed to talk to him, to get over it. People said, 'No, he's manipulative. He'll fill you up with lies.' But I had to go."

Maria Shelton accompanied Susie and the baby on their visit to the county jail. Susie was upset by what she felt were the dehumanizing procedures she and her baby had to go through to visit Ronnie. The guards rudely pulled the combs from her long hair and checked for contraband. They roughly searched through baby bottles, blankets, diapers. She had to leave her purse, baby bottle, and belt behind in a locker.

By the time Susie was escorted to the bare, noisy visiting

room, she was angry that her tiny daughter was inside an atmosphere of so much hate. Then Ronnie came into the room in his orange prison jumpsuit and slippers.

She wanted to say, Here's our baby, jerk. Where have you been? Instead she said hello.

Maria, who had insisted on holding the baby, handed her to Ronnie. He leaned close to Maria and mumbled in her ear as they held the infant between them. Ronnie looked up and could see that Susie was irritated.

Ronnie told Susie, "I want *you* to hand her to me, not my sister."

Susie took the infant and passed her gently to Ronnie. He stared at Susie expectantly, to let her know this was supposed to be a meaningful moment, but she turned away, ashamed to be passing the little girl to her father under such circumstances.

At the end of the fifteen-minute visit, Ronnie told her, "I swear to you, Susie, I'll do everything I can to make this up to you. When I get out—we have family in California, my mother's family—we can move out there where nobody knows us. I'll get a job; we'll settle down. It will be good."

For the moment, she held on to his promise to take her to California. She thought this dream would help her cope with her topsy-turvy life. But it didn't last. Over the weeks, she talked with her older sisters, then made her own decision: to cut him from her life. Ronnie would never get out of prison, and if he did, so what? She decided to go back to high school, graduate, go to college part-time, and make something of her life.

Later in the summer, Ronnie called her from jail and insisted on seeing his daughter. "Bring her to see me, please."

"No," she said.

"I love her."

"What do you know about love?"

For once he didn't have a thing to say. He told himself he just wanted to get out somehow and see the baby.

July–August 1989

Dr. Emanuel Tanay

By July, McGinty had filled two steel-case drawers with files about Ronnie Shelton—juvenile records (which were inadmissible), medical records, interviews with former girlfriends, and on and on. Then he learned that Milano had hired a forensic psychiatrist named Emanuel Tanay to examine Ronnie Shelton, and suddenly McGinty had a secondary target to assault.

Ever since Shelton had entered a plea of not guilty by reason of insanity, his criminal case had turned into a battle of expert witnesses. McGinty was relying on Dr. Michael Knowlan, the young psychiatrist studying at Case Western Reserve University for the year. Milano selected Tanay, a silver-haired, sixty-one-year-old Detroit psychiatrist and Polish-born Jew who had barely survived the Holocaust. Tanay identified with society's outcasts as a result of his wartime trauma and now worked full-time testifying across the country for defendants accused of rape, murder, kidnapping.

McGinty was wary of the Milano-Tanay team. They had first worked together ten years earlier at the trial of a well-to-do killer who stood accused of the aggravated murder of Julius Kravitz, a prominent Cleveland businessman who founded a supermarket chain. At that trial, Tanay, with his eastern European accent and commanding courtroom presence, had taken over the courtroom. He convinced the judge, hearing the case without a jury, that defendant Michael Levine was insane when he shot Kravitz during a botched kidnap-for-ransom scheme. Since then, Tanay

253

had testified as an expert witness hundreds of times. Over the years, he had aided the defense teams of Ted Bundy, Jack Ruby, and others less notorious, pocketing fees of $1,500 a day.

McGinty knew the case would hinge on whether he could destroy the credibility of Tanay. Knock him out and the trial would be over. McGinty became obsessed with digging up dirt on Tanay, and punched out a flurry of phone calls to Detroit and other cities where Tanay had testified as an expert witness. McGinty hoped to uncover Tanay's weaknesses or learn of cross-examination strategies against him that other prosecutors had found effective.

On July 5, Tanay drove three hours to Cleveland to examine Ronnie. The doctor had already read the sanity report and the neuropsychological report prepared by the court's psychiatric clinic. Over his career, Tanay had interviewed hundreds of murderers and rapists, and his guess was that Ronnie was another in a long line of abused children who grew up to be violent criminals. "The killer potential lies in every man," Tanay often explained. Under enough stress or trauma, one snaps, lashes out, maybe kills in a rage. "Dissociative reaction. A sudden, sharp break with reality."

That afternoon Ronnie refused to leave his cell to see Tanay. Milano had not told him about the visit and Ronnie didn't know what to say. He called Milano for instructions, and the lawyer chewed him out: "I brought him in, your family is paying a fortune for this guy, now fucking talk to him."

"Okay, okay, but you never tell me anything that's going on," Ronnie shot back angrily.

The next morning Tanay met Ronnie under guard at the court clinic. The doctor began his inquiry by asking Shelton whether his childhood had been unhappy.

Ronnie paused for a long time. "I don't know what to say on tape," Ronnie replied. "Does this go to the court? To the prosecutor?"

"If I testify on your behalf, they could possibly listen to it or use my notes," Tanay explained. "Suppose I arrive at the conclusion I shouldn't testify—then it would be not accessible to anyone. My job is to help your lawyer defend you, within reason."

Ronnie proceeded to paint a fairly happy portrait of his childhood.

Tanay tried another tack. "Tell me about your first rape."

"I don't know."

"You don't remember the first one?"

"My mind is blank right now," Ronnie said.

Tanay was getting nowhere. How was he going to help Shelton if the young man told him nothing? "Why are you reacting like this?"

"I'm afraid of you," Ronnie replied.

"You know I'm on your side."

"I didn't know that. I . . . I don't know why."

"Isn't it true you did commit rapes?"

"Yeah."

Finally Tanay was getting past Ronnie's stone wall. He kept up the questions for the rest of the one-hour session.

On August 22, Tanay dictated his report. As Milano had expected, the psychiatrist said Ronnie could not refrain from raping. "True enough, he did not experience delusions or hallucinations instructing him to commit these acts," Tanay wrote. "[But] there is no legal requirement for the defendant to suffer from such perceptual disturbances in order to be eligible for the defense of insanity. I do not believe that the fact that the 'defendant resisted raping a woman who was pregnant' or having a menstrual period . . . proves that he was able to resist, as Dr. Knowlan concludes. We know well from his own account that he struggled against the impulse to commit these compulsive acts. Efforts to resist compulsive behavior are the very characteristic of a compulsion. The fact that efforts were made to resist compulsive behavior does not mitigate against the compulsive nature of the activity.

"In conclusion, it is my opinion that Mr. Shelton suffered from mental illness at the time when he engaged in the antisocial activities and that he was unable to refrain from these acts."

* * *

Milano was happy with the report. Now he could put on a defense on September 11, when the judge finally could clear three weeks on his docket for trial. Who knows? Milano thought; maybe he'd get Shelton into Dayton Forensic Hospital after all. That would drive McGinty nuts.

CARLA KOLE

Tim McGinty had a problem. It was late August, only three weeks from trial, and he planned on having thirty rape victims testify at trial against Shelton. But many were terrified, barely willing to cooperate. He needed each woman to be a firm, confident witness who would move a jury to pity and rage. He figured that if the jurors got to know these women, they would be less swayed by the psychological mumbo jumbo of Dr. Tanay and want to punish Shelton in the conventional way. If he did his job right, McGinty felt, the jury would want blood. But how to shape his witnesses?

He reached back to his days of coaching high school football, the first job he truly loved, and remembered a tenet of Vince Lombardi's (he had read every book by the legendary football coach). The first step was to win the trust of your players. The women sort of reminded him of the freshmen he had coached at St. Edward High School—scared, unsure, in new surroundings, a bunch of kids from all over Cleveland who didn't know a thing about each other.

That gave him the idea of holding a group meeting with all the rape victims. Have them bring boyfriends or husbands. Introduce himself, show them the courtroom, explain the process, let them know what psychological support services were available.

It was a dicey strategy. If one or two strong ones stood up to him—said it was all bullshit, that they didn't want to testify, why not plea-bargain—he might have a stampede right out of the meeting.

The other danger was that Milano would probably learn about a meeting of the witnesses and might make a fuss. He'd certainly have a right to. Milano could argue that the witnesses were now all tainted, that the prosecutor had gotten them together so they could compare testimony and make certain each told essentially the same account. Using suggestive questions on cross-examination, Milano easily could twist an innocent meeting into a far-reaching conspiracy; he was a master at it. But McGinty wagered that Milano would not sharply cross-examine victims: It could turn the jury against him in a flash.

McGinty made up his mind to go forward and got in touch with social worker Carla Kole at the court's Witness/Victim Center.

A sign on Carla's office door said, "Gee, Toto, I don't think we're in Kansas anymore." Inside, the narrow room was a pleasing clutter of books, social work texts, and games for kids. A pair of L.A. Gear walking shoes and sweat socks were tucked under Carla's desk.

A wall poster of three cuddly white teddy bears in a hot-air balloon carried the message, "Let your dreams take flight." On a bookshelf below rested three dolls that clashed with the poster's greeting card sentiment. Used for interviewing sexually abused children, the dolls had tongues and sex organs. The mommy doll, for instance, wore a dress that lifted up to reveal bra, panties, and dark pubic hair—tools of a social worker on the battle lines of domestic violence and perverted sex.

Kole had worked with Tim McGinty many times before, and he had impressed her. He was a prosecutor who pumped up crime victims with confidence by savaging their attackers. He made them feel as though he was their stand-in, their justice system proxy, a raging bull determined to punch the legal lights out of their attackers. This in turn made them feel powerful, that they were taking control of their lives again.

McGinty told Carla Kole what he wanted to do—invite the thirty Shelton victims to a Justice Center meeting to get them emotionally prepared for trial. Could she be there?

Carla was familiar with the case. She had marched in protest against Cleveland's rising rape rates, and had moved from her neighborhood because of the West Side Rapist.

She told Tim she wouldn't miss it.

Carla walked into the meeting in McMonagle's sixteenth-floor courtroom, her three-foot-long brown ponytail swinging, and suddenly felt the pain of the Shelton victims envelop her like nightfall. For four years she had helped crime victims, usually one-on-one. But this situation was dramatically different. It was like a tiny emergency room after a plane crash: Everywhere you looked were severely injured people.

McGinty, in a dark suit, waited nervously for everyone to arrive. Two or three victims had telephoned and said they could not make the meeting. He stood next to a large poster board set on an easel—a trial exhibit listing the victims and when and where they were raped. Many of the women had brought their husbands or boyfriends for support.

Outside the courtroom, a lawyer with the Cuyahoga County Public Defender's Office sat with his ear cocked. He had stumbled across the meeting and was eavesdropping on it for Milano, to whom he planned to pass on any useful trial intelligence. He could see McGinty's exhibits—a map with rape locations, some crime photos—but could hear only bits and pieces. He disliked Tim McGinty, feeling he symbolized everything that was wrong with the county prosecutor's office.

Tim introduced Carla Kole to the group. She started with the easy instructions, pointing out locations of bathrooms and telephones. Then she waded into trickier, emotional waters—how to testify.

"It goes on every day in these courtrooms," Carla said. "It won't be as bad as when you were raped. You've already survived this guy. He is not in control. You are."

She could tell these women were traumatized. Many were already in tears. "He is locked up and you're not," she went on. "You can look him right in the eye. He is powerless."

Then Tim began his presentation. He explained the prosecutor's job and how the court system worked.

"Can he get the electric chair?" interrupted victim Karen Holztrager's husband, Lee.

"No, we can't execute him, because he didn't kill anybody," McGinty answered.

"There's more to death than a pulse," Lee said. "In our eyes, he killed our marriage. He killed my wife's relationship with our sons."

Some of the victims said, "Yeah."

"What is the most he can get?" Lee asked.

"Spend the rest of his life in prison," McGinty said.

"What are we testifying for? These life sentences don't mean anything. He'll get time off for good behavior, all that." Others murmured their agreement, and McGinty suddenly felt nervous.

"How do we know he doesn't have AIDS?" someone asked. "We might all have it." Several heads nodded in assent.

Shelton had had his blood screened in jail, McGinty said; as far as he knew their attacker did not have AIDS.

One victim pointed to the huge trial exhibit. "I'm uncomfortable with my name up there. I want privacy. He might have friends who see that. I've been getting threatening phone calls."

"I've been getting them, too," victim Marian Butler said.

"So have I," said another. "Can we find out who's doing it?"

McGinty didn't need distractions like this, but he didn't want to slough off their concerns. Some of the women were already folding up their handouts, shifting uncomfortably, looking like they wanted to run out of the courtroom. Was he losing them?

"I'll see about getting phone traps," he promised.

Connie Bellini, Ronnie's old girlfriend, complained that Maria Shelton had been following her in her car; she felt threatened.

She'd told a friend she couldn't believe she had been talked into testifying. "Tell me if she does it again, and I'll have her arrested," Tim said. Connie looked relieved.

"What about the media?" one of the men asked. "I don't want my wife on TV."

"She won't be on TV," McGinty said. "I'll instruct the cameramen not to film your faces. You don't have to talk to them unless you want to."

By now, more of the victims were quietly crying. Going to trial, facing the man who had raped them, being questioned by· his lawyer—they found the prospects terrifying. For some, just talking about the trial brought back terrible memories of being raped.

"What kind of questions are his lawyers going to ask us?" one victim wanted to know.

"Yeah, why drag these women through this stuff?" her boyfriend asked. "Why not plea-bargain?"

Tim had hoped that question wouldn't be put to him. So far, he had stage-managed everything so that Shelton would go to trial. "Each of you deserves a chance to have your case heard," Tim said. "That is your right. Then, when he's convicted, you will have standing with the parole board. That means when Shelton comes up for parole, by law the parole board has to contact you and let you have your say, why he should or shouldn't get out."

"When can he get out?" a woman asked.

"Believe it or not, after fifteen years," McGinty said.

The crowd reacted with grumbling and curses. Tim didn't want to lose them here, leave them with the feeling that the gut-wrenching emotions testifying would put them through would only result in a fifteen-year sentence.

"But he *won't* be out in fifteen years," McGinty said. "With all of you communicating with the parole board, he'll be like Charles Manson: He'll never get out."

"Why should we come forward?" someone asked.

"You come forward and do this for me, I'll work to change the law," Tim promised. "We can change it so these repeat rapists get life sentences. I'll go to Columbus, pressure the legislators."

"Whose case are you going to throw out if there's a plea bargain?" Karen Holztrager asked. "I want my case kept."

"I'm not going to sell out," McGinty said. "I'm not going to plea-bargain, unless you insist on it."

The group was angry, but the more they talked, the more comfortable they felt with each other. Slowly, they were coming together, focusing their rage on Shelton, as Tim had hoped, not on the legal system that was making them uncomfortable at the moment.

"When I got in the courtroom and saw all the families there, I was overwhelmed," Karen Holztrager would say later about the meeting. "They literally packed that place. I was really relieved I wasn't the only one. While we were waiting in there, the biggest thing was all the men seemed like they were ready to kill. The hostility—you could just feel it coming from the men."

Tim felt that now was a good time to spring his questionnaire. He and Carla passed out a carefully crafted sheet of leading questions, including, "What type of sentence do you feel would be fair and appropriate?" He also asked for up-to-date addresses and work and home telephone numbers.

"You tell me what *you* want to do with him," Tim said. Almost as an afterthought, he said, "We can plea-bargain—if you want to."

One victim, Becky Roth, knew what she felt was appropriate. She wrote, "Put him in a room with all the victims for a half hour. Torture. Death."

The victims, emboldened by each other, spilled out their anger in suggesting appropriate punishment:

"I was held at gunpoint and orally raped. This bastard should never see the light of day!!!"

"Death. Penis cut off beforehand," wrote another.

"Since death isn't possible, the absolute maximum."

"Death or castration."

"I'd love to see death. No parole. Life will do also, 1,000 yrs."

"I do not want to plea bargain. What he has done not only to me but to the other women, we will probably never forget. We will be scarred for life. I feel he should pay for this—with his life."

Near the end of the meeting, McGinty told the women that they could sue Shelton in civil court. "I think in five, ten years, that will be the trend in this country. I don't think you'll recover anything, but if he ever inherits anything, you'll have a claim."

Carla Kole finished up by saying that she was available for free counseling. For the first time in her career, she gave out her home phone number.

The meeting broke up, and the women drifted out, some talking like good friends. They were finding strength in each other already. One or two grabbed Carla Kole and asked to talk to her, and she walked them to her office on the first floor.

Out in the hallway, the eavesdropping public defender grabbed his notes and went to his office to type a report for Milano. He had overheard McGinty tell the victims to sue Shelton, which the public defender felt was clearly improper. He'd also heard McGinty tell the women not to worry if they each used different descriptions when talking about Shelton's voice, that he'd take care of that problem.

In the memo, he offered Milano some suggestions about legal strategy: "Obviously, you may question each person as to the content of the meeting in an effort to create inconsistency and the possibility that the group meeting was inappropriate. Certainly, questions of identity and possible suggestiveness [by the prosecutor] might arise."

When Jerry Milano got the memo, he thought, Good, that dumb fuck McGinty did something stupid. Only Milano wasn't sure how he could use the information to help Ronnie Shelton.

PART FIVE

"Unfinished Murder" Revenged

September 1989

THE TRIAL

On the day of jury selection, September 11, the *Plain Dealer* ran a lengthy page-one story, "Suspect Called 'Compulsive' Rapist." In it, McGinty derisively referred to Ronnie as "this poor defendant" and explained why he had refused Shelton's plea offers: "I want him found guilty of charges related to all the victims so they can contact the parole board when he is eligible and he stays behind bars his entire life." The article noted the meeting of the rape victims two weeks earlier and quoted McGinty again: "It was like a lynch mob, and they are all geared up and ready to go. Usually a rape trial involves one victim, but with thirty of them together they are as ready as any witnesses I have ever seen."

To the Shelton victims, McMonagle's sixteenth-floor courtroom seemed suffocating. It was dark, with no windows. A two-tier jury box lined one wall. Light brown industrial-strength carpet covered the floor, and brown louvers subdued the fluorescent lights ringing the room. Just inside the courtroom doors, which opened at the back of the room, were four rows of padded spectator benches that seated about seventy. The room had all the charm of a modern airport chapel.

Judge McMonagle's "room" was distinguished from the other forty-three courtrooms in the Justice Center tower by the way he arranged its trial tables. The two long rectangular wood trial tables were pushed together to form a large square in the middle of the courtroom. The prosecution team—McGinty and his co-counsel, assistant county prosecutor Frank Corrigan, plus

Detective Bob Matuszny—were to sit on the side closer to the jury; the defense—Ronnie, Jerry Milano, and, this morning, Jerry's lawyer son, Jay—would sit on the other side of the table, facing the jury. McGinty liked the setup; he and Shelton would be just a few feet apart.

The thirty victims met with Carla Kole and McGinty early that day in McMonagle's empty courtroom. Usually at a trial, only the first day's witnesses were found waiting outside the courtroom, because most of them had to take time off from work and because many trials settled just before jury selection. Also, the county had to pay $6 a day for each witness, which made having the entire witness list in attendance unnecessarily expensive.

But McGinty had a grand design, which explained why he had subpoenaed all the victims there. He had notified the TV news departments about the trial and made certain to have on hand Carla Kole as well as Jennifer Wise from the Rape Crisis Center. Many family members had accompanied the victims, and the crowded courtroom was tense with emotion. Ronnie's sister and mom sat in the room, unaware of what was unfolding.

Kole gave the women instructions on testifying. "You don't have to worry about your physical safety. There will be police officers in the courtroom and deputies out in the hall." She wanted to reassure them before giving tougher instructions. "We don't want to make you uncomfortable, but you have to use specific terms in describing what he did to you. If you say 'rape,' it could mean his finger, an object, or his penis. Be as specific as possible, and use the terms 'penis' and 'vagina.' We need to use them because people agree on what they mean. Practice saying them. I know it's going to be awkward at first, but it's just the way it's done."

"Where do we look?" one victim asked. "Do we have to look at him?"

"You have to point him out when asked. After that, you can look anywhere you want to," Kole answered. "You can look at the clock above the doors . . . anywhere."

One of the women asked about the insanity plea. "If he gets out on that in a few years, he can come back and get me," she said nervously. "He promised he would."

Several other victims joined in, voicing the same concern. McGinty could see that they were full of fear. "Please, don't worry about it," the prosecutor said. "The jury is going to find him guilty, you watch."

Then the prosecutor said the judge wanted him and Shelton's lawyer in chambers. The judge was trying to get him to agree to a plea bargain, McGinty said, but he would not sell them out. "Now you'll all have to wait outside the courtroom. Once you testify, you can come inside and watch the rest of it. Thanks."

In the crush of people in the hall that morning were Ronnie's parents and his sister. Some of the women thought Maria was one of the Shelton victims who had missed McGinty's orientation meeting two weeks before.

Then word swept the corridor—he's here! A deputy sheriff had brought Ronnie in by a jail elevator from which you could walk directly into the courtroom through a side door. Security was tight. A deputy uncuffed his wrists.

Ronnie wore a stylish gray suit, red tie, and white shirt. He tried to look nonchalant, as if he had nothing to fear. His hair was long and feathered in the back, and trimmed short on the sides. His skin was jailhouse white.

Most of the rape victims hadn't seen him since the lineup identifications the past winter. Others had never attended lineups, having picked him from photo spreads. The women outside the courtroom pushed to view him through the narrow vertical windows in the courtroom's swinging doors. Marian Butler, on crutches after a foot operation, was having a hard time maneuvering through the crush.

Maria Shelton stood, blocking the windows. "Who the hell is she?" someone wanted to know.

"That's his sister, Maria," Connie Bellini told the other victims. "She's a little crazy."

In obstructing the view, Maria was making a worthless gesture—the women were all going to see Shelton soon enough.

Karen Holztrager persisted in trying to look in, but Maria stood firm in front of the windows, blocking Karen's view.

"You got a fucking staring problem?" Maria hissed.

"No, do you?" Karen shot back.

"My brother needs support," she said.

Maria's remark detonated Marian Butler. " 'Support'? I'll give him support," she boomed out, waving a crutch. "I'll support him with this right up his ass!"

A deputy sheriff at a nearby security desk jumped up. "You!" He pointed to Marian, then to a chair. "Sit right there."

Karen Holztrager went over to Ronnie's parents. "I feel bad for you," she said to them both.

"What's your name?" Katy Shelton asked.

"Karen."

Katy Shelton started to cry.

Maria Shelton told herself she would have to help manage her brother's case and not forget anything during the commotion and stress, so she started keeping a diary. She knew her parents could not cope with it. She tried to talk to Connie Bellini, Ronnie's old girlfriend, but Connie wanted nothing to do with her. "I want him to fry," was what she said.

Now Maria sat down and wrote:

This has got to be the worst experience of my life. I wish this upon no one, not even my worst enemy if I had one. Everyone is so hateful. I have never seen so many go crazy over anything in my life. There have been threats to me like that's Shelton's sister, let's kill her. Everyone said, "I wish she was in my shoes." A lady said she would like to poke my eyes out. Her boyfriend is a Cleveland cop and he said Ron's going to fry anyway and started laughing.

Meanwhile, McGinty noted TV cameras on tripods in a corner of the courtroom and smiled. "I always try to use the news media," he would explain later. "I'll use whatever I can to put pressure on the system. These judges want to settle. Then I pack the courthouse with victims and families and all of a sudden these judges are fighting pricks for victims' rights. I wanted to force McMonagle's hand. So I packed that courtroom. I whipped them up. They took on a life of their own."

Before walking into the judge's chambers, Milano said to McGinty, "You son of a bitch. There's no reason for all these witnesses to be down here today."

McMonagle hadn't put his robes on yet. He still hoped for a plea. "This is not a football game," the judge snapped at McGinty. "You want to hold a pep rally, do it in your office."

Sensing an advantage, Milano offered that Shelton would accept a twenty- to fifty-year sentence, with his first parole review after five to eight years. McGinty countered that he wouldn't accept a plea of less than one aggravated rape felony for each victim and no parole review until fifteen years.

"No way. I'd have to be fucking crazy to agree to a deal like that," Milano told him. "Don't insult me!"

The judge stepped in. "What if the jury finds him *not* guilty by reason of insanity, Tim, then what? He could be out in a year. What about the victims then? They're not going to be happy."

McGinty would not budge. McMonagle, exasperated, started to put on his black robe. He warned the lawyers, "I want no outrageous comments out there, gentlemen."

OPENING STATEMENTS

Shelton felt McGinty, in his quotes to the press, had been trying to make him out to be a Ted Bundy. Now, sitting across from the prosecutor, he struggled to keep from jumping over the table and smashing the sausage-lipped lawyer. But Detective Matuszny, with his mile-wide shoulders and 9-millimeter handgun, sat in the next chair, and Ronnie decided an attack would be a stupid move, for now. He settled into the tedium of jury selection.

After prospective jurors were walked in, Milano and McGinty individually questioned them about employment, education, addresses, whether they had been crime victims. If a juror already knew quite a bit about the case and admitted to having an opinion, that juror was excused, and the strike was not charged to either the prosecution or the defense. Each side, without explanation, could eliminate six jurors. Deciding which juror would be sympathetic to which side was mostly guess-work.

Contrary to popular thinking, McGinty didn't select women as jurors in rape cases. Like most prosecutors, he believed conser-vative men made better jurors, feeling they were more likely to believe a woman's testimony. But in the Shelton case, he went the other way. He wanted older women jurors, preferably divorced, who might have suffered some hard knocks. He also wanted women because they could understand being afraid of a man.

Jerry Milano knew theories for picking a defense-minded jury but relied instead on hunches and gut instinct to make his picks.

By Tuesday morning, the second day, McGinty and Milano had agreed on a jury panel of eight women and four men, with two alternates in case someone fell sick. Most of the twelve were employed, in a range of occupations from secretary to business executive. A third of them were black. Only one juror, a young woman, lived in West Park.

Before testimony began, Milano crafted a surprise motion. To save time and money and spare the witnesses duress, Milano said Shelton would not contest the charges against him; he admitted to most of the crimes.

"It has been estimated that it will take two to three weeks to parade these poor unfortunate women who have been raped by the defendant, and the defendant has conceded that he commit-ted these crimes," Milano wrote. Since Shelton admits the crimes, Milano argued, the only thing left for the jury is to decide whether or not Shelton was legally insane at the time of the rapes. So let us just put on the experts from both sides and let the jury make its decision.

It was a bold move, admitting to all 230 felonies, but worth the risk if the judge granted it. Anything to keep the emotional, inflammatory testimony of the rape victims away from the jury.

Judge McMonagle considered it . . . and decided the women would testify anyway.

By now spectators filled every seat in the courtroom, waiting for the fireworks to explode. The four local television stations— WJW TV-8, WKYC TV-3, WEWS TV-5, and WUAB TV-43— assigned camera crews. Among the spectators this morning were several assistant county prosecutors and criminal defense lawyers who had come to savor the action in what would be the courthouse's main bullring for the rest of the month.

Then the judge did something his fellow judges in Cuyahoga County usually did not do. In an attempt to clear up a popular misconception, McMonagle instructed the jury about the meaning of the insanity plea. "You understand that, in Ohio, when the jury would find and return a verdict of not guilty by reason of insanity, the accused in those matters is not just cut loose," the judge told the jurors. "They are sent down to the Dayton Forensic Center, which is a penal institution, and they remain there. And they, conceivably, can remain there for the rest of their life. Every six months, the matter is brought up for review to the trial court, and we have a hearing to determine whether or not the individual has been returned to sanity.

"Sometimes it's a worry of some people that, Gee, maybe I can find him not guilty by reason of insanity, but that means he's going to be out on the street. That is not the case."

Milano was thunderstruck. He had asked the judge to explain what would happen to Shelton if a verdict of not guilty by insanity were returned, and the judge said he'd think about it. "It's the fairest thing this judge has ever done," Milano whispered to his son, Jay. All of a sudden Milano felt that Shelton might have a shot at Dayton Forensic after all.

McGinty, of course, didn't like the judge's instruction. It made getting a guilty verdict less of a certainty. But he was confident the jury, once it realized how many lives Shelton had crushed, would convict him.

The judge signaled him to commence, and McGinty stood up in front of a large Cleveland area road map, marked with the locations of thirty rapes and the names of the corresponding victims. "For five years, this individual"—he pointed accusingly—"Ronnie Shelton, by our allegations and by our evidence, stalked, waited, terrorized, attacked, humiliated, robbed, and intimidated this list of victims we're giving here."

Then McGinty went down the list in chronologic order and described each rape and robbery, devoting three or four minutes to each. By the second hour it was plain: He wasn't carving up Shelton so much as bludgeoning him, battering the jury time and again with details of the rapes. By the end of his opening, he had risked desensitizing the jurors to the horrors he described. But he knew of no better way to outline his case. He sat down and wondered how the jury felt about Shelton now.

Milano stood and walked toward the jurors, completely at ease. "Ladies and gentlemen, I will not be quite as lengthy," he said. "Listening to the prosecutor's opening statement, I feel now that without having a word from any witness I could argue this case to you and argue to you that what Mr. McGinty has described is a stone lunatic."

The verdict in this case—a not-guilty-by-reason-of-insanity case—will hinge on which psychiatrist you believe, Milano went on. Then he proceeded to build up Dr. Emanuel Tanay, the psychiatrist who would say that Ronnie Shelton, at the time of these crimes, couldn't refrain from raping.

Dr. Tanay was not the kind of psychiatrist who would advocate letting a dangerous criminal out on the street, Milano promised them. To prove his point, Milano told the jury a true story: Dr. Tanay had testified for the defense ten years before in one of Ohio's most sensational cases, the murder of supermarket magnate Julius Kravitz, a trial that many were likely to remember. A couple of years later, Milano said, when new lawyers for the killer tried to get him released from the penal hospital, who do you think the state of Ohio hired to say the killer was dangerous and needed incarceration? "Dr. Tanay," he answered with a flourish. "That is the type of man Emanuel Tanay is"—a man who will do what's right, Milano was saying. Then the manicured lawyer sat down.

As his first witness, McGinty called Keri Hansen, the woman Shelton raped after surprising her while she wrapped Christmas presents. She was the only victim Shelton had beaten, and McGinty had full-color police photos of her face after the December 1987 attack: puffy eyes, bruises, fresh scabs on her face, a lump on her forehead. This would show the jury the truth about Ronnie Shelton, the prosecutor hoped.

McGinty led her through the rape, then asked her to identify the police photos. "To be honest," Keri Hansen said, "these were taken right after it happened, and a few days later I looked a lot worse. A lot of the bruises hadn't come out yet."

A few minutes later, it was Milano's chance to cross-examine the witness, and he approached Hansen as if she were a live claymore mine. After a few perfunctory questions about her statements to police, he said he had nothing further. This would be his approach to most of the women who testified. He said how terribly sorry he was for what had happened to them and asked no questions. For the moment Milano, the skilled cross-examiner, was forced to sheathe his sharpest weapon.

THE SURVIVORS

The next morning, the women were eager to come back to court, even though most knew they would not be testifying against Shelton that day. They were comforted just being with other women who had suffered the same trauma. Two weeks earlier they'd barely spoken to each other at the orientation meeting with Carla Kole and McGinty; now they sat together in a semicircle of chairs at the end of the hall outside the courtroom, drinking coffee from a coffee and doughnut cart that Carla had ordered up from the cafeteria. (She followed this practice every day of the trial, and by the end had spent $150 of her own money—the Witness/Victim Service didn't have a budget for such amenities.)

Their emotions poured out, raw feelings that had been bottled up for years—crazy fears they could not discuss with husbands or boyfriends, rages at the insensitivity of coworkers, whatever —and it felt good.

"I had to tell what happened to, like, five different cops that day, and they were all cold-blooded," said one 1983 victim. "Especially the one who asked about the guy's penis. I can't remember if it was a guy in a uniform or a detective who asked me how big the rapist's penis was. I said I didn't know. What was I supposed to do, measure it?"

The other women laughed.

Jeannine Graham, who was raped in Parma in 1983, piped up. A tall, talkative mother of four who worked part-time as a bartender, she had a lousy experience with a detective to share with the others. She said she was asleep in bed, nude, seven months pregnant, when Shelton broke in. He pulled back her covers, saw she was pregnant, and changed plans—he forced oral sex instead.

After she was treated at the emergency room, a Parma police detective took her to the station for questioning. "He wouldn't let my husband be there," Jeannine went on. "So I told him what happened, about the knife, the whole bit. Then he asks me if I'd take a lie detector test and did this really happen to me. I'm mad now, so I go, 'What are all these questions?' He says he's required to ask 'em because they've had pregnant women make up stories like this so their husbands stay home at night. Can you believe it?"

A couple of the women shook their heads in disgust.

"I told him, 'You think I cut my own phone cord and my own screen so I could come here and go through all this?' Get this: He was driving me back and I said something like, 'He changed his mind when he found out I was pregnant.' And the detective goes, 'What is this guy, a Christian rapist that he doesn't have intercourse with you because you're pregnant?'"

Out in the hallway, a couple of the women gasped. Jeannine worked on her cigarette, then said, "I felt like he slapped me. Who would ever put those two words in the same sentence: 'Christian . . . rapist'? If that was his way of making a joke, it was in bad taste."

That night many of the rape survivors went home feeling for the first time that they had found understanding.

The next day in Courtroom 16-D, seven more rape victims took the stand. McGinty took them through their ordeal, asking them precise, clinical questions about how and when and where they were raped. The details each woman separately provided were remarkably similar. By the lunch recess it was becoming clear to the jurors that Shelton had a distinct pattern of behavior.

The victims, mostly young and attractive, were emotionally devastated. Over Milano's objection, the judge allowed McGinty to ask each woman how the rape affected her life. "I cannot be home alone without fearing that this is going to happen to me again," one of them told the jury. "It has just changed my life. I had to move from a place I loved because of someone that had the nerve to do this to me. My rights, my—my body was violated by someone that I just did not give permission to do this to me. . . . I could not go back to that house. I was afraid that he would come back to kill me."

There were small twists and differences in the finer details. One of the victims felt that Ronnie seemed disgusted with himself after the rape. "After he was done and everything, he told me, 'Close your legs.' And he said it like he was really disgusted with himself for what he had done. And—and I was scared . . . and then he says, 'You know it wasn't you I really wanted. It was your roommate. It was that other girl. But, she left first this morning' . . ."

McGinty asked, "And you described him to police?"

"Yeah," she replied. "He smelled like, like sweat and smoke and he smelled like he had been masturbating or—the odor of semen . . . And he also told me that, he says, 'I kinda like you. And I kinda—I feel kind of attached to you. And I think I'll come back and I'll see you again.' Like he was gonna come back to my apartment again."

McGinty: "Like he'd do you some kind of favor?"

"That's what he was acting like—he was doing me a favor."

CONNIE BELLINI

The next morning, Thursday, September 14, Connie Bellini was scheduled to be the first witness, and she took the day off from work. Connie dreaded having to explain to dozens of people in open court what she had hidden from her parents and boss and friends: that she was raped by Ronnie Shelton and even went back to him afterward. Because of this, she was uncomfortable around the other women, feeling like the biggest fool in Cleveland, the woman who'd *dated* a serial rapist.

The other victims were almost insatiably curious about Shelton, and they peppered her with detailed questions. She was touched that Karen, Jeannine, 1986 victim Janis Wren, and the others invited her for lunch in the cafeteria, and that Karen called her that night to make sure she was okay. And she was relieved that Maria Shelton had stopped following her. Before the trial, Connie had wanted to back out of testifying, and told McGinty so. But now she was glad she had decided to take the stand. The other rape victims were "a beautiful group of women," she told a friend, and she wouldn't think of letting them down.

On the witness stand, Connie calmly answered McGinty's questions, painting a devastating picture of a lazy, selfish, explosive young man who was a master at manipulation: charming one minute, brutal the next.

"When I started getting upset with him for going out and leaving me at home, he became abusive," she said at one point. "At first, he started pushing me around, grabbed my face and

277

pushed me away from him. Eventually, he slapped me. And after that he started using his fists."

She recounted how he took her money using her bank card, how she co-signed for a van that he then fixed up as a bachelor pad, on which he never made a payment. How he threatened to hurt her sisters and nephews if she ever tried to leave him. And how on May 26, 1986, he raped her.

Milano decided to cross-examine Connie Bellini about the rape, and, as she often did when nervous or unsure, she hid behind a tone of sarcasm.

"You tried two times to get him into psychiatric hospitals?" Milano asked.

That's right.

"And you were very much in love with Ronnie Shelton?"

She felt disgusted answering these questions. "At that time," she replied.

Did you see a knife or a gun? Did he threaten to kill you? Did you scream out?

She answered no to all three.

And you didn't go to police or report the rape?

"He threatened me. And my family."

Was that before or after you put on your nightgown?

She couldn't believe the insinuation. She couldn't believe Milano was a fellow Italian. He was such a pig. "That was after, when he jumped on top of me."

After Connie finished testifying, McGinty called Becky Roth as the next witness. Within minutes, she changed the attitude of nearly everyone connected with the case.

BECKY ROTH

Becky was the most fragile witness in the case. Married to an abusive husband, she was haunted by unresolved trauma and guilt from being sexually molested as a girl. Her job, working with mentally handicapped adults, was both poorly paid and emotionally demanding. Desperate to dull the pain of her life, during the four years since the rape, Becky drank, smoked pot, and took antidepressants.

Now the sixteenth floor outside McMonagle's courtroom had become her harbor. Here, among the women who'd survived Shelton, was the only place in the world she felt safe and understood. It was a precious feeling, for she couldn't achieve it at home. Several times during the trial, her husband came up to the other women and demanded to know where she was. He seemed to resent the newfound confidence she had gained from their support. The women hid her in a restroom and brushed him off.

A half hour before Becky Roth was to take the stand, Detective Matuszny, as he had with the other witnesses, ushered her into the interview room, just off the courtroom. There he handed her the statement she had given detectives when she was raped, and asked her to read it. It was a two-page, single-spaced account of the atrocities that she had spent nearly four years trying to obliterate. Reading the report catapulted her back to the attack. She began to hyperventilate, and Carla Kole, summoned for help, ran for smelling salts from her office downstairs.

279

Meanwhile, Becky's husband read the police report and became angry. Becky hadn't told him all the details found in the report. "Why didn't you tell me this happened?" he demanded.

"I just remembered it now, reading it," she said. He began to argue and she told him to leave her alone. She felt as if she was losing her mind. She couldn't testify. Someone asked her husband to leave the room.

As Carla returned, she saw a deputy sheriff move toward Becky, who was sobbing now. Carla could tell that she was reliving the rape, freaking out, and that the worst thing would be for the deputy—a strange man, a power figure with a gun—to touch her, to even put his hand on her shoulder.

The deputy stopped a couple of feet away, as if he knew just what to do, then leaned in. "My wife, she was raped ten years ago," the deputy said. Now he choked up. "They never caught the guy. You have the chance to do something my wife never got to do. You can put this guy away. You've got your shot, and you'll feel better for it."

By now Carla was at Becky's side. Becky, breathing in shallow, rapid gasps, was on the brink of fainting. Carla pressed a brown paper bag over her face and told her to breathe.

After several minutes, Bob Matuszny came out of the courtroom. "Are you okay?" Becky nodded yes. Carla handed him the smelling salts and he walked Becky inside and up to the witness stand. Out in the hallway, they could still hear her sobbing.

She cried through her testimony, just as she had cried during the forty-five minutes Ronnie Shelton had tormented her, raping her four times. "It was so gross," she told the jury, answering McGinty's questions, weeping. "It was disgusting. He told me to say, 'Fuck me, fuck me.'"

Her testimony was pathetic, gut-wrenching, and electrifying. Judge McMonagle's eyes teared up and half the jurors cried openly.

"What effect has this had on your life, Rebecca?" McGinty asked quietly.

"You can sort of look at me and see some of it. It's been hard living in the same house all these years."

"Have you wanted to move?"

"I wanted to move. We haven't been able to. I'm scared. I was unable to take a shower for a year. I couldn't even go"—she broke down—"I had a hard time going in the bathroom. Then after that I would have my mother over and sit with me in the bathroom while I took a shower and constantly talk to me. And if she'd stop talking for a second I'd just panic. I can't—I'll never be able to close my eyes in the shower. I still wear a bathing suit when I shower. I always have to wear something and I'm always—I can't wear pajamas. I'm always wearing clothes. It was hard because I never saw his face and I was always afraid he'd be watching me 'cause he always said he would come back. So, I was living in fear for all these years, thinking that he was watching me, and I couldn't go anywhere without being scared to death."

McGinty asked her, "Did that have an effect on your personal life?"

"My"—she collapsed into sobs again—"my husband and I are probably gonna be getting a divorce because of this."

"Are you seeking counseling and help?"

"I have to. I'm gonna be living with this for the rest of my life." She fixed her eyes on Shelton, a laser gaze shooting anger and hate. "He did this to me and I want him to pay!"

"Thank you, Rebecca. No further questions."

Sitting in the packed courtroom, Carla Kole gave a silent cheer. Becky had never felt safe, so she could never take the first step to recovery. But today, finally, she had taken control.

"I've talked to hundreds of rape survivors," Carla Kole would say later. "This was the closest I've ever come to sensing what rape was really like. Those weren't words—those were all raw emotions."

After Becky Roth left the courtroom with Matuszny's help, Milano approached the bench. He was shaken by her testimony. He felt the jurors' disgust and anger roiling, ready to spill out of the jury box.

"What I'd like to do on the record is, again, move that the prosecutor not put these people through this," Milano pleaded with the judge. "We'll concede [Shelton committed the rapes]. It's stipulated for this record. I've discussed it with my client.

He's in complete agreement. We concede that point and we feel—I don't think that these people should be put through this, other than for *his* show." He pointed to McGinty.

Denied, the judge said, and recessed for lunch.

Meanwhile, as soon as she hit the hallway and the court doors closed behind her, Becky looked at her new friends and said, "Fuck him." Some of the other rape survivors pumped their fists and shouted, "Yeah!" Others ran up and took turns hugging Becky. She was still crying.

Now McGinty strode out, smiling widely. "You were great. You did just great." At this moment, he felt the course of the trial had shifted dramatically.

In the deliberating room, gathering their purses and jackets, the jurors were shaken. Several felt as if they had just witnessed the rape itself. One juror, Valerie Dailey, who lived in West Park and dated a First District policeman, cried openly. She felt Becky was too young to be destroyed. Some jurors didn't leave for lunch, as they usually did: They had to stop crying and get a grip on their feelings before walking past the victims to the elevators.

"Oh my goodness, what he did to her," said Joseph New, a middle-aged man with silver hair, one of the four black jurors. He had served on a murder jury years earlier and at the end of the Shelton trial would be elected jury foreman. So far he had struggled to not form an opinion of Shelton, but now Becky Roth had made that impossible. It must have been pitiful, her crying and sobbing the whole time Shelton raped her. New felt Shelton had to know what he was doing. The man made him sick.

RONNIE

Ever since Ronnie's arrest, Maria had done whatever she could. She interviewed lawyers and found Milano. She sent Ronnie cigarettes, bought him a suit, ferried his girlfriends to and from jail visits. She bought clothes and presents for Ronnie's infant daughter.

She and her mother came to the trial every day, getting there early enough to get seats. It was rough on Katy Shelton. As Ronnie told his friends, she suffered from Huntington's chorea, a hereditary disease marked with involuntary spasms that gradually dismantles the nervous system. Already she twitched and was unable to form complex thoughts. Outside the courtroom, on the way to the elevators or to the women's room, she walked head down, bumping through clumps of people, oblivious. She said over and over again that her son could not have done these terrible things, and she asked him, repeatedly, to tell her she was right. At home, she either cleaned the house compulsively or prayed, her Bible in hand. Her husband was afraid to let her drive the car, and she became increasingly isolated. Maria was her lifeline.

Rodney Shelton attended his son's trial when he could. He sat next to his wife, saying little. The jurors noticed all of this. Sometimes, in the choreography of a trial, defense lawyers hope a subtle psychological message is being sent to jurors that the accused's family is normal, supportive, and devastated by the charges. The idea is to have at least this emotion working on your side during jury deliberations. But to many jurors in this case, the Shelton family seemed disheveled, listless, cold. Some jurors were willing to feel bad for the family, but the Sheltons, on the surface, didn't seem normal enough for the jurors to engage with emotionally.

Becky Roth's testimony before lunch had troubled Ronnie. Usually when the women he raped testified, he glanced at them briefly, then turned away. He wanted to be tough, cool, and unconcerned. But now a victim had pierced his self-pity. He felt ashamed of what he had done to Becky and wanted to hug and comfort her. He was rattled, but, wisely, he sat still and said nothing. Later that afternoon, after the trial reconvened, he decided he'd take the stand. He composed a statement:

I Ronnie Shelton would like to take the stand and save the rest of the remaining victims the burden of having to take the stand and re-live their nightmarish turmoil all over again.

I am of sound mind, and body. I could save the court a lot of agonizing grief and also *time*!

The true reason of this motion is because I too have feelings! Feelings for what I put them through. Feelings for how they are afraid in today's society. Feelings for what I have put their families through and also feelings for the fear that I have put into the community of Cuyahoga County through this time period.

Although this may not be easy, I will try and answer all questions from both sides of attorneys as I remember them. Because I have been reminded of events when I heard testimony of victims, of things that had not happened or was not the way they happened or was led by prosecutor McGinty as to what happened.

Fact: I've never had a police scanner or monitored police activity.

Fact: I don't remember whether or not I said I had a gun or not. But no gun was used or shown to victims. Fact: I do not consider myself a bad looking person. I've never had to rape any of my dates (which includes Connie Bellini). I could have over 50 witnesses themselves come in and testify to that. I didn't have to have sex all the time.

Fact: The reason there was a "West Park Rapist" is because there were a few rapes in that vicinity of the westside and the media sent me over there.

Fact: I couldn't stop from doing these things to women. I don't know why.

Fact: I don't know what happened to me or why I did them.

Fact: Rape is wrong.

This court and the people of Ohio want to know. And for this reason and for my own family, I am asking for this chance on my own behalf. The prosecution tries to explain to the victims and the state why this happened. Only I (Ronnie Shelton) know what happened! They do not!!

If they [state prosecutors] are so good at analizing [sic] what had happened, then why had they let this go on for *5 years* and possibly more? I Ronnie Shelton will be able to tell you why.

No one has suggested or forced me into having written this statement. Thank you.

Jerry Milano was not known for his bedside manner with clients. He preferred the professional criminals of the old days, the bookies and safecrackers, who paid him and let him do his job without a lot of hand-holding. When Ronnie showed him the statement and told him he wanted to take the stand, Milano blistered him. "You asshole, you're gonna blow this fucking thing." Stung, Ronnie turned away and fumed.

TIM McGINTY

Several more women testified that afternoon. About four o'clock, McMonagle recessed until Tuesday. This gave McGinty and co-counsel Frank Corrigan three days to catch their breath and plot the expert witnesses McGinty would present on Monday.

On Saturday, a political sideshow intruded on the trial. It was the Cleveland mayor's race. The primary election was only three weeks away, and leading a field of five was George Forbes, the Cleveland City Council president, a tough, profane, skilled backroom operator who was the most powerful man in northern Ohio. But Forbes had a problem: Women voters didn't like him. Polls showed disastrously negative ratings.

The testimony of the Shelton victims, their faces obscured, had dominated the TV news the past four days. And Forbes, who said he had been moved by the wrenching accounts, drafted legislation mandating the Cleveland City Council to spend $100,000 for counseling and restitution for the Shelton survivors and other sex abuse victims.

McGinty, a Democrat himself, nonetheless felt Forbes was exploiting the trial—Cleveland politics as usual—but kept his mouth shut. "Some of the Shelton victims called him a fraud," McGinty would say later, "but I said take him up on it. Take all your bills to City Hall—your bills for counseling, baby-sitters, security locks. Make 'em pay."

* * *

286

Late Saturday evening, McGinty stepped from the shower to answer a ringing phone. A woman's voice, barely above a whisper, implored: "Help me, Timmy, help me. He's getting me." And the line went dead.

It sounded like Patricia, his younger sister. McGinty ran to his bedroom, yelling to his wife, Ellen, "Call the police! Someone's gonna kill Trisha! Call the police!"

In a second he had called the police and pulled on his clothes. He looked for his gun, but he had put it away years ago and couldn't find it. It was in his office downtown, he suddenly remembered. He ran to the car. "Shouldn't you wait?" Ellen pleaded.

He sped out as his young son and daughter, roused from bed and frightened by the uproar, sank to their knees and prayed to Jesus to make sure their aunt Trisha was okay.

The Lakewood police were at her small apartment building. No one had responded to her buzzer and the police were waiting for the manager to let them in. McGinty told them who he was and kicked in a window to her apartment.

He ran from room to room. There was no one inside. What the hell, he wondered. Was he imagining things? Was the trial getting to him? Or was someone deliberately trying to rattle him?

Later that night, Ellen told him, "You've got to turn it off sometimes." But he couldn't. He was more tightly wound than usual. It seemed like every night he lived this case. Two or three of the rape victims had called him at home this week, crying, wanting to back out of testifying. He'd calmed them down, talking to them forever. While Ellen said she was proud of him, there were times when she seemed ready to cut the phone cord.

THE BOND TAKES HOLD

Over that weekend, more than a dozen of the Shelton survivors participated in a group therapy session at Witness/Victim offices. They sat in the large office of therapist Patrick Nicolino.

They had met Patrick briefly the second day of the trial. Carla Kole had said a psychologist on the staff was coming up, someone who could assist them. But she hadn't prepared them for Patrick. He moved slowly down the carpeted Justice Center hallway, smoking a cigarette and walking a golden Labrador retriever. Patrick Nicolino was short and broad-shouldered, with long dark hair, olive skin, thick black eyebrows accenting a handsome face with a matinee-idol chin. Then you noticed his eyes. His right one stared unblinking. Glass. His left was hidden behind a nearly closed eyelid. Patrick Nicolino was blind.

Lee Holztrager saw him first and wondered, How does a blind guy light his own cigarette? His wife, Karen, thought, If he can't see us, how can he help us?

Carla introduced Patrick to the group of women, and a moment later a couple of them stooped to pet the intelligent-looking dog and ask its name.

"This is Bosco," Patrick said. His voice was soft, almost effeminate. He seemed like the most nonthreatening man in Cleveland.

On Saturday afternoon, Patrick decided to go around the room and ask each woman how she was coming along. He had counseled Vietnam vets, child abuse victims, rape survivors—

but nothing in his studies had prepared him for this group. It was unique: a score of women traumatized by the same attacker. He was working on his Ph.D. in psychology, and the closest thing in the literature for a group suffering from the same trauma were studies of plane crash survivors. But it wasn't the same. Plane crash survivors didn't feel guilty or blame themselves for the accident. Crash survivors did not have to suffer shame or the skittish attitudes of a society too embarrassed to discuss rape. Nicolino was navigating without a map, and apprehensive. At the same time, when he thought about it professionally, he was fascinated.

The women took turns spilling their feelings: Their friends treated them differently; their parents and husbands were afraid to talk about the rape; the trial gave them nightmares and flashbacks; sex with their husbands was a disaster.

Jeannine Graham shared her story: The first night after the rape, her husband Bob had started to make love to her, but Jeannine stiffened, then froze. Hours earlier, in the same room, in the same bed, under the same quilt, a man had raped her.

That night, she needed Bob to just hold her: She was still in shock, and unprepared for any deeper intimacy. But she was so emotionally bruised by the rape that she couldn't tell him how she felt. Everything felt weird. Bob was making love to her, but not talking. It wasn't like him, Jeannine said, not to explain how he felt, what he was doing. She decided he was trying to tell her, without words, that he still loved her and wanted her sexually, even after what had happened. She went through the motions and made love.

Thereafter, sex was always strained.

"To save my sanity, I had to get outside the house, and I took a job tending bar at a nice restaurant," Jeannine told the group. She earned about $10 an hour, mostly in tips. Her customers didn't know her history and treated her just like anyone else. She found this helped her get her life back in order. She talked to people all evening, filling the emptiness she felt at home.

Usually Bob was asleep when she got home, and she would crawl in next to him and drift off. Their sex life was lousy, and Jeannine told the group she blamed the rapist. Before the attack, she thought nothing of slipping into sexy lingerie late at night, prancing into the living room where Bob would be watching TV, snapping off the set, pointing to the bedroom with a smile, and saying, "You and me, now!"

"I'd like to try that again sometime, but it seems too weird now," Jeannine said.

Betty Ocilka said she was angry at McGinty. The day before, he and Matuszny had taken her aside and explained that her charges were being dropped. He was sorry, but since her boyfriend, a Cleveland cop, had shown her Shelton's photo before she'd ever gone to a lineup, it opened her testimony to attack. Milano could nail her on cross-examination, make her identification seem faulty. If that happened, it could possibly taint the state's entire case. Right now, they were so far ahead, McGinty said, he wanted to be overly conservative. Betty said okay. But minutes later her rage at McGinty and Matuszny began to mushroom.

"I was just trying to catch the son of a bitch," Ocilka told the group. "No one told me what was going on. Wouldn't you try to catch him?"

Yes, of course, they reassured her. "Betty, his guilty verdict will be for you, too," someone said.

"Yeah, sure. But I'm still mad. I want mine. If he ever gets out, I'll be there. As soon as my kid is full grown, then I'll be on the hunt."

Nicolino realized Ocilka was still feeling powerless, cast adrift by the justice system. Her revenge fantasy was natural, a way to claim power. Sooner or later, she would get past that.

One woman said she was angry that people had expected her to have cuts and bruises because she was raped. A couple of inches taller than Shelton, she said she sometimes wished she had fought back; Shelton seemed so scrawny in the courtroom.

"You didn't do anything wrong," Nicolino said. "You didn't do anything wrong. You did what you needed to do to survive. And you did. You survived him, and now *he* is on trial."

By now Nicolino's office was filled with cigarette smoke. Coffee cups and soft drink cans rested on nearly every flat surface.

Becky Roth jumped in. She had been proud of herself immediately after testifying at trial the other day, but now her spirits had crashed. "After a great day, then it hit me like a wall," she said, crying. "I feel like committing suicide. I feel like I'm going crazy."

"You're not going crazy, even though you feel like it," Nicolino said. "What you're feeling is natural, normal."

Why even go through it? she wailed. It's too hard.

"The pain gives way to growth, to acceptance," he said. "If you stick with it, the result will be worthwhile. It will. You'll see."

"We'll help you," one of the women said. "We're here for you."

Becky said thanks. Without her new friends, she said, she would never be able to make it.

JOHN DOUGLAS

On Monday night, September 18, Tim McGinty set up a meeting with FBI agent John Douglas, his most important witness. He wanted to run Douglas through the sort of cross-examination Milano would use to discredit him. McGinty suggested they talk over a sandwich at Shooter's, a sprawling restaurant and bar on the boardwalk along the Cuyahoga River.

McGinty noticed that Douglas dressed with a kind of flair rare among FBI agents. Tall, dark-haired, and trim, Douglas used exercise as a release for the draining work of trying to get inside the mind of serial killers or rapists, trying to think as they do in order to catch them.

McGinty threw every tough question he could at Douglas. Under the fading summer light, as the pleasure boats cruised the sluggish river to and from Lake Erie, Douglas parried each thrust as smoothly as any witness McGinty had ever coached. Tim laughed, suddenly happy. Later he warned Douglas that Milano could make Mother Teresa seem like a commie spy. Douglas chuckled and said he looked forward to testifying.

The next day, before the trial started, Tim ran into Maria Shelton in the hallway outside the courtroom. "Have a nice weekend?" she asked him. Usually, Maria only stared at him as if she were going to pluck out his eyes.

Suddenly McGinty thought of the phone call hoax that had terrified his family. "Yeah, real nice," he replied.

"Restful?" she asked.

"Yeah, especially Saturday night."

Maria smiled as if she had scored a touchdown.

"If it happens again, *you* won't have a nice weekend," he warned, and she turned away.

This morning, Tuesday, September 19, before calling Douglas to the stand, McGinty put on his key police witnesses. Detective Mark Hastings of the Sex Crimes Unit explained how he had arrested Shelton and found the Monte Carlo. Hastings vouched for the evidence recovered from the search of the car.

Bob Matuszny explained how he'd tracked Shelton for several years before handing over his files to Ed Gray and Andrea Zbydniewski at Sex Crimes.

Zeb detailed her interviews with the victims. She also told of her forty-minute interview with Ronnie shortly after he was arrested.

FBI agent Douglas was McGinty's closer. He could wrap the cases together so that the strong ones would carry the weak, by testifying that Ronnie had a "signature," a "behavioral finger-print," that was found in each of the rapes. Milano stipulated to all the crimes—not contesting that Ronnie did them. By not contesting the rapes, Milano was playing to the jury, showing sympathy to the victims and speeding up the trial. He also hoped this would lull McGinty into relaxing a little. Despite the stipulation, Milano still could ask the judge to dismiss the counts for which McGinty didn't present sufficient proof.

McGinty was surprised that Milano had not found a reason to oppose Douglas's testimony about "signature crimes." This would be the first time in Ohio such testimony was attempted. Maybe Milano thought it wouldn't matter; Judge McMonagle tended to allow all sorts of testimony and then let the jury decide what was credible.

Douglas took the stand Tuesday afternoon, and McGinty swung for the fences.

McGinty: "What is a signature crime?"

Douglas: "A signature crime is a particular aspect of a crime that the offender leaves as his calling card. It is beyond the scope of, say, modus operandi. Modus operandi is an extremely dynamic feature of a crime and is very, very, very malleable. So consequently you can't really link cases together by modus operandi, so you look for other features.

"And specifically, rape cases, we feel, are much easier to analyze. You have much more information provided to you, because you have a surviving victim. So there's three areas you focus in on: the verbal assault, the sexual assault, and the physical assault of that offender.

"And within those three areas, that's where you'll find the uniqueness of a particular offender. That is called the 'ritual' aspect of the crime, or the criminal's 'behavioral fingerprint.'"

Douglas gave an example of a modus operandi. One rapist he studied would put a teacup in the small of the back of the husband of a victim and make him lie facedown on the floor. The rapist would warn the man that if he heard the cup clatter, he'd kill his wife. Then he'd rape the victim in another room, within earshot. The teacup—essentially a handcuff—was one aspect of the criminal's modus operandi: what he needed to do in order to commit the crime, Douglas explained.

Then he gave an example of a rapist's "ritual," or signature. A rapist in the Deep South had his victim call her husband or boyfriend and summon him to the house. The rapist would tie him up in a chair and rape the woman in his presence. "That is ritual," Douglas explained, "because he is going beyond what he has to do simply to rape the woman. His innate desire is to

293

manipulate, is to dominate, is to control, is to take this woman in the presence of a husband, a boyfriend. So that is a ritual aspect.

". . . The biggest error when you're analyzing cases is if you think that the motivation of an offender in rape cases is strictly sex. That's erroneous. The underlying theme of rapists is anger, it is power, and it's to manipulate and dominate and control victims.

"And it's also erroneous to think that there is a typical rapist in this country or any other country. There are five to six different rape typologies."

McGinty: "And what are they?"

Douglas: "The most common type of rapist, whether it's Cleveland, Ohio, or New York City or in London, England, is a 'power reassurance' rapist. He makes up about eight out of ten of our rapists in this country. He is known in the police circles as a 'gentleman rapist.' He's apologetic: 'I'm sorry. I have personal problems.' He may stay at the scene and have something to drink, take something out of the refrigerator and make himself a sandwich. That's the most common type."

McGinty asked what type of rapist he found in this case.

Douglas: "It's one of the more unique ones, a style of rapist found in only one out of ten rapists—a "power assertive" rapist. This style, matched with Shelton's rituals, makes him very, very unique to Cleveland, Ohio. It would be extremely unique if you had two operating within your community."

McGinty asked what Shelton's primary motivation was.

Douglas: "The underlying theme is the anger. It's the power. It is to manipulate that victim, to dominate, to degrade, to debase, to intimidate this victim. Now, you look through many of the cases and you see there's a theme of money, to obtain monies. Well, I perceive that as a method of diffusing the victim. When a subject breaks into a victim's residence and the victim, for example, is asleep and has a knife at her throat, her goal is now to survive. She must survive. 'I'm going to be killed.' If she begins to scream, if she begins to fight, the subject must now diffuse that. So he—what he has to do is to give that victim the false hope that really his primary motivation is—'I'm not here to rape you. I'm not here to kill you. I want money. I need money.'

"So then what happens is now the victim becomes under control. Then once he does this, now he moves back into his rape mode. Now the victim's primary goal here, because she saw what he was like a few seconds earlier, the propensity for violence, what she's afraid of now is, 'I may be killed, so I'll go along, just hope that he gets out of here and doesn't hurt me.'

"Then the final act is the intimidation, is the threat, 'If you call the police I'm going to get you'. . . . So you certainly don't get any kind of remorsefulness."

McGinty asked him to classify the rapist in this case.

Douglas: "This is a 'power assertive' rapist. . . ."

McGinty asked about the time gaps between the rapes.

Douglas: "Sometimes the subject may physically leave the area. Sometimes the subject may be institutionalized. He could have had a close call with the police. He could be incarcerated or he could just still be out there on the hunt. There is no cooling-off period.

"But what we all see is that with this particular style of rapist here, it's like a predatory animal. The hunt is on, looking for that victim of opportunity." In this case, the suspect was smart, successful, and if not apprehended would have kept raping.

McGinty: "Is marital status or the presence of consensual sexual relationships related to whether a person commits rape?"

Douglas: "No. Most of these types of offenders are having some type of heterosexual relationship at the time. And sometimes that's the underlying problem with the offender: He is having these difficulties, whether it's family members or whether it's other female associates. And what's interesting is, many of these cases, rather than striking out at the person who's causing them the most grief at that particular time, they decide to go out on the hunt. And rather than strike on family or girlfriends, they go out on the hunt looking for a victim of opportunity.

"The underlying theme in this case is not sex," Douglas said. "The underlying theme is anger, is this power. And the method of his sexual assault—masturbating on the victim, performing vaginal sex, withdrawing, ejaculating on the victim's stomach, or masturbating over the victim, masturbating between the victim's breasts—it tells you this is total domination of the victim.

295

"And it has been my experience, of the cases I've done—I've done over five thousand cases in the FBI, all types of cases, but a majority in the area of rape and rape-murder—it is a very, very unique characteristic. These elements of this particular crime are very, very unique—in fact, so unique that there's no hesitation of saying that you have one person operating in Cleveland, Ohio, who's perpetrating these particular crimes in this cluster of cases here. You have one person."

McGinty asked Douglas if he had ever heard the term "compulsive rape syndrome." No, sir, the agent answered.

McGinty turned to the judge. "No further questions."

Milano asked to approach the bench, and the judge signaled okay. Out of the jurors' hearing, the lawyer asked, "What the fuck was that? Jesus Christ, this guy's got more cases than One-A-Day." The judge chuckled softly. Milano said, "I would move that this entire amount of testimony be stricken."

McMonagle said overruled.

"Let's have a recess," Milano said. "I don't think I'm going to ask him anything."

After the break, Milano had no questions for Douglas. McGinty was surprised. That was it? McGinty rested his case and prepared his ambush of the defense's expert, Dr. Tanay.

TIM McGINTY

On Wednesday, September 20, the trial was recessed for five days. Dr. Emanuel Tanay could not travel to Cleveland until Monday because he was busy, set to testify in two criminal cases in other states.

McGinty was glad for the delay. It gave him more time to prepare. His biggest worry was Tanay's interview tape of Shelton. Milano had cleared it with the judge to allow Dr. Tanay to play his recorded interview with Ronnie. The effect would be the same as if Shelton testified under friendly questioning, and McGinty knew he couldn't cross-examine a goddamn tape recording. No way did he want that tape played. And knowing the judge's temperament—allow everything in and let the jury decide—McGinty didn't think he could quash the tape.

Milano was supposed to have given him a copy of the Shelton recording days ago. But what he sent over at first was the wrong tape, and McGinty lost two days of preparation. Nice trick, he thought; I'll have to remember that one.

He prepared for the Tanay cross-exam like it was a playoff game. To familiarize himself with the psychiatrist's courtroom manner, McGinty reviewed videotapes of his past performances. He also obtained a letter from one of Tanay's colleagues, who listed five attack points. The most useful, the colleague said, was that Tanay "is stylistically very arrogant, defensive and argumentative. . . . The main thing that turns off jurors about [Tanay] is his tendency to be easily provoked to battle with a lawyer and to be arrogant or grandiose in terms of his knowledge of law."

McGinty hatched a plan: He would goad Tanay, keep the witness on the stand, pressure him until he lashed out. McGinty honed his feelings to the fine hatred needed to savage someone you don't know. He convinced himself Tanay was a charlatan, a money-grubbing expert who fashioned opinions for whoever was paying his way.

Over the weekend, McGinty did miles of roadwork to cut stress, ate well, and got enough sleep. Monday morning he walked into the Justice Center, rested but intense, his eyes narrowed. This is the entire case right here, he told himself, this one witness. Dr. Emanuel Tanay.

DR. EMANUEL TANAY

On Monday morning before he resumed trial, Judge McMonagle called Milano and McGinty into his chambers. It was a likely day for fireworks—the defense expert was to testify—and McMonagle did not want McGinty or Milano to blow up or fire off improper questions that might create reversible error. McMonagle did not want to chance giving the Eighth Circuit Court of Appeals a reason to order a retrial.

The judge figured that Tanay's fee would be a main avenue of McGinty's attack, so he made certain to warn the impulsive prosecutor to behave. "You can inquire of him if he's getting paid for his testimony and his time and research, but you cannot ask him the amount," the judge said.

McMonagle saw that his point had sunk in.

"And gentlemen, you know, you both have been very nice throughout the trial here. This is getting down to the nuts and bolts, all right? If you have an objection, make an objection. Don't yell and scream. Do you understand?" Both lawyers said all right.

Dr. Emanuel Tanay was sworn in, and then he settled into the witness stand like it was a favorite easy chair. Tanned, wearing an expensive suit and wireless bifocals, his silver hair extending just over his ears, he looked like a successful businessman, save for his thick-soled shoes. McGinty stabbed him with stares, his eyes roving from the jurors to Tanay, wondering what they were thinking.

Milano took Tanay through his impressive credentials: medical school in Munich, Germany, faculty member since 1958 at the Wayne State University College of Medicine, a fellow of the American Psychiatric Association, a fellow of the American Academy of Forensic Sciences, numerous articles, books, and medical conference presentations. All this tedium by Milano was necessary to qualify Tanay as an expert. Now, unlike other witnesses, who could talk only about what they saw or heard, Tanay could offer sweeping opinions on Shelton's motivations, his ability to control his impulses, his sanity, and all matters psychological.

Under Milano's lead, Tanay made the important point that he considered Shelton dangerous, and that the young man should be kept in a penal hospital indefinitely. Tanay also criticized the court clinic's assessment of Shelton—its "preliminary sanity report"—because Dr. Knowlan, the author, had made his determination without having test results that showed whether Ronnie had organic brain damage from his 1983 fall.

Through Tanay, Milano also attacked McGinty for withholding police reports, which Tanay had requested for his evaluation. Milano hoped to create some suspicion about McGinty's motives.

"That's the first time you've been denied police reports, isn't it?" Milano asked his expert.

"I don't believe I've ever encountered a situation in a serious case where I was not permitted to look at the police reports," Tanay responded.

Milano hoped to paint McGinty as someone who would do anything to win, including deliberately withholding information favorable to the defense. It was not that Milano was above such disreputable tactics himself; he just wanted to cast doubt on McGinty and hope that it spilled over to the evidence.

Milano led Dr. Tanay through Ronnie's brain surgery. Tanay had reviewed Ronnie's medical records and now dwelled on the injury and the defendant's three days of unconsciousness. This injury certainly could have loosed Ronnie's impulses to rape, Tanay told the jurors.

Karen poked her husband and whispered, "That is so stupid, so outrageous."

And did the accident occur *before* the first rape charged in this indictment? Milano asked.

All of the rapes occurred after the brain injury, Tanay answered.

There it was: the science for the defense's case. The foundation blocks for Milano's closing argument. The reason, however far-fetched on its face, that Ronnie was a rapist: a severe head injury that had sent him over the edge. Would anyone on the jury be persuaded?

Karen felt ready to explode. She noisily exited the courtroom, and when she looked back, several other victims were following her out to the hallway.

"He fell off a ladder, big F deal," Jeannine Graham said.

"For five years I didn't get any counseling, and now he's supposed to deserve doctors and treatments?" Karen complained. "That's not justice."

"Just the words of it, 'not guilty' by whatever, that makes me furious," said another. "Not guilty, bullshit."

The women were too unsettled to go back inside, and instead watched the trial from a TV monitor set up in an interview room.

Meanwhile, in the courtroom, as casually as if he were asking for a cup of coffee, Milano said he'd have Tanay play the Shelton tape now if it was all right with the judge.

McGinty objected showily. The judge dismissed the jury so he could hear the lawyers argue on the record. McGinty, aware of the reporters and rape survivors in the courtroom, did some grandstanding.

"This is hearsay, in the sense that you have a defendant, in effect, testifying to the jury through a tape, through a doctor, without having the guts to walk up to the witness stand and be subjected to cross-examination," McGinty said. ". . . How do I cross-examine a defendant? It's impossible, through his agent who he's hired to come up here and testify for him. It's misleading, it's self-serving, what we have on this tape. And it was presented to me Friday afternoon after they presented the wrong tape to me. I finally found out the tape they presented to me was a bunch of screaming gypsies threatening to kill each other. . . .

"They can't play the tape and talk about 'poor Ronnie' crying and blaming it on his father, or he didn't get taken to the ball game enough, or whatever his problem was. To hear this guy's voice sniffling and crying for long periods on this tape is certainly not within the purview of proper discretion from a trial court. It just isn't right."

The judge listened to the defense's arguments and decided the tape could be played for the jury.

The rape survivors were electrified by the sound of Ronnie's voice as it played in the hushed courtroom. To many, it seemed horribly familiar. Others didn't recognize it. His parents were rattled as the sound of their son's voice blanketed a roomful of strangers. They listened carefully, hoping that this nationally known psychiatrist—they had given Milano $7,500 for Tanay's retainer—could pull off a miracle and somehow help their troubled son.

By now the jurors were extremely alert. They leaned forward in their seats, eyes focused, with a minimum of fidgeting. After two weeks of watching Shelton sitting silently at the trial table, they were finally getting to hear his voice, learn about his background. This was the trickiest moment so far in the trial. How would his words and emotions play on the jury?

On the tape, Tanay asked about troubles at home.

Ronnie: "I've always had a temper. I think that's from my father. I've been in fights."

Tanay: "How about stealing?"

Ronnie: "I wasn't really into that until recently. I didn't do it when I was a child. I did it when I became mature enough to know when it's wrong."

Tanay: "How about any type of sexual difficulties, sexual transgressions?"

The jurors heard a pause on the tape, then sniffles.

Tanay: "What are you getting upset about?"

Ronnie: "I'm not. I really, I—"

Tanay: "Well, you got teary-eyed. Now, what happened? What feeling went over you? Here, I don't know if we have any Kleenex here."

Ronnie: "It was just me and my sister—my parents always tried to give me everything. Something happened when I was a juvenile, and it's not brought up yet. My parents moved me around to keep me and my sister out of busing and all that. We went from the inner city of Cleveland to the suburbs to get a better education and climate. And I don't know what happened to me. I got worse."

Tanay: "Why did you react with tearfulness when I asked the previous question?"

Ronnie, through his tears, told the story of trying to rape the woman next door in Brunswick Hills. "I thought she liked me. She always used to have dirty books and stuff like that. And she treated me like an adult."

Tanay asked about his first rape.

Ronnie explained that the first one he was charged with was in October 1983, three months after his head injury. But he insisted he couldn't have raped then, that he was still recovering.

Tanay asked about the head injury.

Ronnie: "I went to work. We were putting up a new roof on this auto body shop. And it's three days later. I didn't feel nothing. I didn't know I was in an accident. I remember going to work. I remember something about we were getting ready to do a roof and I remember it's three days later."

Tanay: "You wake up where?"

Ronnie: "St. Alexis Hospital."

Tanay: "So far as the police say—even though you don't accept it—according to the police, not according to you, the first was in October of '83."

Ronnie: "Yeah, yeah. That's when they say it starts."

Tanay: "And you say it starts when?"

Ronnie: "I don't know. I'm, I'm being charged with a lot of things I didn't do. I know I couldn't have done them."

Tanay asked how many women he raped, but Ronnie didn't want to be pinned down. He avoided the question.

Tanay: "Well, tell me the first one you can remember."

Ronnie: "I'll be—I'll be open, but I can't—I can't remember."

Tanay was used to such seeming memory lapses from criminal defendants. Reading from Dr. Knowlan's report, Tanay asked Ronnie about his arrest for voyeurism. "What was involved in that?"

Ronnie: "I was looking in somebody's window."

Tanay: "For what purpose?" No answer. "Is it difficult for you to answer right away or are you just deliberating—"

Ronnie: "I'm thinking. I'm thinking."

Tanay: "You're thinking about what? If you should answer or not?"

Ronnie: "Which time—no. Which—yeah. If I should answer, if I—"

Tanay: "Are you reacting to me as if I were a policeman who interrogates you?"

Ronnie: "I am afraid of you, if that's what you want to know."

Tanay: "Well, why are you afraid of me? After all, you know that I'm on your side with—"

Ronnie: "No, I didn't know that. I know my attorney hired you. I just know that you're a doctor who, who knows—who can—who—who tries to find out the problem."

Tanay changed the tape to the second side, where Ronnie complained that the TV stations and newspapers were exaggerating his crimes.

Ronnie: "They made me like one of the biggest . . . I'm supposed to be the worst rapist Cuyahoga County's ever seen. They told people that's who I am. I'm told that McGinty wants to get public attention to become judge off my case, using my case for his benefit."

Tanay: "Isn't it a fact, however, that you did commit a number of rapes? Isn't that true?"

Ronnie: "Yes."

Tanay: "Well, how did they find out it was you?"

Ronnie: "They said they were looking for me for five years. I've been a very irresponsible person; I've been arrested a number of times. And they're telling me that they've been looking for me for five years, from '83 to '88, like I'm a master criminal. They made my case out to be like Ted Bundy's. Like I'm the Bundy of Ohio.''

Tanay: ''Well, let me tell you, *I* examined Ted Bundy and my impression would be that you're not.''

Ronnie: ''You met him?''

Tanay: ''Oh, I—yeah, I was the expert in the Ted Bundy case.''

Ronnie: ''Well, that's who they've made me out to be.''

Tanay: ''Well, do you think they're right?''

Ronnie: ''I've never hurt nobody. . . . The problem is I don't know what I did. . . . And it's like I start sweating, but there's an excitement there. It's like I know what's gonna happen but I don't want it. I try not to do it. . . . Then I sit there, on the ground, or I smoke cigarettes and debate whether I should do it or not.''

Tanay: ''Now what goes on in that debate?''

Ronnie: ''It's like I'm—it's—it's like—the only thing that I ever did in drugs is cocaine. There's a difference between snorting cocaine and smoking it. And I smoked it for a while. That difference in high is the high that I have while I'm outside waiting. It's like—I'm light-headed, I'm sweaty, and half of me tries to fight this half, saying not to do it. He told me to be honest with you. You just told me you're here for me. There could be fifty, sixty more rapes on this sheet that I stood over.''

Tanay: ''That actually took place or—''

Ronnie: ''No. That I watched while she slept and I left. . . . I tried not to do it. I did one of these when I just got through having sex with my girlfriend. I've got the prettiest girlfriends that you, that you could watch walk down a beach. I have, I can go to any bar and I can get any girl.''

Tanay brought him back to something that had bothered him earlier. ''You keep repeating that 'I never hurt nobody.' You know, when you rape a woman, you hurt her. She's terrified. You threaten her. And she doesn't want to have sex with you. That's hurting her, isn't it?''

Confronted with this painful truth, Ronnie avoided the question, and talked instead about his compulsion to drive and look for victims.

Tanay: ''But you didn't answer my question. I was saying to

you that what you did *did* hurt women. Would you agree with that?"

Ronnie: "Yeah. I would never want nothing like that done to my sister or my mother."

Tanay: "All right. So you would want to change your statement, what you said before, that you didn't hurt these women. You mean you never hurt them physically?"

Ronnie: "Right."

Tanay: "Did you beat any of them?"

Ronnie: "There's some that said I did. I didn't have to."

Going into the interview with Ronnie, Tanay had guessed there was only a slim chance that a jury would find him not guilty by reason of insanity. He had committed so many rapes, and Shelton's inability to refrain was, at best, borderline. Still, Tanay pressed on with his examination, and asked about problems such as depression or having "your mind play tricks on you."

Ronnie: "No. I've always been—when I was a kid, always depression. I'm depressed now. I was, I was no good. I was just no good for nobody. I mean my friends, I had fake friends. But you know my dad never let me do what—the things I wanted to do. He didn't let me join the navy. My dad used to be my buddy. My dad used to be my baseball coach when I was a little kid. Then when we moved, it's all different, we're having troubles.

"The only reason you're here is because of my mom. My mom says he loves me. He don't. He's my natural father—and he hung up the phone yesterday when I called. . . . I've always had this hate for my father. I don't know why. My mother, if something happened to my mother, I would kill myself. But I never, all my life my dad's told me I was no good. My dad was respected. My dad was somebody, and he is somebody now. Except he didn't have a son that was anybody. He had a daughter that was somebody.

Tanay: "And you get upset about that?"

Ronnie: "He says he loves me. He don't. 'Cause it's—'cause it's—I think it's my dad's fault that I did—that I did some of these things."

The courtroom spectators who knew what Ronnie's parents

looked like now scanned the room for them. Rodney sat next to his wife and daughter, stone-faced. A lifetime of concealing his anger wasn't going to be overturned today.

Tanay: "Your dad's fault? How's that?"

Ronnie: "Because I think I took out on some of these girls where my dad took things out on me. My dad stopped me from accomplishing a lot of things I wanted to do in my life. And I used to get mad and sometimes I did go and do a couple of things just out of anger. And before I did it, I told my dad, 'Watch, just watch.' But I would never tell him what I did."

A minute later in the courtroom, the thin sound of Ronnie's tearful voice clicked off. The hour-long tape was over. It was half past noon and the trial was recessed for lunch.

Milano was pleased that he had staged the tape so that it ended just before lunch break. The jury would have seventy-five minutes without new courtroom distractions, and the sounds they'd take to lunch would be the crying of Ronnie Shelton. Now, Milano needed Tanay to wrap it all up, convincingly and simply. He felt the doctor had been impressive so far.

VALERIE DAILEY

For juror Valerie Dailey, a lot of pieces of the Ronnie Shelton puzzle snapped into place after hearing the audiotape of his interview with Tanay. She was a twenty-two-year-old receptionist at the Cleveland Clinic, the world-renowned hospital complex, and had caught Ronnie's attention right away. She was cute, slender, with stylish brown hair. Ronnie gazed at her, and

Valerie, unafraid, stared back. She felt he was trying to read her or convince her that he was okay, and she refused to let him charm or scare her.

She was surprised to be on the jury in the first place. She lived in West Park and, until Shelton's capture, didn't make a move at night without thinking about the mystery rapist being out there, prowling her neighborhood. She didn't know it until after the trial, but she and her girlfriends had probably run across Shelton as they danced and drank at the Rampant Lion and Flash Gordon's, two of his haunts. Ever since the publicity about the West Side Rapist began in the mid-1980s, Valerie and her girlfriends wouldn't let each other leave a nightclub alone. They dropped each other off, then called when they got home to make sure they were all safe. One night, Valerie ran so fast to her house in the dark she tripped and crashed through a storm door. She was lucky she wasn't seriously cut.

During jury selection, the lawyers learned that her boyfriend was a First District cop assigned to a zone car. He had been briefed repeatedly at roll call about the West Side Rapist, and in the weeks before Ronnie's capture, had been shown the bank surveillance photos of the suspect's rusted Monte Carlo. Milano figured that Dailey, through her boyfriend, might have a more sophisticated knowledge of police work, with its frailties and foul-ups and constant pressure to round up a suspect. Depending on how the testimony unfolded, she might be the juror, during deliberations, to dispel storybook notions about men in blue, to understand that they might lie on the stand to win a case. Milano kept her on the jury.

Throughout the early days of Ronnie's trial, Valerie Dailey hoped he was the West Side Rapist. Otherwise, a terrible criminal was still on the streets, and she hated the thought of that. Now, after listening closely to Shelton's interview with Tanay, she was not moved toward sympathy. When she heard Ronnie blame his father for his crimes, she wanted to jump up and say, That doesn't cut it. Sorry. Seen it before. Lot of people had it rough. If it was so bad at home, why did you move back in with your folks? You coulda got help if you really wanted.

But another juror, Lila Hohenfeld, a sixty-four-year-old grandmother, felt sorry for Ronnie after hearing the tape. "I abhorred what he did," she would reveal later, "but I felt sorry for anybody in that situation. It's such a waste of life. I knew he had a problem. You see these movies that show both sides. What causes him to do this? There's a reason he was doing this. I was thinking of how they tried to say it started after he fell off the roof. He was not normal, anyone who would do this."

CROSS-EXAMINATION

After lunch break, Dr. Emanuel Tanay was called back to the stand. He settled comfortably into the witness box, smiled at the jury, then looked out at Milano.

Milano asked him a few questions about the court clinic's reports before inquiring, "Doctor, in examining the reports, did you read of the many times Ron Shelton refrained from raping?" Milano was referring to the many times the accused admitted breaking into women's homes, only to masturbate, then leave.

Tanay: "I certainly have."

Milano: "Is that of psychiatric significance to you?"

Tanay: "Oh, it clearly is psychiatrically significant that he had these persistent recurrent impulses to terrorize, intimidate, render women helpless, and that he recognized that this was something he shouldn't do. He went through these, sometimes hours, of struggling with this recurrent impulse, and on many occasions he did *not* succumb to the impulse. He was able to resist, overcome, control it—whatever term you wish to use.

"He tells us pretty clearly that this compulsion was a persistent one and was operating for five years and continues to operate even now, when he is in jail, in the form of dreams."

Milano needed the jury to believe that sometimes Shelton couldn't stop himself. "Doctor, based on the entire amount of work you've done in this case, the documents you've examined, the taping and evaluation of Ronnie Shelton, do you have an opinion as to whether or not this young man could have refrained from committing these crimes he's indicted for?"

Tanay: "In my opinion, he could not have. He was driven by the underlying pathology, by the combination of the personality disorder that he has, aggravated by the organic brain syndrome. He may have had such impulses before, but I think the organic brain syndrome certainly weakened, in my judgment, his ability to cope with his antisocial impulses which he has demonstrated earlier in life."

Milano: "Is that to a medical certainty, Doctor?"

Tanay: "That is to a medical certainty, yes."

Milano looked toward McGinty. "You may inquire."

In the morning session, it had seemed that Tanay was well received by the jury. With his Polish accent, open face, and grandfatherly manner, Tanay displayed charm as a witness. Like Jerry Milano himself, Tanay seemed to come to life in the courtroom. Now, faced with a hostile questioner in prosecutor McGinty, Tanay leaned slightly forward. He seemed on the balls of his feet, ready to parry and counterpunch.

"Doctor, you've had considerable experience in the courtroom, have you not?"

McGinty's tone was derisive. He stood in front of the witness stand, squared off, his chin out. McGinty felt he had a few surprises for the good doctor, things he'd uncovered that Milano was not expecting.

"You've been in the courtroom many hundreds of times testifying, have you not?" McGinty demanded.

"Oh, I don't know if many hundreds of times, but I have been in courtroom on many occasions," Tanay answered. He often dropped articles before words, common among eastern Europeans speaking English as a second language.

"Let me ask you one more time, Doctor: Hundreds of times would be a fair estimate, would it not?"

"You have my answer, sir," Tanay replied.

". . . Now, Doctor," McGinty said, dripping condescension, "I want you to listen closely to my questions, okay? If you don't understand my questions, stop me and ask me to repeat them. But if you do understand my questions, Doctor, will you give a straightforward, simple answer to it?"

Tanay smiled.

"That's a question, Doctor. Can you answer that?"

"I will make every effort to do so."

"Can you promise that you'll make that effort, Doctor?"

"I have given you my answer, sir."

"Will you listen to the question and answer the question only, sir? Will you do that, sir?"

"I have already given you an answer. Now—"

"We're starting already, aren't we, Doctor?"

Milano shouted an objection as Tanay said to McGinty, "Sir, stop intimidating me."

It was only minutes into the cross, and outright hostility was wafting from both men. They hated each other already.

Tanay had weathered many vicious cross-examinations and felt he could handle McGinty. He would have to push the prosecutor off-balance somehow.

McGinty moved in a bit closer to Tanay, then read from an old law review article of Tanay's in which he congratulated himself on having helped a plaintiff win $75,000, saying he deserved an Academy Award. "Did you write that in the *Wayne County Law Review* in 1969, yes or no?" McGinty asked.

Tanay asked to see what he was reading from, but McGinty said, no, he was asking the questions here. Tanay admitted yes.

McGinty looked to the jury, as if to say, See, the guy's an actor. He puts on an act to win money.

McGinty then sprang a trap that he'd been given by a Detroit prosecutor who had battled with Tanay. McGinty asked Tanay if he had once covered his ears with his hands in court and refused to testify because he hadn't been paid his fee.

Tanay: "That was a symbolic gesture out of respect to the court." He glared at McGinty. "That is a trick on your part, sir. That is—"

McGinty: "A trick that you were—"

Milano: "May he finish?"

McMonagle admonished McGinty, "Don't interrupt him, please."

Tanay: "That is really embarrassing for an officer of the court to play a trick like this before the jury. You take those two pages. You know very well what the subsequent pages show."

McGinty: "Hold it, Doctor."

Tanay: "I know exactly what you're trying to do here. You're trying to play dirty tricks, and that kind of behavior is a disgrace to your profession."

McGinty: "This is a speech you use in every trial, isn't it, Doctor? We have the verbatim transcript. When you don't like what the prosecutor is saying—"

The judge broke in. "Wait a minute, wait a minute, wait a minute." He stopped testimony for a moment to bring order.

McGinty, turning the screw, moved in close to Tanay. He stood just to the left and behind the witness stand. "All right, Doctor, do you remember *State versus David Reuben McPeters*—"

Tanay: "Go stand there, first of all." He pointed in front of the witness box. "I don't want you to stand next to me."

McGinty: "You're going to have to ask the judge if you want to give orders."

Tanay: "Get over there. Get over there. Don't stand behind my back!"

McMonagle finally jumped in. "Mr. McGinty, would you stand over there, please. Doctor, I'll tell him. Just wind down, all right?"

Tanay had been cross-examined hundreds of times, but he had never seen anything as aggressive and obnoxious as McGinty's attack. Tanay seemed perplexed. This judge was very loose. He was allowing everything. The prosecutor, not the judge, appeared in charge.

McGinty read from two transcript pages from the McPeters

trial, a Detroit case in which Tanay had refused to give an expert opinion on the defendant, even though he'd interviewed him briefly on tape. To force the issue, the judge had played excerpts of the tapes to refresh Tanay's memory, and Tanay had covered his ears in protest.

McGinty asked, "Now, Doctor, is that transcript accurate, yes or no?"

Tanay: "The transcript is accurate. The next pages show that this is untrue what you have just created. . . . I was asked by a lawyer to provide testimony where I had no opportunity to prepare. I was given a subpoena without a court appointment and my position was upheld by an appellate court. So this whole line is absolutely disgraceful, trying to show that I did something improper. I am extremely proud of what I did in this case for justice."

The bickering went on for hours. McGinty attacked him for being a highly paid witness: "The check controls you, doesn't it, Doctor." Tanay: "This is an insult!"

McGinty attacked the doctor for having examined Shelton for only one hour, then forming an opinion. He attacked him for writing in his 1976 book, *The Murderers*, that every man is capable of murder or having murderous impulses. McGinty's idea was to make Tanay's professional opinions seem far-fetched.

McGinty pushed too far occasionally, and McMonagle knocked him down a peg in front of the jury for improper questions: "I'm telling you how to do this, Mr. McGinty, do you understand?" Another time, at a sidebar, the judge told McGinty that he had seen this sort of attack create sympathy for the expert.

But McGinty kept up the battering and Tanay kept lashing back aggressively. As the hours dragged on, Jerry and Jay Milano felt the value of Tanay slip away. The man was brought down to the gutter, besmirched, his reputation and credentials and explanations were minimized. McGinty did not hurt him with rapier thrusts or devastating questions, but simply neutralized him by putting him through hours of mud-wrestling.

Tanay was still on the stand when the judge recessed late in the afternoon. McGinty said he had more questions for the doctor.

By now, some of the jurors wished McGinty would move on to another witness. He had been rude to Tanay, and they had even begun to feel sorry for the doctor, as the judge had predicted they might. But they did latch on to one fact McGinty underscored repeatedly: Tanay had only examined Shelton for one hour. Could a psychiatrist determine that Shelton was insane simply on the basis of the hour-long interview that they had heard played in the courtroom? The tape had not consisted of any testing, merely an interview in which the psychiatrist had asked questions the jurors themselves might have thought to ask. The tape seemed to demystify Tanay's profession.

The next morning, McGinty resumed cross-examining Dr. Tanay. Sometimes, swinging wildly, McGinty gave Tanay openings to counterpunch effectively.

For instance, the prosecutor tried to establish that Ronnie had lied to the doctor during their July 6 interview in order to avoid going to prison.

McGinty: ". . . Now you're aware the defendant has expressed an aversion to going to jail and would prefer to be hospitalized, where he can have fellow patients—"

Jay Milano: "Objection."

McGinty: "—be given privileges, not be forced to work?"

Jerry Milano: "Judge, that's an objection and a stone lie."

Judge: "Just a minute. The jury will disregard that question."

McGinty: "Doctor, are you aware that in his social worker report, this individual specifically stated he didn't want to go to jail?"

Tanay found a mile-wide opening. "Oh, you know a man of his background in jail would be victim of rape, you know very well."

McGinty: "Doctor, I didn't ask you additional—"

Tanay: "I am telling you that, in my knowledge and experience, this man within few days is gonna be victim of homosexual

313

rapes in jail, and he knows it. We didn't talk about it, but he knows it, you know it, and everybody who deals with law enforcement knows it."

McGinty: "You're stating for a fact that everybody who goes to prison is raped in three days, is that what you're telling us?"

Tanay: "No, sir. I didn't say that. I'm saying that a young man with his history, his appearance, when he goes to penitentiary, within a very short time will be, if he wants to survive, somebody's patsy."

McGinty: "That's strictly your theory, your off-the-wall theory again, isn't it, Doctor?"

Tanay knew he had scored sympathy points for Shelton. He smiled. "No, sir. You asked me if he's afraid of going to prison and I am giving you an answer."

McGinty: "Do you recall my question? He's making a very rational decision, isn't he, when he says he would prefer going to an institution, where he can meet nice nurses or patients and have privileges, to jail?"

Tanay: "He didn't say that. And a great many criminals are horrified of going to a nuthouse, as they call it. Many of them prefer to go to prison. I have seen that many times."

McGinty tried another tack. "This guy discussed whose fault it was. He tried to blame it on his father. There is no rational reason to put it on his father, is there? No indication from your knowledge that his father ever did anything to this guy, correct?"

Tanay: "We don't know that. You know from the tape that whenever something came up about his childhood, he began to cry. . . . If you have a person like this who has a lifelong history of disturbed behavior, then you do want to know about his childhood. So that his blaming, as you put it, his father might refer to items that neither you nor I know about."

A few minutes later, McGinty said he had no more questions.

REDIRECT

Milano stood up and worked quickly to repair the damage. This was "redirect," a chance to restate his case, but only about matters challenged during the cross-examination.

Milano asked, "Mr. McGinty said Shelton may have lied to you during your interview with him, Doctor. Now would that have changed your opinion that he was insane?"

No, Tanay answered.

"What is the significance psychiatrically that he may have refrained from committing rapes and other times he was compelled to rape?" Milano asked.

"It's indicative of the illness I'm talking about," Tanay said. "There is a common notion that people who suffer from sexual deviation have no conflict about it. That's not the case. There is a struggle. Mr. Shelton was driven, emotionally driven, to commit these acts."

Milano asked about Tanay's work with serial killer Ted Bundy, knowing Tanay's decision would likely impress the jury favorably. "I determined that he had no basis for the insanity defense," Tanay said. ". . . I testified in that case as the judge's expert."

Then Milano quoted from an article about abusive cross-examiners that Tanay had written for a professional journal. "'An abusive cross-examiner is someone who tries to humiliate and degrade the witness without a realistic basis . . . Abusive cross-examination is a gamble and is usually undertaken by lawyers who feel that they do not have much to lose. Obviously, there are those cross-examiners whose personality makeup gives them little choice but to be abusive, even when there is no rational reason for such a technique.' "

"Did you write that, Doctor?" Milano asked.

"I did."

Milano went back to the article. " 'Abusive cross-examination, in order to be effective, must be prolonged, persistent, and relentless.' Did you write that, sir?"

"Yes, I did."

"Did you write that the primary purpose of abusive cross-examination is to confuse the jury and neutralize the effect of the direct examination, which, presumably, was an effective one?"

"Yes, I did."

"Would you say, sir, that that describes what went on in this courtroom?"

"I believe so," Tanay answered.

DR. MICHAEL KNOWLAN

After Dr. Tanay's testimony, the judge recessed briefly. The courtroom was still jammed with rape survivors, court watchers, and the press. With the showdown over, McGinty was feeling relieved and playful. He believed his cross-examination had gone well; he felt Tanay had lashed back at his provocations, full of bluster and self-importance, making himself appear unprofessional.

While Milano walked the psychiatrist to the bank of elevators, McGinty caught Shelton's attention across the trial table, then ceremoniously picked up two M&M's. "You know what these are?" the prosecutor asked Matuszny.

Matuszny smiled, knowing something was up. "No, what?"

McGinty rattled the candy across the hardwood table toward the detective. "These are little Ronnie's balls. He doesn't have balls big enough to take that twenty-foot walk." McGinty pointed to the witness stand.

Shelton's eyes darkened and his face changed tone. "Fuck you, asshole." He seemed ready to jump over the table.

Milano was back now and rushed over to calm his client. "Don't listen to 'em. He's just trying to manipulate you."

Shelton said, "I wanna take the stand." The jury was coming in soon. Milano quickly sought out the judge, and fumed, "I need ten minutes, Judge. McGinty, that son of a bitch, is doing it again. My client wants to testify and I need some time to yell at him."

The judge said okay. In the adjacent holding cell, Milano blistered his client, his booming profanities carrying inside to the spectators, bringing smiles.

Now it was the rebuttal part of the trial for McGinty, and he called Dr. Michael Knowlan, the naval hospital psychiatrist, to the stand. Knowlan had examined Shelton in the spring as part of his court clinic fellowship. He found Shelton sane, and McGinty wanted the psychiatrist to contradict or at least blunt whatever favorable points Tanay may have made. Knowlan, a lieutenant commander, was lean and controlled, his face hidden by a close-clipped beard, the picture of rectitude. His fellowship at the court psychiatric clinic had ended and Knowlan was to report back to his ship by midnight that night.

Knowlan testified about the seven-plus hours he spent examining Shelton and how he believed the young man did indeed have control of his criminal behavior, thereby fulfilling Ohio's legal definition of sanity. Shelton could have refrained from raping, Knowlan said; indeed, the young man admitted he had done so on fifty or so occasions when he broke into women's apartments, watched them sleep, masturbated, and left.

Dr. Knowlan also noted that he referred Shelton to a

neuropsychologist. He wanted to see if he had sustained brain damage when he fractured his skull in a 1983 fall.

McGinty asked him whether having a personality disorder meant you were mentally ill. Knowlan said no.

Have you ever heard of the term "compulsive rape syndrome"? No.

During your seven and a quarter hours of interviews with Ronnie Shelton, did he tell you about having attacked and attempted to rape a woman *before* he had his head injury?

Milano objected strongly, and the judge overruled.

Knowlan answered that Shelton never admitted trying to rape a woman before suffering a head injury.

Your witness, McGinty said to Milano.

Milano stood. His legal pad, open on the table, displayed questions he had crafted and arranged, all carefully printed in block letters. He approached Knowlan.

"We chatted briefly this morning, did we not?"

"Yes."

"And I said to you that I think you are a fine psychiatrist and I have no quarrel with your motives in this case, is that not correct?"

"Yes."

"And I in no way, sir, intend to embarrass you. We talked about that, didn't we?"

"Yes, sir."

Milano was playacting for the jurors. He didn't care about Knowlan, but he did care that the jurors not think he was rude or a bully. He had studied Knowlan's sanity reports over the past week and, with Tanay's help, had fashioned a lengthy cross-examination, his first in the trial. Milano fired his questions quickly. "Are you certified by the Board of Forensic Psychiatry?"

"No, I am not. The process takes—"

Milano slapped him down immediately. "Sir, you have answered my question."

Then Milano contrasted Knowlan to Tanay. "Have you received any special honors or awards from any psychiatric organizations?" No.

318

"Did you know Dr. Tanay was honored and awarded by ten? Did you know that, sir?" No.

"Are you a member of any editorial board?" No.

"Did you know that he was a member of three editorial boards?" No.

"Doctor, do you have any publications?" No.

"Did you know that Dr. Tanay has authored books and has publications of twenty-three? Did you know that, sir?" No.

And on and on. With each question Knowlan came up short when compared with Tanay.

Yes, Knowlan had to answer, he was part-time with the court psychiatric clinic. Yes, he was in training—a trainee, so to speak. Yes, he had seen videotapes of Tanay that were used as a teaching aid.

Then it was on to the sanity report, which Milano began to challenge. "Tell the jury the day you dictated that report."

"April 25, 1989," Knowlan replied.

"And on April 25, 1989, you had not consulted with any neuropsychologists, had you?"

"No, that's not true," the doctor replied.

"Had you?" Milano asked.

"Yes, I consulted with Dr. John Kenny, a neuropsychologist in our clinic, regarding Mr. Shelton."

"Does that appear in your report?"

"No, it does not, because—"

"I did not ask you 'because,' Doctor," Milano snapped.

McGinty objected. "Can the witness finish his answer?"

Knowlan explained that Kenny's report was not typed by April 25, so he asked Dr. Kenny for an oral evaluation, which he'd taken into consideration when he wrote his sanity report.

"And you told Kenny you had found the man sane and to write you a neuropsychological report, isn't that the way it went down, Doctor?" No.

Milano's strategy was perfectly plain: He wanted to suggest that Dr. Kenny, knowing that Dr. Knowlan had found Shelton sane, would do likewise. Now Milano's questions came rapid-fire:

"Are you telling the jury that Dr. Kenny at the time of his

examination didn't know that you had found the man sane?"
No.

"Are you telling this jury that Kenny didn't have your report prior to writing his report?"

"My report may have been done," Knowlan said.

"Sir, my question to you is: Are you telling this jury that Kenny didn't have your report before writing his report?"

"He probably did at that point," Knowlan admitted, backing off.

Later, Milano brought out Kenny's report.

"Now you said that you talked to Kenny about his evaluation of Shelton *before* you wrote your report, is that correct?" Yes.

"Your report was April 25, is that correct?" Yes.

Milano asked Knowlan to read the date of Kenny's evaluation of Shelton. "May 11, 1989."

Then you could *not* have talked to Dr. Kenny about his opinion of Shelton because *he hadn't seen him yet,* isn't that right, Milano demanded.

Knowlan stuttered a bit, then admitted that yes, that was true; he must have made a mistake.

Milano would not let go of Knowlan's misstatement. For the next few minutes he used it to call into question Knowlan's entire report. The psychiatrist couldn't wait to get off the stand.

Minutes later, in the hall, some of the women discussed what had just happened.

"Oh, no," one of them moaned.

"It won't matter," someone else insisted.

Still, the feeling was that their side had stumbled.

Closing Arguments

After the trial was recessed in midafternoon, Karen Holztrager, Jeannine Graham, Janis Wren, and about ten other women decided to pay an unannounced visit to the city hall office of George Forbes, the city council president.

Forbes was trying to quickly pass through the Cleveland City Council a $100,000 relief bill for them, but they felt the money should go to other rape victims, that it was too late to reimburse most of themselves anyway. They wanted the money to go to new rape victims. And now they were going to tell the most powerful man in town in very clear terms that that was what he should do.

The women, along with Carla Kole, marched across Lakeside Avenue and down one block to city hall. A week earlier, this impromptu display of political involvement would have been unthinkable; these women had been isolated, frightened, barely able to say the word "rape." Now they confidently announced themselves at Forbes's office. They were told he wasn't in. An aide came out. The women told him they hoped the new rape victims bill wasn't just a political ploy.

Oh no, he assured them, it was not.

If Mr. Forbes was serious about getting money for women who had been raped, that was fantastic, the women said. But we want it to go to other victims, not to us.

The aide promised to tell his boss what they wanted.

* * *

321

The next morning, Thursday, September 28, there was a slight tang in the air from Canadian winds pushing in over Lake Erie. The mayor's race was swirling into an unpredictable finish. On the sixteenth floor of the Justice Center, closing arguments were set in the trial of the West Side Rapist.

McGinty, in a dark suit, had outlined his close on a yellow legal pad. He limited himself to thirty minutes, but knew he would probably go well over it. His friends were always telling him he didn't know when to shut up.

He faced the jurors and said, "This experience is one you'll never forget, one which is going to leave an impression on you your entire life. This took a lot more sacrifice than you probably thought. It had to be emotionally trying for you to deal with these victims of sexual assault."

Then McGinty went through each victim and sketched in the evidence and the similarities, editorializing as he went. "We know Shelton's a liar from his own tape. We even get this guy [Tanay], the hired gun, to admit he's a liar. It took hours to soften him up, it took a long time to get something out of Tanay, but even he conceded that this man he was here serving is a liar."

McGinty did not worry about leaving anything out; he would get to address the jurors again—during rebuttal—after Milano's closing arguments. McGinty got to present his argument twice to the jury, since the state had a higher burden to prove its case. He enjoyed rebuttal; by that point, he had the defense's closing arguments to attack, which suited his prosecutorial style.

"The guy is no genius," McGinty said of Shelton. "And it's hard to be a genius when you're out drinking alcohol every night and combining with it cocaine and smoking cocaine, where your head gets puffed up and you think how powerful you are. So his plans weren't perfect."

But what Shelton was good at, McGinty pointed out, was intimidation. The fear, five years later, was still present, he said; the fear was as if it had all happened today. "This guy is an urban terrorist in Cleveland."

Then the prosecutor slipped. He was talking about the rape of Roxanne Lincoln. "The girl who lived on West Tenth off Brookpark," he reminded the jurors. "She vomited during this process of humiliation that the guy put her through. And what does he say? It's caused by her husband, something her husband did. Can you imagine that? Can you imagine the vengeance, and the planning and the cunning, to the demented plans this individual engaged in to get back at her husband?"

Jerry Milano smiled and leaned over to his son. "I always said McGinty would fuck it up." He sent Jay out for a dictionary; he would need it as a prop.

Meanwhile, McGinty continued. He referred to Becky Roth and a few other women, taking his shots at Shelton, appealing to common sense. "And don't forget this: We hear these theories about trying to look for an excuse psychologically for this guy. Many times many criminals do have some excuse. That's the judge's job in sentencing—to take into consideration his background, to see if there's an excuse, such as he was beaten as a baby, or he lived in a cage the first ten years of his life, or whatever."

But Shelton has no excuses, nothing, McGinty went on. "Just a typical criminal concept to blame everybody but yourself. Assume no responsibility. Try to blame it on his family, who's done nothing to this guy. People look for an environmental issue, but some people just fail in terms of conscience and morality. Some people are evil. Some people are plain mean. Some people are bad. And that describes Ronnie Shelton. He has no excuses environmentally. He can't blame it genetically. There's no history of mental illness in the family."

McGinty ridiculed Tanay's theory of impulsiveness, that Ronnie couldn't control himself. He pointed out that the defendant stole money after the rapes. "Does he have an impulse for a hundred dollars? Did you ever hear that one? Of course, everybody has an impulse for money! Every crook has an impulse for money. He wants a hundred dollars to put right up his nose or whatever his particular expenses are when you're not working. He needs that money. God knows he's not going to break a sweat and do something when he can leech off somebody else."

Then he brought up the Teresa O'Brien rape. "Now we have the photo at the ATM where he's disguised. Very rational behavior. He's got the sunglasses on, smoking his cigarette right there, and wearing broad sunglasses in the middle of the night. Obviously, he's disguising himself. And we have the jacket right here. And then there's his little callbacks. His little thank-you calls. His little thank-you-for-the-rape calls, I'll-kill-you calls. Further intimidation. And he has the audacity to tell her to put more money in her account. That's how bold and brazen this guy is and how confident he is that he won't get caught."

McGinty brought his argument up to the last victim and to Vic Kovacic, who was "sitting back and he's charting and he's putting his map up and he's accumulating reports, and he's using the twenty-seven years of experience and the brain God gave him and the intuition that followed from those combinations. And he knows there's going to be a mistake. Kovacic knows, and he springs like a cat when there is a mistake.

"And this guy, his demise was right there." McGinty pointed to the bank photo. "He didn't anticipate it, and who would have? He put that car in the background. And whoever would think the bank machine would have been able to get the whole parking lot . . . ?

"Kovacic starts on his own time. And he's not going to get paid a dime more. He's a superintendent. He's already put his years in. And he goes out and finds his car because he sees the pattern, he sees the activity."

And when Shelton gets caught, what does he do? McGinty asks the jury. The detectives ask him the location of his car, the Monte Carlo in the photo, and he lies. Says it's in Brunswick Hills when it was really on West 68th. "Very rational, very good process for a criminal. You lie to the police because you don't want all this junk coming out." He gestured to the evidence table, strewn with incriminating materials taken from Shelton's car: a knife, a flashlight, the jean jacket seen in the bank photo.

Then McGinty switched from sarcasm and the colloquial to a lofty tone and referred to the Founding Fathers and the burdens of citizenship. "This case will be going to you. Our democracy depends on the twelve of you in that deliberating room, the decision you will make. Thank you."

The judge announced a five-minute recess, and Milano took the opportunity to ask court reporter Debbie Baer to read something back to him.

After the recess, Jerry Milano stood and seemed to glide to the center of the courtroom, his tiny feet encased in imported loafers. He waited until he had the jury's attention.

"In listening to Mr. McGinty talk to you and explain these terrible things to you that we've already told you we agree he's done, something just struck me when he talked to you. And I think it puts this whole case in perspective."

His voice boomed, but his manner was more fluid than McGinty's head-butting style.

"His language, as Debbie read to me, that he used in his closing argument, ladies and gentlemen, was this." He paused dramatically. "'To . . . the . . . de-MENTED plans . . . that this individual engaged in.' 'Demented plans' is what the prosecutor told you, and I think it's what we all know." He turned to his son. "Jay, you got the dictionary. Give me that."

McGinty: "Objection."

Judge: "Overruled."

Milano: "It's what this—"

McGinty: "Objection!"

Judge: "Overruled!"

Milano: "It's what this case is all about. I almost don't have to read it, it's so simple." He read the dictionary definition of "demented": "Condition of deteriorated mentality. Two, madness and insanity." He looked at the jury and said as convincingly as he could, "It means madness and . . . insanity! Those words came from *his* mouth. It's not Tanay. It's not Milano. It's not the judge. That's what *he* told you, and that's what this case is."

Sitting next to Matuszny, McGinty scowled, irked that he had given Milano an opening to exploit. He hated to admit it, but his opponent was good.

Milano reminded the jurors of McMonagle's instructions the first day about the insanity plea, and he reread from the transcript: If they returned a verdict of not guilty by insanity,

Shelton would go to a penal hospital, not be set free on the streets, and possibly remain in the prison hospital for the rest of his life. The judge would decide.

"We told you in the beginning he did it to these poor, unfortunate young women—it's just terrible," Milano went on, and he was looking at Becky Roth as he spoke. She was sitting up straight near the back of the courtroom. "But to me, it's demented. To Tanay, it's demented."

Milano turned to his old nemesis, Judge McMonagle, the man who suspended his law license for a year and sent him tumbling into debt. Now Milano praised him extravagantly as the fairest, finest judge in town. "We on our side of the trial table hope that this fine jury allows you to decide where this man will serve his time, how long he'll be there in an institution where he can be studied, analyzed by teams of psychiatrists, and maybe something good can come of this. That psychiatrists in these penal institutions can look at him and find out what makes people do these things, and then, perhaps, at some time, be able to nip these things in the bud."

For the past three weeks Milano had tried to read the jurors, to pick up signals: the slightest nod of agreement, an impatient look. He now glanced at Joseph New, with his silver hair, but New's face was still as a pool.

"Dr. Knowlan," Milano said derisively. "You'll remember at the beginning I said to him, 'I think you're a fine gentleman.' My opinion of him has since changed. I think he's a liar, but a liar within reason, which I will explain to you."

Knowlan, the part-time trainee on leave from the navy, gave his expert opinion without having all the facts, Milano argued. He didn't know that at police lineups twenty some women had successfully identified Shelton, who was supposed to be so devious, covering up his face.

Further, Milano said ominously, the doctor dictated his sanity report without having the results of Dr. Kenny's eleven neuropsychological tests. Yet Knowlan swore under oath that he had the benefit of an oral report from Kenny. But we all know that to be a lie, Milano said; the psychiatrist has admitted it.

"Now, that's not a mistake, that's a lie. It's not a lie just to hurt Shelton or to hurt the defense. It was a cover-up—a cover-up because Knowlan did a bad job evaluating Shelton." Now you, as jurors, have to decide who did a more credible evaluation of Ronnie Shelton, Milano said. Whose expertise do you believe: the part-time psychiatrist in training who didn't tell the truth, or the nationally known Dr. Tanay?

Milano closed by stroking the jurors again, thanking them in advance for their honesty, fairness and common sense. And he reminded them of McGinty's slip—calling Shelton "demented." The definition of "demented" isn't difficult to remember, Milano said. "Demented" means mad or insane.

Milano sat down, and without a break, McGinty stood for rebuttal. "Ladies and gentlemen, I'd like to thank you for your attention again, and good afternoon."

"Good afternoon," they chorused back.

He took that as a good sign. "The word 'courage' was defined once by Ernest Hemingway as grace under pressure. Now we have an individual here—I'm going to start with the word 'courage', I'm going to finish with the word—we had a career naval officer and a public servant, an honest man, versus a hired gun, the ultimate dodger, here in this courtroom—"

Milano interrupted deliberately. "Judge, if that remark, sir, was directed at me, I'm going to object to it. And if not, I'll apologize to Mr. McGinty."

McGinty: "Perhaps—"

Milano: "Was that directed at me, sir?"

McGinty: "No, sir."

Milano: "Well, who was it directed to?"

McGinty: "And, Judge—oh, if he can't figure it out—"

Judge: "Overruled."

McGinty: "If this guy can't even figure it out—"

Milano: "Objection."

Judge: "Overruled."

Milano: "Objection!"

McGinty: "I'm not going to sit here and argue with the guy. It's real simple: the hired gun, the dodger. He'll have to sit here and listen if he can't figure out the obvious, the career naval officer and public servant versus the man who's been hired to come in and give the testimony."

McGinty was off-stride and irritated. He would start and Milano objected, objected, objected. Finally, McGinty found sure footing attacking Emanuel Tanay. "ET, that's what we'll call that doctor—his initials, ET, because he's that bizarre and he's that far out. He is completely out of it. He is completely in his own planet."

Matuszny tried to hide a laugh from the jurors.

McGinty went on, appealing to the jurors' common sense: Who doesn't get dates mixed up? Especially when you have Milano confusing the doctor, poor guy, with badgering questions and then blowing up an honest mistake into some sort of conspiracy. Remember, Milano didn't attack any of the findings in Knowlan's sanity report, right? He just wants to throw out this red herring "to divert your attention to try to make this a trial of Dr. Knowlan instead of the trial of this guy, the serial rapist."

And as far as using the word "demented," so what? McGinty asked. What about Ted Bundy? He murdered and raped from coast to coast. Of course that was demented behavior. It was depraved, it was degenerate. But that doesn't mean a person is insane. Insanity means not responsible for his actions. And of course, Bundy *was* responsible for his.

McGinty circled back to courage. He read from *Profiles in Courage*, the best-selling 1956 book by then-Senator John F. Kennedy. He selected from the last chapter Kennedy's ghost-written definition of courage, and read, "The courage of life is often a less dramatic spectacle than the courage of the final moment, but is no less a magnificent mixture of triumph and consequences. . . . In whatever area of life or where we go, this challenge of courage will come. The stories of past courage can teach, they can offer hope, they can provide inspiration, but they cannot supply courage itself. For this each man must look into his own soul."

During this reading, the judge swore he heard McGinty slip into a slight Boston accent as he put his hand inside his coat in a Kennedyesque pose. A few of the Shelton survivors, realizing that the trial was finally ending and moved by the moment or by McGinty's words, quietly cried.

McGinty looked up. "These ladies looked into their own souls. They looked into their hearts. It has been a distinct honor and privilege to have been present, merely present, in this courtroom when these women defied fear and courageously testified and faced this man and gave their evidence." He gazed full-faced at the jury. "I thank you."

The judge gave instructions to the jurors. Just after two o'clock on Thursday he sent them to the windowless deliberation room where they would decide Shelton's fate.

THE VERDICT

On Friday afternoon, September 29, the jurors were on their way back to the deliberating room when one of them, a man nearing sixty whom the others felt was odd, stopped Judge McMonagle in passing. He asked the judge if he could be excused. McMonagle told him no, he couldn't. The juror said thank you very much and continued on to the deliberating room.

Later, the judge told lawyers from both sides what had happened. "I just wanted to let you know," he said. "I'm not going to do anything, unless I get a note from them that they're fighting or hung up."

Jay Milano didn't want to say it, but he knew this might be a good sign for Ronnie Shelton. The jury apparently was divided. Once that was the case, anything was possible.

McGinty didn't know how to take the juror's mysterious request. When deliberations had begun Thursday, he had expected the jury to come back quickly, certainly before the weekend started. He felt sorry for the women in the hallway: A weekend wait would be hell.

Out among the semicircle of chairs at the end of the hallway, Karen, Jeannine, Janis, Betty, Becky, and the others waited for the verdict, talking, sharing fears, expecting the worst. Karen's husband Lee stewed.

"Somebody must be holding it up in there," he said. "Somebody is in there arguing that he's crazy."

"All they need is one to ruin it," Karen said.

"That's all it ever needs." Lee could not shake from his mind a scene in a movie whose name he had forgotten. It was set in Chicago. An el train squealed outside the window of a jury room. People argued back and forth for days, filling ashtrays to the brim with butts. Is that what was happening here?

"Some asshole in there is going to find something to cut him loose with," Lee said. Then: "No way that guy is crazy."

The others griped bitterly. Lee turned to a friend. "The guy stole away my sex life for the rest of my life. I will never be able to have it spontaneous like it used to be when we first got married. That son of a bitch stole that, and I will never let him forget that. I don't care what the judicial system says, if he gets out he ain't going nowhere else. I mean they are still looking for Hoffa, and they *want* to find him. They dug up golf courses and housing developments looking for that guy, and nobody gives a shit about this Ronnie Shelton."

"Maybe his mother."

"Yeah, maybe his mother."

Everytime someone came out of McMonagle's courtroom, the door squeaked loudly, grating on the nerves of everybody sitting in the semicircle of chairs at the end of the hallway. The judge's docket had gotten backed up because of the long trial. Now lawyers, deputies, court reporters, and other parties were streaming in and out of the courtroom and the judge's chambers.

To break the tension, the women wondered what kind of

sentence McMonagle might give Shelton. They were betting on a heavy one.

"I'll tell you what I'd sentence him," said one woman. "Put his dick in a vise."

They laughed at the image, but one survivor said that wasn't punishment enough. "Put it in a vise like in a garage somewhere and then set the garage on fire."

"Yeah, right!"

"No, how about this?" said another. "It's in a vise, the garage is on fire, and he has a knife."

"He'd have to decide whether to cut it off or fry."

"Oh, yeah, I like that."

Everyone was laughing now, throwing in contributions to the group revenge fantasy, spinning it out as far as they could.

The deliberations broke for the weekend and resumed Monday morning. Lee brought an oilcan and doused the courtroom door hinges, but when it swung open with the next visitor, it squeaked just the same. The women laughed. Nothing was going right. They hoped this wasn't an omen.

Monday dragged on, then ended with no verdict being reached. Tuesday was another day of torture. "If it's a hung jury, there's no way I can testify again," Karen Holztrager said. "I can't go through this again."

Several others agreed, saying they could not go through it again, either. It would have to be a plea bargain; this process was just too painful. Janis Wren said she was also worried about losing her job because she had taken so much time off. No way could she ask for more leave time. "Tell me about it," another survivor said.

On Wednesday morning, Judge McMonagle came out to the hallway outside the courtroom. The jury had been deliberating for four days. There were only eight or nine rape survivors present this morning. The rest were at home or work, waiting for a call.

"We have a verdict," the judge said.

Everyone jumped up and took a few steps closer. "Can you give us kind of a preview hint?" Lee asked.

"No, sorry. Absolutely not," the judge said. "You'll have 'til about noon before we can get the lawyers and everybody back here." Then he left.

There was a dash to the phones and to Witness/Victim offices to tell Patrick Nicolino and Carla Kole to use the extra phones there to phone the other survivors. Within moments, from all across town, they came racing down to the Justice Center.

Two rows of seats were reserved for them, but still some of their husbands and boyfriends had to fight for a seat. Reporters lined the walls and the TV cameras were ready to film. The scent of violence hung in the air like cordite. Extra deputies positioned themselves along the walls and near the railing separating the spectators from the lawyers and Shelton.

Janis Wren's fiancé, Kevin, and Jane Lamb's boyfriend, Michael, both vowed to fly over the railing and smash Shelton should the verdict come back not guilty by reason of insanity. They said they didn't care if they went to jail; it would be worth it.

"Okay, guys, we don't want anything to blow this for us," Patrick Nicolino told the group. "I don't want any outbursts. We've come too far. You don't want a mistrial, anything like that." He took Lee Holztrager aside. "I want you to sit by Kevin, okay?" he said quietly. "Hold his hand or put your arm around him. I don't want anybody jumping that rail. After the judge slams his gavel down, I don't care what you do. But until then, you've got to watch it."

Lee said he'd try.

By now the courtroom was packed and Shelton, dressed in his gray suit, was brought through the side door by a deputy. Milano had spent thirty-five years waiting on jury verdicts. He felt these jurors had been out so long because McGinty's remark about Shelton being demented had given them pause.

He noticed McGinty peeking in through the courtroom door. "Look," Milano said to Shelton, "the asshole is gonna make a grand entrance."

In a moment, McGinty walked in and the Shelton survivors burst into applause. He grinned widely; he felt like he was gliding on clouds. "It was the high point of my career as prosecutor," he would say later. "The most exhilarating feeling was when I walked in that courtroom for the verdict, and the girls clapped. That just felt good. I was really proud. But I still had the nerves."

McMonagle came in, his black robe swirling. He seemed relieved to see the number of deputies along the rail that separated the crowd from the prisoner and the lawyers. The women had all linked hands, a daisy chain of rape survivors snaking across the courtroom.

The jurors filed in and sat in the box.

"Mr. New, you've arrived at a decision?" McMonagle asked the jury foreman.

"Yes, we have."

It seemed like the air had been sucked out of the courtroom. Everywhere you could hear shallow, fast gasps. The spectators seemed frozen in place.

McMonagle looked at the thick stack of verdict forms. "Is it the same verdict on each count here?" Yes, the foreman said.

"All right," McMonagle said. "The jury in this case has found Mr. Shelton"—the judge looked up—"guilty of every count."

A covey of murmurs skittered along the back of the courtroom.

"Is that your verdict, Mr. New?" Yes.

"All right, Mr. Shelton, we're going to sentence you at one o'clock. Anything further, counsel?"

Milano looked at the jurors and said, "Thank you and I think you're a darned good jury."

The bailiff said all rise, and that was it. It was over in an instant, almost before the women could react. No one screamed, no one jumped over the rail. They didn't feel free to let go until they learned what was going to happen to Ronnie Shelton. How was Judge McMonagle going to sentence him?

THE SENTENCE

Jerry Milano went back to the jury room and invited all the jurors to lunch with him and Jay. He always invited jurors to lunch or dinner after a verdict. He wanted to know how they'd made their decision, what had worked and what hadn't. He stored it away for future trials.

More than half the jurors followed the lawyers across the street to the Lincoln Inn. Once they got settled at a big table, Milano said to New, "The whole trial I was trying to read you."

The jury foreman smiled.

"I tried to read you and I didn't see one damn thing," Milano said.

"That was my card-playing face," New said, smiling.

"Hell, I don't want to play cards with you," Milano said.

It gradually came out: The jurors didn't buy Dr. Tanay. It seemed like he hadn't spent enough time with Shelton, only an hour, to have come up with his opinion. It also seemed like he was out to make a buck, someone said.

Dammit, McGinty's attacks had worked, Milano realized.

"Why didn't you cross-examine the FBI guy?" someone asked Milano. "We were waiting for it."

Another miscalculation, Milano realized. By not questioning Douglas, Milano gave his testimony credibility.

When he left, New told Milano he'd hire him if he ever needed a good lawyer.

"You call me," Milano said. "I'll take care of you."

* * *

After the lunch break, nearly all the Shelton survivors who lived in Cleveland were present in the courtroom. They were nervous, some near tears, wondering if the judge could still send Shelton to a mental hospital where he could get out soon.

The judge said, "Mr. Shelton, would you step up here with your lawyers, please."

Jerry Milano was in another courtroom for a hearing. Jay Milano stood next to Ronnie.

"What do you have to say before sentencing?" McMonagle asked him.

"Can I say what I want to say?" Ronnie asked Jay Milano, who said go ahead.

"Okay," Ronnie said, "I thought about what I wanted to say. As I understand the verdict morally, there's a lot of things that the jury doesn't know because I didn't take the stand. Regardless of what I was found guilty of, believe it or not I am not the West Side Rapist. I am responsible for West Park. I have an easy case for an appeal, but hand in hand, just thinking about it, none of the girls who I am responsible for deserved what happened to them, and then I thought about appealing it, and my honest-to-God wish is that I wish to be injected with sodium pentothal and given a lethal injection until I am dead."

Judge McMonagle waited a moment for quiet. Then he said he felt transformed by this trial. The crimes, the terror suffered by the women, the fear in the community—he had no idea. "I am very conscious of this now." He looked at Shelton. "You are a menace to the community, and these women should be commended. They've got a lot of courage to stand here like this."

Then he read each victim's name and the crimes committed against her—and imposed the maximum for each count, ten to twenty-five years. He specified "actual time," which meant no probation until the full minimum sentence was served. And most significantly, he strung the sentences consecutively.

When McMonagle came to the Becky Roth counts, he stopped and looked down at Shelton, and, with his voice cracking, said, "There's nothing I can give you that would be enough for this case."

Shelton was found guilty of forty-nine rapes (he raped some of the victims more than once during an assault), twenty-nine aggravated burglaries, eighteen felonious assaults, sixty counts of gross sexual imposition, twelve kidnappings, nineteen counts of intimidation, three counts of cutting telephone lines, two thefts, and twenty-seven aggravated robberies. He was convicted on 220 counts of the indictment. McMonagle gave him 3,198 years—the longest sentence in Ohio history.

"If the parole board ever considers you for parole, they should all be probated," McMonagle said. He stood to leave, and then the noise began.

Pandemonium. The survivors could not hold their emotions a moment longer. The trial finally was over, and nothing they did now could change its outcome. The sweet release of emotion shot like a geyser, showering the courtroom. A mass of people, sobbing, hugging.

A uniformed deputy sheriff moved quickly to take Shelton through the door that led to the prisoners' elevator down to the jail. A line of brown uniformed deputies tightened up between Shelton and the crowd.

Betty Ocilka, her long black hair flying, ran up and got as close as she could to Shelton. "You son of a bitch!" she spat. He did not turn his face.

As the door leading to the corridor to the prisoners' elevator was opened, Karen Holztrager called out to Shelton, "Bye-BYE-eee." Everyone laughed, then exploded into applause.

A minute later, in the hallway, Karen saw Rodney Shelton standing at the doorway. She walked over and gave him a hug and said she felt sorry for him and his wife.

Rodney Shelton was blurry-eyed. "I don't know what to say. I'm sorry it all happened."

CELEBRATION

That evening, in the Appalachian foothills of southern Ohio, Mary Gooding was idly watching the news on CNN, the national cable news network. The announcer told of a stunning jury verdict in Cleveland, Ohio, in which a serial rapist was sentenced to more than 3,000 years in prison for raping twenty-nine women.* She focused her attention, since she had lived in Cleveland as a girl. As Ronnie Shelton's name and photograph came on the TV screen in Gooding's small living room, she jumped up, stunned, and hugged her surprised husband. "Yeah! Yeah! Yeah!" she shouted.

"What? What?"

"'Member the guy I said raped me when I was twelve? That's him! Oh, sweet Jesus, yes!"

Her husband was shocked. He had heard her stories about living with the Sheltons on War Avenue and felt sorry for her, but had no idea he would ever see the face of the young man she hated so much.

"I always wished I coulda blown his head off his shoulders," Mary Gooding said, "but this will do." She started to cry. "Oh, thank God, thank God, thank God."

One of the strongest-willed rape survivors, Marian Butler, held a victory party that night at her second-floor apartment in a

---

*By withdrawing Betty Ocilka's case because of possible tainted ID, prosecutors reduced the original thirty cases to twenty-nine.

two-family home she rented in Parma. She invited her fellow survivors, friends, Jennifer Wise from the Rape Crisis Center, and others.

Marian had the apartment decorated by the time people got to the party that night. Hanging from the apartment ceiling of the living room was a life-size cardboard cutout of a man, dressed in jeans and a T-shirt, emblazoned with a drawing of Shelton's face. In case the guests missed the point, the effigy had a name tag and twenty-nine yellow ribbons—one for each survivor who testified—tied around its neck.

As the night wore on, the music got louder and the drinks flowed more freely. The tensions and inhibitions of Marian and the others slid away, and anger seeped out. They began to taunt and attack the effigy. Around one in the morning, Marian carried the cardboard figure out to the front lawn, and a friend doused it with lighter fluid and ignited it. As flames shot up, Marian and her friends danced around the burning effigy, chanting, "Burn, Ronnie, burn! Burn, Ronnie, burn!" Marian ran back inside and came out holding a gun high, and the crowd cheered. She moved in close and shot the Shelton figure through the crotch, and everybody howled.

Not used to such an uproar in their quiet neighborhood, several residents called the Parma Heights police. Within moments, a patrol car arrived and an officer came over and asked the celebrants just what the hell they thought they were doing.

"We're victims of the West Side Rapist," Marian said without shame. "He was convicted today. That's him." She pointed to the flaming mass of clothes and cardboard.

The policeman chuckled. Everyone in the department knew about the case. After some conversation, he suggested they put the fire out.

Marian said okay and got a bucket of water and doused the flames. The women laughed and moved back into the light of the house as the smoke drifted up past the orange-tipped maples and faded into the October sky.

Author's Epilogue

The trial was over. Carla Kole's coffee urn and doughnut cart were trundled back to the Justice Center cafeteria. The polite sheriff deputies with the big revolvers on their hips moved on to other chores inside the courthouse. The survivors of Ronnie Shelton returned home or to work, where many had to explain for the first time why they had taken days off. Their bank accounts were drained from weeks of unexpected bills for baby-sitting, lunches, and downtown parking.

Fortunately, they had each other and the free counseling of Cuyahoga County's Witness Victim Center. There, with continued group therapy under Patrick Nicolino, they pushed themselves down the path to recovery, building their comebacks on the proud feeling that they had had the courage to get up on a witness stand and tell everybody what Ronnie Shelton had done to them.

Now, confronting fears and exposing feelings that could hurt their spouses and family was turning out, not surprisingly, to be hard, upsetting work, but it had to be done.

In November, they took another step: Prodded by Patrick Nicolino, they actually began using the word "rape." Until now, they had referred to it as "the incident," "the assault," "the attack"—everything but "rape." It was a breakthrough, as if they had defeated the word itself. If they could say it, then they were going to be okay. "The group gave me the strength to leave my husband," Becky Roth would later explain. "The girls, they really helped me bring out the courage inside of me that I didn't know I had. To say, 'Hey, I deserve better.'"

It was at this point that I entered the lives of these women. As a senior editor of *Cleveland* magazine, I had resisted writing about the case. It seemed exploitative. The daily news media had covered it like a flood. At my editor's suggestion, however, I made a quick study of it and made an interesting discovery: that police in various suburbs and in the city of Cleveland had arrested or detained Ronnie Shelton at least fifteen times during the course of their hunt for the West Side Rapist. Now a magazine story had merit, for an important point could be made: Law enforcement should adopt a task force approach to serial criminals so that they could be chased across jurisdictions. Equally important, police should consider voyeurism as a likely gateway to serial rape.

It wasn't that Shelton was so devious. Certainly, he hid his face and stashed his car. But many times, locked into his rape fantasies, he was careless, particularly by 1988. Suburban police, with their rapid response time and willingness to answer petty-crime calls, picked him up several times. But they failed to realize that voyeurism can be pathological foreplay to serial rape. Street cops aren't taught this at the academy, nor is voyeurism mentioned in the popular police handbooks on investigating rape. In this so-called age of sex crime awareness, the popular image of the Peeping Tom carries all the menace of a dirty old man in a raincoat, not that of a possible rapist in waiting.

I came to know many of the Shelton survivors and learned how they had bonded into a remarkable sisterhood of strength. Never before had so many rape survivors taken the witness stand against a serial rapist. By the first day of trial, with Carla Kole's encouragement, the women were helping one another recover, each one refusing to be just another rape victim, an "unfinished murder," a dead soul. I was moved by their struggles, and decided their stories had to be told. Far from feeling exploited, many insisted I use their real names in this book. "He's the one who has something to be ashamed of, not me," said Betty Ocilka. Hers was a common sentiment.

* * *

As a journalist, I rarely bring comfort to the people I interview. It is the nature of the craft: wading into riots and crashes, crime scenes and courtrooms, hostage dramas and financial fraud. In the course of research for this book, with its more than one hundred interviews, many of them requiring rape survivors and their spouses to recall in painful detail the darkest moments of their lives, I was able to bring good news to one person, at least.

It came while I was seeking to pin down Ronnie Shelton's earliest rape, a crime that he still refuses to discuss. Because he holds hope that he may get a new trial someday, he doesn't want to admit to any rapes before his June 1983 brain injury, the crux of his insanity defense. However, I knew his first rape had to be earlier; he had hinted at it and, after all, he had first attempted rape in 1978, unsuccessfully targeting the woman next door.

Combing through Cleveland's reported crimes of early 1983, I found a six-sentence newspaper brief about a twenty-year-old West Side woman who had been raped in April by a man with a gun who left fingerprints on a beer can. Neither her name nor address was mentioned, which made it almost impossible to find the old crime report. But Vic Kovacic of the Scientific Investigations Unit checked the fingerprint log for the April date and turned up a cross-reference to a police report number and to a set of "lifts" from the crime scene. I asked Kovacic if he would compare the lifts to those of Shelton. He did—and they matched.

The victim's name was Kathleen Bond. Matuszny and McGinty had not located her during the pretrial investigation, when they'd searched for as many cases as possible to pin on Shelton. Her crime-scene address on Marne Avenue was outside Shelton's three main rape clusters in Cleveland. By the time of my investigation, the rape of Kathy Bond was outside Ohio's seven-year statute of limitations and Shelton could not be prosecuted for it.

I called Kathy Bond and told her that I was writing a book about the West Side rape case and that I knew for dead certain that her attacker was serving a 3,000-year-plus prison sentence. When I met with her and explained how I knew, she nearly broke down. She said she had lived in daily fear since the rape—he had promised he'd come back and kill her if she called the police—and indeed had given up hope of finding relief in her lifetime. "Today is the best day since my son was born," she exclaimed. And in that instant I understood why detectives and prosecutors and rape crisis workers endure their emotionally and physically hazardous work.

Kathy Bond, like the other women survivors, asked why Ronnie Shelton turned out to be a serial rapist. He wasn't born that way, or was he? What were the forces that had shaped him into an adult who deliberately raped and then deluded himself about his crimes?

I believe Shelton's family life holds a key. There were criminal convictions on both sides of his parents' families. Several of his uncles, his mother's brothers, the Taveras of Santa Cruz County, California, were prison-hardened felons; Shelton told me they were associated with the Mexican Mafia.

On his father's side I unearthed an astounding history of which Ronnie had no clue, a story that goes back to June 8, 1964, when an old man fishing at a spring-fed gravel quarry near Tipp City, in southwest Ohio, snagged a human arm chopped off at the shoulder joint.

While fire pumpers tried to empty the spring-fed quarry, police divers dragged the bottom, and found another arm. By the next day, a crowd of several hundred people from Miami County's farm towns gathered just off the banks, many with picnic hampers, ghoulishly waiting for divers to surface with the rest of the body. Four days later, in a stretch of the old Miami-Erie Canal, a torso was found tied in a burlap feed sack. The county coroner determined that the victim was a short woman, about thirty to forty years old, weighing 100 pounds, most likely strangled by her killer, who then cut her up with a saw. Except for the left thumb, the hands were too decomposed to yield fingerprints. The next day, a woman's head, swaddled in a patterned dress, was fished out of the canal downstream.

Over the next few days, the nation's newspapers splashed Tipp City's grisly story across the front pages. Headline writers abbreviated the bizarre story to the "Torso Murder" or the "Gravel Pit Case."

Thirteen miles to the south, in Dayton, Dorothy Lochner, the sole female deputy in the Montgomery County Sheriff's Department, had a hunch the victim was Daisy Shelton—Ronnie's grandmother. Lochner handled women prisoners for the county and knew every female with a record in Dayton. As I later learned, Dorothy Lochner had special pity for Daisy Shelton, a petite woman whose life married to Harvey Shelton had been very rough. In contrast to Ronnie's idealized memories of him as the only man who had ever showed him love, Harvey Shelton was a demanding husband prone to fits of rage. When summoned by police, Harvey would come out of his car or through the front door brandishing a bat, yet minutes after an outburst, he could be charmingly apologetic, a winsome good old boy.

By the late 1950s the Sheltons' marriage had collapsed and Daisy was drifting along the skid row bars of downtown Dayton, attaching herself to men for protection and comfort, occasionally getting back together with Harvey, who held a decent job as a tool-and-die maker.

Both Ronnie Sheltons' paternal grandparents had long rap sheets. Harvey had been arrested more than a dozen times, for public intoxication, assault, disturbing the peace, making lewd and threatening phone calls to the police. A judge once sent him for observation to Dayton State Hospital, an institution for the mentally ill.

Daisy had been arrested sixteen times in the Dayton area, mostly for public intoxication, disorderly conduct, and morals charges, including a 1959 conviction for contributing to the delinquency of a minor. She too was sent to Dayton State Hospital, where she underwent two months of evaluation and treatment.

When Dorothy Lochner obtained the Miami County coroner's report of the unidentified torso, she was struck by a flat recital on page two: ". . . the external genitalia show mutilation. The labia majors have been removed, apparently by cutting. Only an inch or some fraction of an inch of the vagina remains." To her, it looked like a crime of sexual jealousy.

Later that summer, the county coroner used medical records to identify the torso. Its cracked ribs and the steel sutures from a hysterectomy perfectly matched Daisy Shelton's old X rays. Next, detectives focused on murder suspects, including Harvey Shelton, who lived in Cleveland, where his son Rodney had just moved with Katy and three-year-old Ronnie.

When Ronnie's grandfather called the county coroner's office for the release of his wife's body, a secretary said he might have to wait a day. He called her a slut and blistered the coroner with epithets. He said he was coming down to claim the body and would kill the coroner or anyone who got in his way.

When Ronnie's grandfather arrived at the coroner's office, he was arrested and sent once again to Dayton State Hospital for psychiatric observation. He quickly quieted down enough to tell detectives he hadn't seen his wife in a long time. He said she had been living with another man.

That man, a flower shop worker, told detectives that when he and Daisy lived together in California, her husband Harvey had sent threatening letters with cutout newspaper headlines that said, "Man Kills His Wife."

Detectives weren't sure what to believe.

After ten days at Dayton State Hospital, Ronnie's grandfather was released to the Miami County sheriff. There detectives interrogated him, then released him. Days later the press was told that Harvey Shelton wasn't a suspect in the gruesome killing, a crime which today is still unsolved.

A few days after his release, Harvey wrote a letter to one of the detectives and gave a new version of events:

Dear Sir:
After getting away from that silly Sheriffs department, I have had time to clear my head and think straight. Now I remember my wife (Daisy) calling me and asking me to take her back and make a home for her. I tried, but it wasn't working and my family in Portsmouth was afraid if they took her in it might cause trouble in their home, so I called her back and told her I couldn't find a place for her. That was sometime in October 1963 or maybe early November. (It was getting cold weather) I just thought this might narrow things down and help you.
Chief, I would like to take this opportunity to thank you and *all* of

the officials of Miami County for working so hard on this case. I wish you God speed until it is solved!

Yours truly
Harvey E. Shelton
3311 E. 55th St.
Cleveland, Ohio

Despite his family history, Ronnie Shelton was not born a serial rapist. But by young boyhood he clearly was a sex criminal in the making. How did it happen?

I turned to an independent expert, Candace Risen, codirector of the Center for Human Sexuality at University Hospitals, Cleveland's highly regarded teaching hospital complex connected with Case Western Reserve University's School of Medicine. A board-certified clinical social worker and an assistant professor at CWRU's medical school, Risen has treated and counseled scores of sex offenders since the late 1970s. She conducts group and individual therapy sessions with pedophiles, voyeurs, rapists, obscene phone callers, exhibitionists, and pornography addicts, among others. Many of these men are convicted sex criminals who come to her as a parole requirement after serving prison sentences in Ohio. She is a widely known expert. Sometimes the FBI and local police ask her for advice during investigations.

An attractive woman in her early forties with a soothing voice, Risen had followed Ronnie Shelton's trial in the newspapers. She was professionally curious about him and volunteered to interview him at Warren Correctional Institution, where he was incarcerated, about forty-five minutes north of Cincinnati in southwestern Ohio. Before we drove, Risen read Shelton's psychiatric evaluations by Drs. Knowlan and Tanay, a neurological evaluation, the social history prepared by court social worker Rita Haynes, and portions of my numerous interviews with him.

Shelton was nervous about talking to a woman about rape, and afraid of what he might say about his family. The night before the interview, perhaps in an attempt to avoid Risen's probing questions, he cut off an ID bracelet and was thrown in "the hole" for punishment. That meant no visits. The warden's office called that morning to cancel the interview, but we had already started on the three-and-a-half-hour drive from Cleveland to Warren Correctional. When we arrived the warden graciously permitted the interview.

One of the first areas Risen probed was Ronnie's first sexual intercourse.

Ronnie: "When I lost my virginity I remember I didn't want to do it. I hated that feeling of doing it. It was my friend's girlfriend and she had a baby with him. I used to call her and we used to talk all the time and one time we went for a walk in the park and she more or less came on to me. We are at a park, daylight, and she had sex with me and I wasn't expecting it. I didn't like it, it was an ugly feeling."

Risen: "What didn't you like?"

Ronnie: "The actual intercourse."

Risen: "Do you remember what you didn't like about it?"

Ronnie: "A lot of things. Number one, it was out in broad daylight. Number two, it was—I was very depressed this is what sex was all about. The actual intercourse, I didn't like the feeling."

Risen: "What do you think on looking back that you didn't like about it?"

Ronnie: "It was ugly. The whole thing about it was ugly. It was more or less pull the pants down, lay on the hill out in broad daylight, and have sex. I didn't like it."

Risen: "What did you think about her?"

Ronnie: "I thought she was a slut."

Risen: "This is your friend's girlfriend?"

Ronnie: "Yes. I didn't turn it down."

Risen: "So it wasn't the arousal that made you feel bad—you were saying you like that feeling of being aroused, excited—but something about doing it with her?"

Ronnie: "It was her. It was ugly. I didn't like it."

Risen: "Did you feel used by her?"

Ronnie: "Yes. I felt dirty too. I felt that I wanted to get in the shower. She used to call all of the time. She lived right on West Twenty-fifth and Denison Avenue, where a lot of my cases are."

Risen: "Is that just a coincidence, that she lived there and this
is where a lot of your rapes are?"
Ronnie: "I don't know."

That day Candace Risen's interview stretched into six hours
over two sessions. She made a few general observations:

> He has a feeling that women are more powerful than men. He
> is slight. He has an obsession with his hair. He longs to be
> female and he is resentful toward women who are holding the
> cards.
> He believes he is feminine and they'll see through his macho
> bravado.
> He has a lot of negative feelings about sex. In his description
> of his first sexual experience—his best friend's girlfriend
> coming on to him—he is saying that women betray men. That
> it's not safe to be connected to women.
> His need to rape is his need to restore the balance of power.
> So he gets a masculine tattoo, boxing gloves, to shore up his
> masculinity. When he rapes, he's the boss.

These were her broad strokes. She went on to conjecture that
Ronnie Shelton, as a preschooler, never "separated" from his
mother. "Most of us start off identifying with our primary
caretaker, which for most of us is our mother," Risen explained.

> The baby doesn't know the difference between mother and
> himself. They are one and the same. Sometime in the first
> eighteen months to three years the child then begins to
> separate from mother and understand that the child is differ-
> ent, a separate person. The boy has a special task of relinquish-
> ing the feminine identification and acknowledging the
> differences between mother and himself. The girl doesn't have
> to do that. It is much harder for a boy to become a boy than for
> a girl to become a girl. The differences have to be stressed,
> which may have to do with aggression, with strength, certainly
> with differences in bodies. To the extent that the mother values

those differences and rewards the child for being different, the boy is able to then establish a separate identity. . . .

To the extent that a mother can reward the boy for being a boy, or there is a father there pulling for that, the boy will do fine. He becomes a boy. If, however, the boy is so tied to his mother that she continues to value the tie, the sameness, and doesn't particularly value masculinity, there can be problems. Maybe she doesn't like men. Maybe she hates aggression. Maybe she hates everything men stand for. She is not going to then value a lot of what masculinity is all about. Or she may value masculinity, but values more keeping him close to her. You get a momma's boy.

Which was the taunt from his father that Ronnie grew up with and bitterly resented.

"Ronnie said, 'My mother and I are like one. She loves me more than she loves herself,'" Risen said.

He suggests identification with each other where they merge and they are one. There is a tremendous attachment to his mother. At one time he says, "My mother doesn't believe I could do these things. My mother believes in my innocence." He is really saying my mother cannot see me as a separate person. She cannot see me as a man who did this, even though the evidence was overwhelming. The price a boy pays for that—if there is no father figure pulling him the other direction and the boy doesn't have the makeup to pull himself that way—is that he doesn't feel like a boy.

He is very close to mom and that feels real good. But he has a price to pay. He gets confused. He feels ashamed and so he hides the identification to mother because he senses from the culture that those things are not valued. You better not go around saying you want to stay home with her. Then you are a sissy. He learns to hide that piece of himself and he senses that there is something wrong with him. . . .

At the heart of Ronnie's sexual compulsiveness seems to be

an unmasculinity, a sense of a defective or shaky masculinity. With some sex offenders there's a clear wish to be feminine, not with all of them. Some of it is just a defect in being a boy; for others it is also a wish identification to be a girl. Ronnie makes allusions to some of that. He talks about his sister being the favorite child, the beautiful one, the smart one, the parents' favorite. "I love her and I hate her," he says.

Then there's this huge struggle between him and his dad over his hair. His dad calls him a sissy because he goes to a beauty parlor, has long hair. That is an attack on his masculinity. He alternates between being this macho "I am the greatest gift to women and I am superman" and at other times he is saying "I have always avoided a fight, I don't like to fight."

He is not feeling good enough about himself as a man in real life and needs to construct a script in fantasy that restores his manhood. That makes him feel powerful and like a man. Along with that is an anger at women and a need to make women feel as bad about themselves as he feels about himself. "I am going to do to you what I think you have done to me."

And he becomes a rapist.

"He doesn't hate women," Risen clarified. "I use three sentences in terms of how some rapists feel about women: 'I love you, I need you, and I hate you for making me so dependent on you.'" She went on:

Ronnie says, "I love women, my best friends are women, I get along with women, I would help any woman." He is right. He would. He identifies with them. He is more comfortable with them. That is his own feminine identification; but then he has a tremendous need to restore his sense of being a man. He feels that women take that away from him, just as his mother did with her closeness, in his perception. So he feels, "I am going to control you. I am going to make you scared. I am going to show you who is boss. I am going to show you who's the man." It only works for that moment of the attack, and then he feels worse. Now he feels he's defective as a man, because a real man wouldn't do this, wouldn't rape. That is the cycle. . . .

Maybe someday we are going to find, for example, something physiologically different about guys like Ronnie Shelton that makes them more susceptible to sexually aggressive arousal. Maybe we are going to find there is something hormonally different about them. . . . When you give them the drug Depo Provera, a female hormone which lowers testosterone, the deviant urge goes away. If they have conventional fantasies as well, those seem to be relatively unaffected. So we don't know whether we are tampering with sexuality, which is testosterone-linked, or aggression, which is testosterone-linked, or both. But the fact remains: If lowering testosterone alters this deviant urge then we cannot explain sex offenders in totally psychological and environmental terms. There has to be a medical or biologic component to this. We just don't know what it is.

Finally, Risen said that the case of Ronnie Shelton didn't have to have become such a tragedy.

Had he been picked up as a voyeur and treated then, he might have—in a comfortable setting—revealed the rape fantasy before he did it. Now we know that if there is a ten- or twelve-year-old boy who is doing what Ronnie was doing, we would take it seriously. We would be trying to get to them. . . .

Ronnie should have been on Depo Provera years ago. Then he would have been able to be treated—before he raped so many women that he was never going to be treated.

———————————

When I first met Ronnie Shelton in prison I was struck by his boyish good looks and nonthreatening manner. In a polite, deferential way, he exhibited surprising charm. I could understand why he made favorable first impressions on police and parole officers, and especially on attractive young women. He had perfected a soft sell so convincing that my wife, a seasoned litigator who occasionally answered the phone when Ronnie called, commented that if she didn't know him she would have thought he was a perfectly nice young man, someone whom you'd let date your daughter.

My challenge was to try to understand him, to untangle his twisted motivations, to discover why he turned out the way he turned out. I put myself in his place to try to see the events of his life through his eyes. I crawled inside his sickness, and soon felt contaminated.

In our scores of interviews, Ronnie Shelton not only provided an inventory of his crimes but also recounted his everyday experiences and normal sexual fantasies. These stories, not the aberrant ones, turned out to be insidious. Steeped in his life story, I found that the most commonplace things—a look, a song, a phrase—triggered memories of Shelton telling me about similar details in his life. He infected my sleep, my daydreams, my relationship with family. I was becoming what counselors in the sex crimes field call a "vicarious victim." I hated the feeling. On the other hand, it helped me to better understand rape survivors.

After four years of talking to Ronnie Shelton, studying him, uncovering family secrets, examining report cards and love letters and family diaries, I cannot say for certain why he turned out the way he did. But by twelve he exhibited the peculiar markings of a future criminal. His parents, both coming from families that hid shameful secrets, denied his juvenile problems. And the so-called social service "safety net" of the public schools and the county welfare department took note of his welts and were told how he molested a girl, but did not intervene. He slipped through the net and eventually attacked scores of victims.

He will not say how many women he raped; that would be putting the tape measure around the monster. He clings to his denial, to his belief that he is not a Bundy or a Manson. If only one in three rapes are reported to police, as some studies suggest, then Shelton's victims number about a hundred. "I never hurt any of the girls," he still insists, meaning he never cut or killed them. He is oblivious to the fact that his rapes constituted "unfinished murder."

Could a Ronnie Shelton develop again today in Cleveland or elsewhere?

A Cuyahoga County welfare director tells me that reports of child and sex abuse are now taken much more seriously, here and across the country, that the system would most likely snag the next Ronnie as a boy, or at the latest by the time he acted out as a teen. He insists that today something would be done to prevent another Ronnie Shelton from developing.

I wish I could believe that.